"We're all so fortunate for Nite's hustle and dedication to Cambodian cuisine, from her beloved San Francisco restaurants to homes across the country with her beautiful new cookbook, *My Cambodia*. This is clearly a deeply personal book filled with dreamy photography and recipes that are approachable for those, like myself, who are diving into the world of cooking Cambodian food for the first time."

—CALVIN ENG, chef and owner of Bonnie's and author of *Salt Sugar MSG*

"Chef Nite's *My Cambodia* is what I'd imagine if our parents and ancestors hadn't lost all their recipes and memories during the Khmer Rouge regime. Her stories and recipes amplify the many voices of refugees and children of refugees. This love letter to traditional Khmer dishes as well as Cambodia is a must-have not only for anyone wanting to connect with our culture but also for the Khmer American kids who feel disconnected from their identity."

—KARUNA LONG, chef and owner of Sophon (2025 James Beard semifinalist)

"Nite has epitomized what it means to be a proud Asian American in this generation. Her love and respect for her culture flows through everything she does on and off the plate. She captures the soul of Khmer cuisine, shares its lineage and food history, and brings it together flawlessly in *My Cambodia*. Her flavors are bright and bold, and her techniques are confident and precise—there's a reason she has been the leading light in bringing Khmer food to the main stage."

—GABY MAEDA, chef of Friends and Family Bar

"Nite and her restaurants have gathered all the attention around the country. Nyum Bai and Lunette are considered some of the best Cambodian food experiences in the United States. I first got to experience Nite's food at Nyum Bai back in July 2018. It nourished my soul and was so comforting and satisfying. With this cookbook, I look forward to learning more about Khmer history and the rich, delicious flavors produced in Nite's kitchens."

—EARL NINSOM, chef and cofounder of Langbaan (James Beard Award–winner for Outstanding Restaurant), EEM, Yaowarat, and others

MY CAMBODIA

MY

NITE YUN
with Tien Nguyen

A KHMER

4c
4 COLOR BOOKS
An imprint of TEN SPEED PRESS
California | New York

CAMBODIA

Photographs by
Nicola Parisi

Illustrations by
Nak Bou

COOKBOOK

CONTENTS

INTRODUCTION 11

LET'S GO SHOPPING AT ARUN MARKET! 15

THE KHMER KITCHEN 25

- Master Kroeung 27
- Tuk Ampil / Tamarind Water 30
- Bok Mtes / Chile Paste 31
- Somlaw Mu-anh / Chicken Broth 32
- Tuk Trey Mtes / Fish Sauce + Chile 33
- Chrouk Mtes Khtoem / Pickled Garlic Chile 35
- Tuk Krauch Chhma + Ambel + Mrech / Lime + Salt + Pepper Sauce 36
- Tuk Trey Piam / Fish Sauce Dressing 37
- Chrouk / Pickles 38
- Chrouk Khtoem / Pickled Garlic 41
- Khtoem Jien / Crispy Garlic Oil 42
- Khtoem Krahm Jien / Crispy Shallots 44
- Poung Mu-anh Jien / Crispy Fried Eggs 45
- Poung Mu-anh Jien Ka-Lok / Egg Ribbons 47
- *Essay: Rice Is Life* 48
- Bai / Steamed Jasmine Rice 52
- Bor Bor / Plain Porridge 53
- Bai Kadang / Rice Crackers 55

PART I STOCKTON

- Sach Mu-anh Jien / Fried Chicken Wings 65
- Sach Ko Ang / Kroeung Beef Skewers 66
- Nom Pow / Steamed Pork Buns 68
- Sa-Om Poung Mu-anh Jien / Sa-Om Omelet 71
- Tuk Kroeung / Tinned Mackerel with Prahok 72
- Tuk Prahok / Prahok Dipping Sauce with Seared Rib Eye 73
- Bok La Hong / Green Papaya Salad 76
- Plea Sach Ko / Beef Carpaccio Salad 77
- Pleay Trey / Khmer Ceviche 79
- Somlaw Kraung Chnuk / Soup Outside the Pot 82
- Somlaw Machoo Kroeung / Tamarind Kroeung Soup 85
- Somlaw Chap Chai / Celebration Soup 87
- Curi Sach Mu-anh / Chicken Curry 91
- Cha Mee Sou / Peppery Stir-Fried Glass Noodles with Yuba 92
- Mee Ka-tung / Stir-Fried Egg Noodles with Gravy 94
- Trey Jien Juen / Whole Fish with Ginger + Salted Beans 97
- Cha Sach Mu-anh Kyai / Chicken + Caramelized Ginger 99
- Sach Chrouk Ang / Garlic + Pepper Pork Ribs 101

PART II CAMBODIA

- Cha Port / Stir-Fried Corn 109
- Prahut Trey / Lemongrass Fish Cakes 110
- Bangkea Dot Tuk Kampot / Grilled Freshwater Prawns in Kampot Sauce 113
- Prahok Kop / Buried Prahok 115
- Natang / Coconut, Pork + Dried Shrimp Dip 117
- Nom Pung Jien / Crispy Toast with Pork + Jicama 119
- Trey Prama / Pork and Salted Cod Loaf 120
- Jien BawnKwang / Crispy Shrimp Fritters 121
- Trey Jien Svay / Green Mango Salad with a Crispy Fish Fillet 123
- Ngyom Svay / Green Mango Salad with Dried Smoked Salted Fish 124
- Ngyom Mee Sou / Potluck Glass Noodle Salad 127
- Nom Pachok Somlar Khmer / Rice Vermicelli with Fish Chowder 129
- *Sidebar: Nom Pachok Noodles* 131
- Somlaw Koko / Stirring Soup 133
- Somlaw Prahor / Countryside Soup 135
- Curi Saraman / Saraman Curry 137
- Kuy Teav Kho Ko / Caramelized Beef Stew 139
- Nom Pachok Kampot / Kampot Noodles with Coconut Fish Sauce Dressing 143
- Cha Mouk Mrech Baitang / Stir-Fried Squid with Green Peppercorns 144
- *Sidebar: Kampot Peppercorns* 146
- Bor Bor Sach Mu-anh / Chicken Porridge 148
- Bai Mu-anh / Poached Chicken + Ginger Rice with Spicy, Limey Fish Sauce 150
- Mu-anh Doat Cola / Coca-Cola Chicken 153

PART III SF LOVE

Pot Ang / Grilled Corn with Coconut Milk + Green Onion 160
Cha Dau Fu Kh-Chai / Quick Stir-Fry with Fried Tofu + Chives 161
Kapeek Pow / Smoked Fish + Shrimp Tapenade 163
Sach Mu-anh Boungk / Stuffed Chicken Wings 164
Cha Trek Sak / Stir-Fried Cucumbers with Black Pepper + Egg 167
Sgnor Sach Mu-anh / Chicken Lime Soup 168
Sgnor Chuong Kho / Cozy Oxtail Soup 169
Somlaw Machoo Ktiss Ban Kong / Shrimp Tamarind Coconut Soup 170
Sidebar: Re-creating Nearly Lost Dishes 172
Mee Cha / Student Noodles 174
Mee Kola / Cold Noodles with Cucumber Relish + Dried Shrimp 175
Kho Trey / Caramelized Fish with Tomatoes 179
Cha Kdam Kroeung / Stir-Fried Crab + Kroeung 181
Cha Kroeung / Stir-Fried Kroeung 183
Cha Krom Tuk Ampil / Stir-Fried Mussels in Tamarind Sauce 184
Bai Sach Chrouk / Coconut Pork 187

PART IV NYUM BAI

Prahok Ktiss / Prahok Coconut Pork Dip 195
Jien Cho-Yah / Crispy Pork Egg Rolls 196
Ngyom Kroch Thlong / Pomelo Salad with Fish Sauce Dressing 199
Ngyom Trayong Jenk / Banana Blossom Salad 200
Sidebar: How to Slice Banana Blossoms 202
Ngyom Sach Mu-anh / Chicken Cabbage Salad 203
Cha Tra Koun / Stir-Fried Water Spinach 205
Cha Troup / Charred Eggplants with Pork + Shrimp 206
Cha Lapov / Stir-Fried Pumpkin with Pork 209
Essay: The Golden Era 210
Kuy Teav Phnom Penh / Pork Noodle Soup 213
Amok / Fish Soufflé 215
Trey Jien Ban Pouh / Crispy Fish with Simmered Summer Tomatoes 219
Kho / Caramelized Pork Belly 221
Prahut / Pork Meatballs 222
Loc Lak / Stir-Fried Beef Cubes 223

PART V THE DONUT SHOP

Bai Treap / Palm Sugar Sticky Rice 228
Sidebar: Fresh Coconuts Are the Best 229
Nom Pla Ai / Mochi with Palm Sugar + a Lot of Coconut 231
Nom Ansom Khnor / Coconut Sticky Rice with Jackfruit + Beans 232
Jeak Ktiss / Banana Tapioca Pudding 235
Nom Lapov / Pumpkin Pudding 236
Nom Krouk / Savory Coconut Custard 239
Nom Poum / Coconut Waffles 240
Nom Bak Ben / Cassava Cake 241
Nom Kong / Palm Sugar–Glazed Donuts 243
Nom Krouch / Sesame Balls 244

SOURCES + FURTHER READING 246

ACKNOWLEDGMENTS 247

ABOUT THE CONTRIBUTORS 249

INDEX 250

RECIPE INDEX

FOUNDATIONS

Master Kroeung 27
Tuk Ampil / Tamarind Water 30
Bok Mtes / Chile Paste 31
Somlaw Mu-anh / Chicken Broth 32
Tuk Trey Mtes / Fish Sauce + Chile 33
Chrouk Mtes Khtoem / Pickled Garlic Chile 35
Tuk Krauch Chhma + Ambel + Mrech / Lime + Salt + Pepper Sauce 36
Tuk Trey Piam / Fish Sauce Dressing 37
Chrouk / Pickles 38
Chrouk Khtoem / Pickled Garlic 41
Khtoem Jien / Crispy Garlic Oil 42
Khtoem Krahm Jien / Crispy Shallots 44
Poung Mu-anh Jien / Crispy Fried Eggs 45
Poung Mu-anh Jien Ka-Lok / Egg Ribbons 47
Bai / Steamed Jasmine Rice 52
Bor Bor / Plain Porridge 53
Bai Kadang / Rice Crackers 55

SNACKS

Sach Mu-anh Jien / Fried Chicken Wings 65
Sach Ko Ang / Kroeung Beef Skewers 66
Nom Pow / Steamed Pork Buns 68
Cha Port / Stir-Fried Corn 109
Prahut Trey / Lemongrass Fish Cakes 110
Bangkea Dot Tuk Kampot / Grilled Freshwater Prawns in Kampot Sauce 113
Prahok Kop / Buried Prahok 115
Nom Pung Jien / Crispy Toast with Pork + Jicama 119
Jien BawnKwang / Crispy Shrimp Fritters 121
Pot Ang / Grilled Corn with Coconut Milk + Green Onion 160
Kapeek Pow / Smoked Fish + Shrimp Tapenade 163
Sach Mu-anh Boungk / Stuffed Chicken Wings 164
Jien Cho-Yah / Crispy Pork Egg Rolls 196

DIPPING DISHES

Tuk Kroeung / Tinned Mackerel with Prahok 72
Tuk Prahok / Prahok Dipping Sauce with Seared Rib Eye 73
Natang / Coconut, Pork + Dried Shrimp Dip 117
Trey Prama / Pork + Salted Cod Loaf 120
Prahok Ktiss / Prahok Coconut Pork Dip 195

SALADS + VEGGIES

Salads

Bok La Hong / Green Papaya Salad 76
Plea Sach Ko / Beef Carpaccio Salad 77
Pleay Trey / Khmer Ceviche 79
Trey Jien Svay / Green Mango Salad with a Crispy Fish Fillet 123
Ngyom Svay / Green Mango Salad with Dried Smoked Salted Fish 124
Ngyom Mee Sou / Potluck Glass Noodle Salad 127
Ngyom Kroch Thlong / Pomelo Salad with Fish Sauce Dressing 199
Ngyom Trayong Jenk / Banana Blossom Salad 200
Ngyom Sach Mu-anh / Chicken Cabbage Salad 203

Veggies

Sa-Om Poung Mu-anh Jien / Sa-Om Omelet 71
Cha Dau Fu Kh-chai / Quick Stir-Fry with Fried Tofu + Chives 161
Cha Trek Sak / Stir-Fried Cucumbers with Black Pepper + Egg 167
Cha Tra Koun / Stir-Fried Water Spinach 205
Cha Troup / Charred Eggplants with Pork + Shrimp 206
Cha Lapov / Stir-Fried Pumpkin with Pork 209

SOUPS

Somlaw Kraung Chnuk / Soup Outside the Pot 82
Somlaw Machoo Kroeung / Tamarind Kroeung Soup 85
Somlaw Chap Chai / Celebration Soup 87
Curi Sach Mu-anh / Chicken Curry 91
Nom Pachok Somlar Khmer / Rice Vermicelli with Fish Chowder 129
Somlaw Koko / Stirring Soup 133
Somlaw Prahor / Countryside Soup 135
Curi Saraman 137
Kuy Teav Kho Ko / Caramelized Beef Stew 139
Sgnor Sach Mu-anh / Chicken Lime Soup 168
Sgnor Chuong Kho / Cozy Oxtail Soup 169
Somlaw Machoo Ktiss Ban Kong / Shrimp Tamarind Coconut Soup 170
Kuy Teav Phnom Penh / Pork Noodle Soup 213

NOODLES

Cha Mee Sou / Peppery Stir-Fried Glass Noodles with Yuba 92
Mee Ka-tung / Stir-Fried Egg Noodles with Gravy 94
Nom Pachok Kampot / Kampot Noodles with Coconut Fish Sauce Dressing 143
Mee Cha / Student Noodles 174
Mee Kola / Cold Noodles with Cucumber Relish + Dried Shrimp 175

SEAFOOD

Trey Jien Juen / Whole Fish with Ginger + Salted Beans 97
Cha Mouk Mrech Baitang / Stir-Fried Squid with Green Peppercorns 144
Kho Trey / Caramelized Fish with Tomatoes 179
Cha Kdam Kroeung / Stir-Fried Crab + Kroeung 181
Cha Krom Tuk Ampil / Stir-Fried Mussels in Tamarind Sauce 184
Amok / Fish Soufflé 215
Trey Jien Ban Pouh / Crispy Fish with Simmered Summer Tomatoes 219

CHICKEN + PORK + BEEF

Cha Sach Mu-anh Kyai / Chicken + Caramelized Ginger 99
Sach Chrouk Ang / Garlic + Pepper Pork Ribs 101
Bor Bor Sach Mu-anh / Chicken Porridge 148
Bai Mu-anh / Poached Chicken + Ginger Rice with Spicy, Limey Fish Sauce 150
Mu-anh Doat Cola / Coca-Cola Chicken 153
Cha Kroeung / Stir-Fried Kroeung 183
Bai Sach Chrouk / Coconut Pork 187
Kho / Caramelized Pork Belly 221
Prahut / Pork Meatballs 222
Loc Lak / Stir-Fried Beef Cubes 223

SWEETS + DESSERTS

Bai Treap / Palm Sugar Sticky Rice 228
Nom Pla Ai / Mochi with Palm Sugar + a Lot of Coconut 231
Nom Ansom Khnor / Coconut Sticky Rice with Jackfruit + Beans 232
Jeak Ktiss / Banana Tapioca Pudding 235
Nom Lapov / Pumpkin Pudding 236
Nom Krouk / Savory Coconut Custard 239
Nom Poum / Coconut Waffles 240
Nom Bak Ben / Cassava Cake 241
Nom Kong / Palm Sugar–Glazed Donuts 243
Nom Krouch / Sesame Balls 244

INTRODUCTION

Mom, when you eat this, what do you remember?
Did you learn how to make it from Grandma?
What was Cambodia like back then?
What did you do?
Before the war.
And, Mom.
Do things become easier after you have faced death many times?

Phnom Penh, 2012. I'm at a stall, chopsticks and soup spoon in hand, at complete peace, devouring a bowl of kuy teav. This is my third trip to Cambodia, and I'm home. I love the morning mist, the dusty pathway behind the wat that leads to an amazing view of the sunrise, the hues of oranges and purples. I love seeing my relatives, most of whom I met for the first time just a few years ago. It feels like the answers I want in life are waiting for me to stumble upon them: who my parents were before the war, who they became, who I am . . .

And, of course, the food: bright and fresh, herbaceous and light, full of color and textural contrasts, balanced among sweet, tart, and umami. There are two main stars of Khmer cooking that show up everywhere: prahok, the fermented fish paste that gives so many dishes a savory depth of flavor, and kroeung, a paste that can take a few different forms but often includes lemongrass, turmeric, galangal, makrut limes, garlic, and shallots as its base.

Every time I eat anything here, I think, *This is just so good, so fucking good*. The prahok ktiss I had the other day—a platter of raw vegetables served with a savory dip of fermented fish paste and pork—so good. This kuy teav, rice noodles dropped into a clear pork broth topped with herbs and a few solid squeezes of lime: so good.

I'm about halfway through the bowl, mid-slurp, when it hits me. This is it. *This is it.*

I am going to learn how to cook this food.

I *need* to learn how to cook this food.

My parents miraculously survived the charom[1] created by the Khmer Rouge when the party seized power in Cambodia in 1975, and only then by escaping to a refugee camp in Thailand. That refugee camp was

---

[1] Forced labor camps.

where I was born. We immigrated to the United States in 1984; I was just two years old. And as far back as I can remember, my parents never got along. Their fights carried the weight of a burden I couldn't put my finger on. At night, they had hushed conversations and sharp arguments. During the day, a mysterious aura enveloped their very beings. I knew they were hiding something. Maybe to protect me and my brothers. Maybe because it was the only way they could move on.

But maybe if I talked to them about our food, maybe they'd open up, even a little bit, about their life before. Maybe through food, we could connect, and I could learn about them and myself—and maybe even help us heal.

And as much as my decision to learn how to cook Khmer dishes was driven by my own personal journey, I knew it wasn't just going to be about me. With dominant narratives about Cambodia still focused on the war or on the genocide, being able to share my cooking would be an opportunity to help widen that lens and reshape conversations about Cambodia's past, present, and future. Through food, I could help bring visibility to the Khmer people and shine a light on other aspects of Khmer history and culture, so whether someone was Khmer or not, they could taste and feel and see and hear how lively and beautiful and bright Khmer culture is.

When I set out to learn how to cook Khmer food, I called my mom a lot, asking her how she made her kuy teav, what she put in her somlaw machoo kroeung,[2] and how she cooked other dishes I craved but couldn't find anywhere. I drove two hours from the Bay Area, where I lived, down to Stockton, where I grew up, to cook with her. I traveled to Cambodia, too, to cook with relatives there. Between that, my own taste memories, and any other source I could find, I slowly taught myself how to make the dishes I grew up with and ones I tasted in Cambodia.

Since then, I've been so fortunate to be able to share my cooking with so many people through my pop-ups and my restaurants, Nyum Bai, which closed in 2022, and Lunette Cambodia, in San Francisco—and now, this book. This book in particular is special to me: As I've learned and cooked more and more, I've come to feel a real urgency to preserve these recipes, as I know them, on paper. Like many cuisines, Khmer recipes and culinary techniques are traditionally passed down orally, from generation to generation. That's how my mother learned how to cook, and that's how I learned, too. But not everyone has that opportunity to learn this way, and that's especially true as history has violently disrupted that tradition. So much simply vanished after the wars, and the more time passes, the more memories fade. It doesn't help that this cuisine is extremely underrated and way too often overshadowed by, or entirely confused with, the food of its neighbors, including Vietnam

[2] A beef and water spinach soup in a tamarind broth (page 85).

and Thailand, even though many Khmer dishes predate the existence of those countries.

And so, this book is a Khmer American celebration of the food I grew up with and the dishes I fell in love with over the years, including kuy teav Phnom Penh[3] and prahok ktiss,[4] of course, plus other fun dishes like green mango salads and stir-fried noodles. In cooking these recipes, I hope you will fall in love with Khmer food and culture, too! I hope it also will be a way for Khmer culture to be remembered and documented, and that in turn will inspire new, joyful creations. And if you want to connect with your parents, grandparents, friends–anyone, really–I hope this book will help you create the space for conversations both loving and difficult.

LET'S COOK!

This book is divided into a few big sections. After picking up ingredients in Let's Go Shopping at Arun Market!, we'll prepare kroeung and other bases, condiments, sides, and garnishes that form the foundation for many of the other recipes in the book. From there, the recipes follow the big chapters of my life, from growing up in Stockton, to traveling to Cambodia, to learning how to cook Khmer food in my San Francisco apartment, to starting Nyum Bai. And, to end, I have a chapter on sweets and treats. For easy reference, I've also listed all the recipes, organized by type, on pages 8–9.

When you cook from this book, I highly suggest that you have Khmer oldies but goodies playing in the background, too. If you need some guidance, each chapter includes playlists of my favorite tunes, all of which are in the public domain and easily found online. Queue it up and let's cook!

A QUICK WORD ABOUT THE WORD KHMER

In this book, as in my everyday, I generally identify myself as Khmer or Khmer American rather than Cambodian or Cambodian American. The term *Khmer* (pronounced "Khmai"; the *r* is silent) predates colonial rule: Before Cambodia became a protectorate of France in 1863, its Khmer name was Kampuchea. When France came along, it referred to Kampuchea by its French name, Cambodge. Then, in English, Cambodge became Cambodia. So while technically it's not incorrect to say I'm Cambodian or Cambodian American, they are not terms I fully embrace. To me, identifying as Khmer is one way to reject the remnants of colonialism, at least in how it has been imposed through language.

[3] Rice noodles in clear pork broth (page 213).
[4] Prahok Coconut Pork Dip (page 195).

LET'S GO SHOPPING AT ARUN MARKET!

Arun Market was the OG, one of the first Khmer markets in Stockton. It sat at the corner of a strip mall that was also home to a laundromat and a donut shop. You know, the essentials. Arun was tiny but somehow still managed to carry everything in its cramped aisles. It was our family market as much as it was everyone else's; every day and especially on weekends, you'd run in for, say, prahok or dried fish and inevitably run into someone you knew. I always felt such joy for my mom when we shopped there, because it was one of the few places outside our immediate neighborhood where she could chat about home.

Arun was just one of so many tiny markets all over the country that catered to an immigrant enclave, and it became a hub for community. Arun closed years ago, but I often think of it when I shop. Cambodian ingredients are easier to source now than they were back then; almost everything you need for this cookbook can be found at a Southeast Asian market. I hope you'll find your own version of Arun in your city!

If you don't have a Southeast Asian market near you, many ingredients can be found at well-stocked Asian markets like 99 Ranch or H-Mart. However, they may not carry certain produce or pantry goods like prahok. The following shopping guide will hopefully help you source and prepare the ingredients I use most often.

PANTRY GOODIES

Coconut cream and milk

I use the Mae Ploy brand for coconut cream and Chaokoh for coconut milk. Look out for unscrupulous imposters! Double-check the spelling of the brand name and review the ingredients: Neither should have sugar or any other sweetener. Use or freeze both within a day of opening. When freezing, label the container with the date and how much you're storing—your future self will thank you. They'll keep for up to 1 month in the freezer.

Dried shrimp

Dried shrimp (without shells) can be found at Asian markets, at local fish markets, and online. Generally, the more expensive, the higher the quality, so buy what you can afford. If in doubt, look at the color: The shrimp should be naturally pinkish, without any artificial coloring. Also, extra-large sizes tend to be made with better-quality shrimp. Once opened, refrigerate them in an airtight container for up to 3 months.

Fish sauce

I use Three Crabs fish sauce in this book.

Noodles

Glass noodles. Glass noodles (also called cellophane noodles or bean thread noodles) can be made with a variety of starches; in my recipes, I use glass noodles made with mung bean starch. For convenience, I like packages where the noodles are pre-portioned into 6 or 9 bundles. Each bundle is usually 1½ to 2 ounces, or just what you need for a single serving.

Rice noodles. There are two types of rice noodles I use in this book, both defined by their shape:

Flat rice noodles can be thin or wide, and which one to use depends on the dish. At Asian markets, they're available fresh or dried. Fresh noodles (labeled "bánh phở tươi") are found in the refrigerated section; the dried, in the dried noodle aisle. Dried rice noodles always need to be soaked in water to soften before use.

Rice vermicelli are dried round noodles. Packages will indicate the size of the noodle; for this book, choose small.

Oyster sauce

I use a Thai brand called Maekrua, which is easier to pour and much less salty than many other major brands. If you use another brand, such as Lee Kum Kee, be mindful whenever you add more salt to the dish: Taste as you cook, and adjust the seasoning as needed.

Palm sugar

Palm sugar—not to be confused with coconut sugar or coconut palm sugar—is made from the sap of the palmyra tree, a tree so ubiquitous in Cambodia that it's the country's national tree. Palm sugar is milder and more rounded in flavor than white sugar, with hints of caramel, vanilla, and hazelnut. It's found at most Asian markets, packaged into small pucks or disks or in tubs for scooping. I prefer the pucks because they're more manageable and easier to portion than the tubs. If absolutely necessary, an imperfect substitute for palm sugar is dark brown sugar. Start with a little less than I call for in the recipe and add more to taste.

Peppercorns

Freshly ground, always. In addition to the peppercorns you use every day, I recommend peppercorns from the Kampot region of Cambodia, too; they're distinctly aromatic and fruity, with a warm spice. See page 146 for more about these special peppercorns.

Prahok

Many Asian cultures have some version of a fermented fish paste; prahok is ours. Prahok was developed as a way to preserve fish during the dry seasons, and records show its use going all the way back to the Angkorian era in the fifteenth century. Typically made with freshwater fish like mudfish, prahok is used as an ingredient and a condiment to give a dish a unique body and depth of flavor. For recipes where there isn't much cooking involved, like dips, I might first cook the prahok in a piece of foil to enhance its flavor before combining it with the rest of the ingredients (cooking the prahok in the foil prevents it from burning and makes it easier to transfer once it's done). Khmer food would not be the same without it, and it cannot be substituted.

Look for prahok in glass jars at Southeast Asian markets or online. If you can't read Khmer, the jar may be labeled "mud fish sauce" (or something similar). The paste will either be creamy and smooth, or coarse with pieces of fish; I always use the smooth paste. Make sure the only ingredients are fish and salt; there shouldn't be any rice, rice flour, or oil. Generally, the price will reflect the quality of the prahok, so buy the best you can afford. When you work with it, be careful of bits of bones or skin that may be present, even in the smooth versions; if you find any, pick them out and discard.

Rice

The most important dish on the table! I steam fragrant white jasmine rice for everyday meals, and my preferred brand is Three Ladies. It'll make your whole house smell like jasmine! Some dishes, especially desserts, call for glutinous rice, also called sticky or sweet rice.

Rice flour and glutinous rice flour

I mostly use Thai rice flour, which is sold in plastic 1-pound bags at Asian markets. Due to different processing methods, rice flour from Thailand is much finer than American brands like Bob's Red Mill. As a result, each absorbs liquid differently, so the two aren't easily interchangeable.

Salt

I use Diamond Crystal kosher salt in all my cooking. It has less sodium per volume than other brands of kosher salt, so if the recipe calls for kosher salt and you use another brand, halve the amount, then adjust to taste from there.

Shredded coconut

I much prefer freshly shredded coconuts, because the flavor is so, so much better than anything store-bought (see Fresh Coconuts Are the Best, page 229). The next best option is to check the produce section of an Asian market for bags of shredded coconut; if those are unavailable, use frozen shredded coconut. This won't be as vibrant as grating the coconut yourself, but it'll be more flavorful and fresher than the dried shredded coconut in the baking supplies aisle of the supermarket.

Shrimp paste

Made of fermented shrimp and salt, shrimp paste can vary in texture, flavor, and saltiness depending on where it's produced. For my recipes, use a Thai brand of shrimp paste and review the label to ensure that it contains just shrimp, salt, and sugar. If in doubt, look for the Twin Chicken brand, in a pink container, which lists the percentage of each ingredient: Shrimp should constitute at least 95% of the paste, with the remaining split between salt and sugar. Before using, remove the top layer of wax. A little goes a long way, so buy the smallest tub and it'll keep practically forever in the fridge.

Thai seasoning soy sauce

The soy sauce I use the most is a seasoned soy sauce from Thailand called Golden Mountain Seasoning Sauce. It provides good soy flavor and has some sweetness, thanks to the addition of sugar. It's widely available at Asian markets.

PRODUCE

Banana leaves

Banana leaves aren't edible, but they can be shaped into bowls, used as plates, or spread on a table for a pretty presentation. Find fresh banana leaves at markets that serve Asian and Latin American communities. Frozen leaves also work. Wipe both sides of the leaves with a damp towel before using.

Fingerroot

Fingerroot is a rhizome related to ginger and usually found frozen (and sometimes labeled under its Thai name, kra chai) at Southeast Asian and some Asian markets, or pickled in jars at both markets (the jars sometimes are labeled "rhizome in brine" or "pickled rhizome"). Unless otherwise specified, use frozen fingerroot. Whether frozen or pickled, chop it into small pieces so it'll be easier to pound in a mortar or pulse in the food processor.

Galangal

Galangal is a rhizome with a fragrance reminiscent of ginseng. Found in Southeast Asian markets, it tastes of ginger and citrus layered with the sharpness of mild horseradish. Choose firm pieces without any bruising. Avoid pieces that are slimy or dark where they've been cut, as they've likely been sitting in the bin too long.

    When working with galangal, be careful, as it is very tough and fibrous and can have an oddball shape difficult to keep stable on the cutting board. To prepare, trim away any bruised spots, then use a very sharp knife or a cleaver to peel and smash it, or slice it into thin coins or strips (no need to peel otherwise).

    There is no great substitute for galangal. I prefer to omit it than to swap it out for its step-cousin, ginger. The two have completely different flavors, so if you swap ginger for galangal, the dish will not be the same!

Garlic

I spent a lot of my childhood on the floor of our kitchen, peeling garlic for my mom. I quickly learned the quickest, easiest way to peel several cloves is to trim the tip off the bulbs, peel the outer layers of papery skin to separate the cloves, then smash them with the side of a cleaver or another heavy knife to loosen their skins.

Ginger

Ginger should be firm and aromatic, and its peel smooth without any bruising. I prefer larger pieces of ginger, as they're easier to prep than small, individual segments.

Green onions

Use the whole stalk (green and white parts) unless otherwise specified.

Green mangoes and papayas

Unripe mangoes and papayas are delicious in salads and as crunchy sides to dips. To shred, use a serrated T-peeler specifically designed for that very purpose. I use one by the Kiwi brand, and many others can be found in Asian markets or online. If you don't have the tool, slice the fruit into thin slabs or planks, then stack and slice them into thin matchsticks.

Lemongrass

To prepare lemongrass, remove its tough outer layers, then trim about ½ inch from the base. From here, it can be smashed with a cleaver, mallet, or pestle, or thinly sliced into rings by cutting up the stalk about 4 inches, or until the stalk becomes noticeably woodier and tougher. Discard the unsliced portion of the lemongrass, or steep it in hot water to make some tea.

THE KHMER KITCHEN

To make Khmer food, start here! These are the fundamentals of Khmer cooking. Some recipes, like kroeung,[1] are basic building blocks for other dishes. Some are dressings and garnishes that I use time and time again to finish a dish. Some are condiments, because Khmers are big on condiments, which is another way of saying we're big on customizing our dishes. And still some others, like pickles and rice, are the dishes that make a meal complete.

Many of these can be made in large quantities and frozen for use later, which I encourage you to do so you'll always have them when you need them.

Playlist

"Mou Pei Na,"
SINN SISAMOUTH

"Give Me One Kiss,"
DARA CHOM CHAN

"Don't Speak,"
PEN RAN

"Jombang Jet,"
PEN RAN

"Flowers in the Pond,"
ROS SEREYSOTHEA

---

[1] Page 27.

MASTER KROEUNG

Makes 2 cups

It's all about the kroeung! *Kroeung* translates to "ingredients," but that literal translation doesn't quite capture the significance of kroeung in Khmer cooking. A fragrant paste made by smashing together lemongrass, galangal, turmeric, garlic, shallots, and lime leaves, kroeung traces back to Angkorian times. It's the foundation for Khmer cooking and the base for the vast majority of Khmer dishes not influenced by China, India, or France. In short, you simply cannot talk about or cook Khmer food without it.

Every Khmer cook has their own version of kroeung; it is that important and that personal. This recipe is mine. I also use this recipe as the base for a few different variations, which follow this master recipe. Because I use kroeung so often, and it is a bit of a project to make, I like to make a big batch of it, then freeze what I won't use right away. Then it's RTG (ready to go!) whenever I need it. Invite a friend over and make it a kroeung party!

8 large or 12 small lemongrass stalks, trimmed (see page 23) and thinly sliced (2 cups)

3-inch piece galangal, thinly sliced (½ cup) (see page 22)

½ cup chopped garlic (15 to 25 cloves, 1 to 2 heads garlic)

1 small shallot, chopped (¼ cup)

10 makrut lime leaves, center veins removed, thinly sliced

Place the lemongrass in a mortar and smash it into a paste with the pestle (see Note). Add the galangal and smash it with the lemongrass until it has the consistency of a paste. Add the garlic and smash, then repeat with the shallot. Finally, add the lime leaves a little bit at a time, smashing as you go. The ingredients should barely come together into a paste.

To finish, stir everything together. Doesn't it smell lovely? It's ready to use. To store, refrigerate the kroeung in an airtight container for up to 3 days. To freeze, portion the kroeung into ½-cup containers or resealable bags. It'll keep for up to 2 months.

Note: The key to great kroeung is in the smashing of the ingredients. Crushing each ingredient in the mortar will break down the fibers and release aromatic oils and flavors in a way that tearing and shredding will not. That said, if you don't have a mortar and pestle, a food processor is the next best thing: Place all the ingredients in the bowl of the processor and pulse several times until it turns into a paste. If the ingredients aren't combining, add a little bit of grapeseed or another neutral oil to help things move along.

THE HOLY DUO: PRAHOK + KROEUNG

Kroeung and prahok (see page 19) are foundational to our dishes. Often, they're found in combination with coconut milk, which plays a supporting, but no less important, role. They've been used for centuries, and many of our oldest recorded recipes contain all three of these ingredients. If you don't have prahok, kroeung, or coconut milk when a recipe calls for it, I highly suggest cooking another dish. They are so important in every dish where they're used that they are irreplaceable.

MASTER KROEUNG, CONTINUED

Variations

YELLOW KROEUNG

Turmeric is added to the kroeung, turning it a beautiful yellow.

To make it: Peel and thinly slice a 3-inch piece (¾ ounce) of turmeric (wear gloves, so the turmeric won't stain your hands orange; alternatively, use 1 teaspoon turmeric powder). Add it to the mortar and pestle after smashing the lemongrass. Crush them together into a paste. Then proceed with the rest of the recipe to make the kroeung.

Use it in: Somlaw Machoo Kroeung / Tamarind Kroeung Soup (page 85), Nom Pachok Somlar Khmer / Rice Vermicelli with Fish Chowder (page 129), Sach Mu-anh Boungk / Stuffed Chicken Wings (page 164), Cha Kroeung / Stir-Fried Kroeung (page 183), Prahok Ktiss / Prahok Coconut Pork Dip (page 195).

RED KROEUNG

Chile paste and shrimp paste add depth, funk, warmth, and a beautiful red hue to the kroeung.

To make it: Before pounding the lemongrass, add ¼ cup Bok Mtes / Chile Paste (page 31) and 2 tablespoons shrimp paste to the mortar. Then smash away!

Use it in: Curi Saraman / Saraman Curry (page 137).

GREEN KROEUNG

If you can find lemongrass leaves from a local farmer or market, use them for kroeung! The leaves, plus some fingerroot, give the kroeung a pronounced lemongrass flavor and a vibrant green color. Use leftover leaves to make tea. Just steep them in a cup of hot water for several minutes.

To make it: If the lemongrass leaves are long, cut them into smaller pieces. Add 1 cup leaves to the mortar with the lemongrass. Smash them together, then add ¼ cup chopped fingerroot and a 3-inch (¾ ounce) piece of peeled and thinly sliced turmeric (or 1 teaspoon turmeric powder) and smash that, too. Add the galangal and continue with the rest of the recipe.

Use it in: Nom Pachok Somlar Khmer / Rice Vermicelli with Fish Chowder (page 129), Somlaw Koko / Stirring Soup (page 133).

ដឹកអម្ពិល
TUK AMPIL
TAMARIND WATER

Makes 2½ cups

Water flavored with tamarind is a great way to add a little bit of sourness and tartness to a dish. We use it a lot in Khmer cooking, like in Somlaw Machoo Kroeung / Tamarind Kroeung Soup (page 85) and Cha Krom Tuk Ampil / Stir-Fried Mussels in Tamarind Sauce (page 184). To make it, you'll need tamarind pulp, which is usually sold in blocks at Asian markets.

4 ounces seedless tamarind pulp

3 cups water

Combine the tamarind pulp and water in a medium pot over medium heat. Bring to a boil, then use a fork or a whisk to completely break up the pulp. Turn off the heat, cover, and let it sit for 20 to 30 minutes so the pulp softens even more.

Place the pulp in a fine-mesh strainer set over a small bowl. Use the back of a spoon to firmly press down on the pulp, straining the liquid into the bowl. Be sure to scrape and press any pulp clinging to the sides of the strainer to extract the liquid. Discard the solids. Use the water right away, or cool and pour it into an airtight container and refrigerate for up to 2 weeks. Alternatively, pour the water into ice-cube trays, then store the cubes in an airtight resealable bag or container in the freezer for up to 1 month.

ម្ទេសបុក

BOK MTES
CHILE PASTE

Makes a little over 1 cup

Chile paste is one of the first things I learned to make. It was my job to open up the dried chiles, pick out their seeds, then soak the chiles in warm water. Once the chiles were rehydrated, my mom would blend them with a bit of oil to make a paste. The paste itself offers a little warmth but not much spice; it's used more often for color, to give certain dishes an attractive bright reddish hue. I use it, for example, in my Kuy Teav Kho Ko / Caramelized Beef Stew (page 139) and Prahok Ktiss / Prahok Coconut Pork Dip (page 195). If you can't find the dried California chiles (also called Anaheim chiles) I use here, any other large dried chile like a chipotle or ancho chile will do, though the color of the paste may vary depending on which chile you choose.

3 ounces dried California chiles, seeds removed

1½ teaspoons grapeseed or other neutral oil

Place the chiles in a small pot, completely cover with water, and turn the heat to low. When the chiles soften, about 5 minutes, transfer them, along with ½ cup water from the pot, to a blender. Add the oil to the blender and blend until smooth. It's now ready to use. To store, cool the paste, place it in an airtight container, and refrigerate for up to 1 week. To freeze, portion the cooled paste into small resealable frozen food bags and freeze for up to 1 month.

ដីកស៊ុបមាន់
SOMLAW MU-ANH
CHICKEN BROTH

Makes 3½ quarts

This is a lovely, all-purpose chicken broth flavored with charred onion, fish sauce, ginger, garlic, and cilantro stems. It's a great way to use up any stems that you otherwise would throw out! This is so good all on its own or with a little bit of Khtoem Jien / Crispy Garlic Oil (page 42), especially when you're sick. You also can use the broth for any recipe that uses chicken stock, like in Mee Ka-tung / Stir-Fried Egg Noodles with Gravy (page 94). The chicken from the broth is delicious with steamed rice, or save it for my Ngyom Sach Mu-anh / Chicken Cabbage Salad (page 203), Ngyom Trayong Jenk / Banana Blossom Salad (page 200), or any recipe that calls for poached chicken.

1 yellow onion, trimmed

4 quarts water

6 garlic cloves, smashed

1-inch piece ginger, peeled and smashed

Kosher salt

1 tablespoon + 2 teaspoons fish sauce

1 (4- to 5-pound) whole chicken

1 bunch cilantro, stems only

Khtoem Jien / Crispy Garlic Oil (page 42; optional)

If you have a gas stovetop, turn the heat to medium and place the onion right on the burner grate above the flame. Alternatively, either char the onion in a medium cast-iron skillet over high heat for 5 to 8 minutes, using tongs to turn it often so it chars evenly, or broil the onion on a sheet pan on high, rotating it every few minutes until it's evenly charred on all sides, about 5 minutes.

Place the charred onion in an 8-quart stockpot. Add the water, garlic, ginger, 1 tablespoon plus 2 teaspoons of salt, and the fish sauce. Stir, then add the chicken, making sure it's fully submerged.

Bring the water to a boil, then immediately reduce to low, cover, and simmer for about 40 minutes, occasionally skimming and discarding any foam or scum that rises to the top.

After 40 minutes, turn off the heat. Carefully taste the liquid and add a little more salt if you'd like. Add the cilantro stems and steep for 5 minutes, then remove and discard (otherwise, they'll become slimy and affect the color of the broth). Both the broth—with a bit of garlic oil right on top if you'd like—and the chicken are ready to enjoy immediately. If you're not using one or both right away, store the chicken and broth in separate containers.

To store the chicken: Place the whole chicken breast side down in a large container. (If you don't have a big enough container, you can break down the chicken and store the pieces separately.) Add just enough broth to cover the breast to keep it from drying out. Cool, then cover and refrigerate for up to 3 days.

To store the broth: Strain and pour the broth into a jar or other airtight container, cool completely, then cover. The broth can be refrigerated for up to 3 days, or frozen for up to 2 months.

TUK TREY MTES
FISH SAUCE + CHILE

Makes ½ cup / Serves 4

This is a condiment you always see on tables in Khmer households and restaurants because it goes with everything, from stir-fries to soups, and it's an easy way for everyone to customize their meal with a bit of umami and heat. It's also very quick and easy to make; you can even stir it together on the fly, right before you're about to sit down. Make only as much as you need, as leftovers won't store. You can prepare it in advance, though; combine just the fish sauce and chiles in an airtight container and refrigerate it for up to 2 days. Right before serving, add the lime juice.

½ cup fish sauce

3 to 4 bird's eye chiles, chopped

Wedge of lime

Combine the fish sauce and chiles (add more chiles if you like things spicier) in a small bowl and stir. Right before serving, squeeze in the lime. Spoon about 2 tablespoons per person into small saucers and serve alongside the meal.

ខ្ទឹមជ្រក់ម្ទេស
CHROUK MTES KHTOEM
PICKLED GARLIC CHILE

Makes 1¼ cups

Like Tuk Trey Mtes / Fish Sauce + Chile (page 33), this pickled garlic chile is a very common condiment on the table. There are many variations; some recipes use one type of chile, some call for coarsely chopped chiles or for leaving them whole, some are distinctly sweet and spicy. I personally like the flavor from combining three different chiles (if you can't find Fresno chiles, you can use jalapeños instead). I also like to blend the chiles so the paste is a little bit smoother and its flavors balance with the umami from the fish sauce. That said, it's still spicy, so for a milder paste, use fewer chiles. The paste can be treated like a universal hot sauce; it's especially good with Poung Mu-anh Jien / Crispy Fried Eggs (page 45), any noodle soup, Cha Troup / Charred Eggplants with Pork + Shrimp (page 206), ribs (see page 101), or roast chicken (see page 153).

4 to 6 ounces bird's eye, serrano, and Fresno chiles, stemmed

½ cup garlic cloves (12 to 18 cloves, or a little more than 1 garlic bulb)

½ cup unsweetened rice vinegar

¼ cup water

¼ cup fish sauce

½ tablespoon sugar

Bring a small pot of water to a boil. Add the chiles (the more chiles, the spicier this will be!) and boil for 5 minutes (this cuts down their heat). Drain and set aside to cool completely.

Rinse out the pot, then add the cooled chiles, garlic, rice vinegar, water, fish sauce, and sugar. Bring to a boil, stir until the sugar dissolves, then turn off the heat. Cool completely.

Pour 2 tablespoons of the cooled cooking liquid into the bowl of a food processor, then add the chiles and garlic. Pulse until it's at your desired consistency: Fewer pulses will give you a chunkier sauce; more pulses, a smoother one. If you'd like it thinner, add a little more cooking liquid. I usually pulse mine about thirty times, or until it's finely minced but still has some texture.

It's ready to use right away. It'll be pretty spicy but will mellow out in a day or two. Store the mixture in a jar or other airtight container and refrigerate for up to 3 months.

ក្រូចឆ្មារ + អំបិល + ម្រេចជ្រលក់ម្រេច
TUK KRAUCH CHHMA + AMBEL + MRECH
LIME + SALT + PEPPER SAUCE

Makes about ½ cup

There are just three ingredients in this dipping sauce, but it's full of brightness and flavor. It goes great with dishes like Loc Lak / Stir-Fried Beef Cubes (page 223), Jien BawnKwang / Crispy Shrimp Fritters (page 121), or anything fried. Kampot peppercorns really shine here, but you can use any other black peppercorns you have on hand. This recipe easily doubles or triples, so make as much as you need to serve your party. But since it won't keep, make only as much as you think you'll use.

½ cup fresh lime juice (4 to 5 limes)

2½ teaspoons kosher salt, plus more as needed

1 teaspoon freshly ground black pepper (preferably Kampot peppercorns; see page 146), plus more as needed

Pour the lime juice into a small bowl. Add the salt and pepper, give it a good stir, then taste and adjust the salt and pepper to your liking. Serve immediately.

TUK TREY PIAM
FISH SAUCE DRESSING

Makes about 1½ cups

A bit tangy, a bit sweet, and a bit spicy, this dressing is in my fridge at all times. It is my go-to dressing for most of the salads I make, including Ngyom Sach Mu-anh / Chicken Cabbage Salad (page 203) and Ngyom Mee Sou / Potluck Glass Noodle Salad (page 127). It's also a great base for other sauces and marinades, such as Trey Jien Ban Pouh / Crispy Fish with Simmered Summer Tomatoes (page 219), or use it as a dipping sauce for crispy egg rolls (page 196). Note that it does need to be refrigerated for at least 30 minutes before using so the flavors can meld together.

½ cup unsweetened rice vinegar

⅓ cup sugar

3 tablespoons water

⅓ cup fresh lime juice (3 to 4 limes)

⅔ cup fish sauce

5 garlic cloves or Chrouk Khtoem / Pickled Garlic (page 41), minced

1 shallot, minced

2 bird's eye or Fresno chiles, chopped

Combine the rice vinegar, sugar, and water in a medium bowl and stir until the sugar dissolves. Add the lime juice, stir, and let it sit for 10 minutes.

Stir in the fish sauce, garlic, shallot, and chiles. Refrigerate, covered, for 30 minutes before using. Store leftovers in an airtight container and refrigerate for up to 3 days.

CHROUK
PICKLES

Makes 4 quarts

This pickle of papaya and carrots goes with everything, but it's especially good with Sach Ko Ang / Kroeung Beef Skewers (page 66) and other grilled meat, chicken wings (see pages 65 and 164), and Prahut Trey / Lemongrass Fish Cakes (page 110). You'll need only a portion of the papaya to make this pickle, so save the rest to make a salad like my Bok La Hong / Green Papaya Salad (page 76). To store the papaya for use later, wrap it tightly in plastic wrap or place it in an airtight container and refrigerate for up to 2 days.

1 cup sugar

½ cup rice vinegar

½ cup fish sauce

3 garlic cloves, thinly sliced

2 bird's eye or Fresno chiles, thinly sliced

1 shallot, thinly sliced

3 carrots, peeled and shredded (1½ heaping cups)

1 green papaya, shredded (4 packed cups; see page 23 for shredding tips)

1 tablespoon kosher salt

6 Persian cucumbers, or 2 English cucumbers, unpeeled, cut into 2-inch segments and quartered (2 cups)

Mix together the sugar and rice vinegar in a large bowl until the sugar dissolves, about 1 minute. Stir in the fish sauce, then add the garlic, chiles, and shallot. Set the brine aside.

Place the carrots and papaya in a large bowl. Toss and massage the salt into the carrots and papaya for 1 minute, then set aside for 5 minutes so the salt can draw out their moisture. Rinse to remove the salt. Taste a piece; if it still tastes salty, keep rinsing. Squeeze out as much water as you can.

Add the carrots, papaya, and cucumbers to the brine. Mix well. Transfer everything, including the brine, to a clean gallon-size glass jar or other nonreactive container. Cover tightly, and place on the counter overnight. The next morning, it'll be ready. To store, cover and refrigerate for up to 1 month.

CHROUK KHTOEM
PICKLED GARLIC

Makes 2 cups

It takes a month to pickle this garlic, but it's worth the wait. It's delicious in porridge (see pages 53 and 148), sliced into an omelet, or served alongside Sach Ko Ang / Kroeung Beef Skewers (page 66) or any other grilled meat. Or try substituting it for the fresh garlic in Tuk Trey Piam / Fish Sauce Dressing (page 37) or in the Kampot sauce with grilled prawns (see page 113). You can even eat it by itself! It's that good. The longer the garlic ferments, the more its flavor and umami will develop and deepen.

8 whole garlic bulbs
4 cups water
1 tablespoon kosher salt

BRINE
2½ cups water
⅓ cup + 2 tablespoons unsweetened rice vinegar
¼ cup + 1 tablespoon lightly packed light brown sugar
1½ teaspoons kosher salt

Using scissors, cut off the tip of each garlic bulb and remove the papery layers of skin just until the cloves are visible. With a good grip on the bulb, slice off the root on the bottom, but keep the bulb whole.

Stir together the water and salt in a large bowl. Submerge the garlic in the salted water and soak overnight at room temperature.

THE NEXT DAY, MAKE THE BRINE

Combine the water, rice vinegar, brown sugar, and salt in a medium pot over high heat. Boil and stir until the sugar dissolves, 4 to 5 minutes, then cool the brine completely.

Transfer the garlic to a clean jar with a lid. Discard the soaking liquid. Pour the brine over the garlic and place the lid on the jar. Leave it on the counter for about 1 month. During that time, the garlic will ferment and release gases, so every day or two, unscrew the lid just enough to release the gases (if you don't, they will build and build, and the jar may explode!). After a month, try it: If you like how it tastes, it's ready. Store it, covered, in the refrigerator. Otherwise, let the garlic continue to ferment on the counter until it tastes good to you, then refrigerate. It'll keep for up to a year.

ខ្ទឹមបំពង

KHTOEM JIEN
CRISPY GARLIC OIL

Makes 2 cups

Fried garlic is close to my heart. When I was around eight, my mom set me up on the kitchen floor with a big cleaver in my hand. Bam! I'd bring the side of the cleaver down on the cloves. That was usually enough to loosen their skins so they could be peeled. There was always a lot of garlic to peel, and when I was done, my fingers would feel like glue from the starch oozing out of the cloves. My mom then minced and fried the garlic, and I came to love its fragrance as it permeated the house. And when there was garlic being fried, there for sure was a pot of Kuy Teav Phnom Penh / Pork Noodle Soup (page 213) on the stove, too. But we'd also add it to noodle dishes like Mee Kola / Cold Noodles with Cucumber Relish + Dried Shrimp (page 175), Bor Bor / Plain Porridge (page 53), and Kuy Teav Kho Ko / Caramelized Beef Stew (page 139). You can mince the garlic with a cleaver or speed up the prep by using a food processor to pulse the cloves a few times. In either case, do make sure the garlic is evenly minced or it won't fry evenly.

Grapeseed or other neutral oil, for frying

2 cups garlic cloves (about 6 bulbs), minced (see page 22 for tips on quickly peeling garlic)

Heat 2 inches of oil in a 4-quart saucepan, wok, or other shallow pot over medium-high heat to 375°F, 5 to 8 minutes. If you don't have a thermometer, sprinkle some minced garlic into the oil: If it sizzles, the oil is ready. If not, wait another minute and try again. If the oil begins to smoke, though, it's too hot. Lower the temperature, wait a minute, and test again.

Once the oil is at the right temperature, carefully add all the garlic. Stir until the garlic no longer sticks to the bottom of the pan and the pieces are evenly spaced out and not overcrowded or clumped together (otherwise, the garlic will steam instead of fry). Fry for 5 minutes, leaving the garlic undisturbed the whole time. After 5 minutes, the garlic should be a light golden brown. If not, set the timer at 2-minute intervals and keep checking until the garlic turns light golden brown. Turn off the heat and take the pot off the burner. Leave the garlic to finish cooking in the hot oil. It will go from light to golden brown, about 5 minutes.

Cool the fried garlic completely, then transfer the garlic and its oil to a glass jar with a lid. Store, covered, at room temperature on the counter. It will keep for up to 3 months.

ឈ៊ីមក្រហមបំពង់
KHTOEM KRAHM JIEN
CRISPY SHALLOTS

Makes 2 cups

Fried shallots go on top of everything, but I love them especially on salads and curry. The oil that you fry them in is another gift: Infused with the flavor of the shallots, it can be used in dressings and any time you need cooking oil. Do your best to slice the shallots into similar-size strips; otherwise, the smaller pieces will cook faster than the bigger ones. The key to frying (and not burning) the shallots is to remove them from the frying oil *just* as their color starts to turn from purple to light golden brown. The residual heat will then finish the cooking process and will crisp them up even more. Oh, and fry the shallots in batches so you don't crowd the pan. Everything good takes time.

Grapeseed or other neutral oil, for frying

13 ounces whole shallots (about 8 small shallots), sliced into 1-millimeter strips

Kosher salt

Heat 1 inch of oil in a 4-quart or larger saucepan over medium-high heat to 375°F, about 5 minutes. If you don't have a thermometer, drop a few shallot strands into the pot. If they sizzle, then the oil is ready. If not, wait another minute and try again. If the oil begins to smoke, though, it's too hot. Lower the temperature, wait a minute, and test again.

While the oil heats, place a cooling rack on a sheet pan. Layer a few paper towels on top of the rack and set aside.

Working in batches to avoid overcrowding the pan, carefully add the shallots into the oil. Stir constantly, keeping your eye on the pot at all times: Because of their sugar content, the shallots can burn extremely quickly if you don't keep them moving.

Fry the shallots until they start to turn a light golden brown color, about 4 minutes, then use a skimmer or a strainer to transfer the shallots to the paper towel–lined rack. Sprinkle the shallots with a big pinch of salt, carefully toss, then spread them in a single layer so the paper towels soak up the excess oil. Once they've completely cooled, they're ready to use. Store leftover shallots and oil in separate airtight containers: The shallots can stay on the counter for up to 2 weeks, or up to a month in the fridge. The oil will keep, refrigerated, for up to 1 month.

ពងទាចៀន
POUNG MU-ANH JIEN
CRISPY FRIED EGGS

Serves 1

Why do I even have this recipe? Well, everyone has their favorite, nostalgic ways to make fried eggs; this one's mine. This was the first dish I cooked for myself, often after school when I didn't want to eat whatever my mom had on the stove. I ate the eggs with a little bit of soy seasoning on a bowl of jasmine rice—the best combo—and watched *Oprah*. I'm sure there's at least a handful of Khmer kids who have similar memories. I like my eggs with crispy edges, which aren't difficult to achieve, but you do need to cook the eggs in hot oil, so take care to avoid the oil splatter. In addition to rice, these eggs are great with stir-fried noodles and any other time you want a fried egg over anything.

1 tablespoon grapeseed or other neutral oil

2 eggs, preferably pasture-raised organic (see Note)

Thai seasoning soy sauce or Maggi Seasoning, for drizzling

Bai / Steamed Jasmine Rice (page 52), for serving

Note: Pastured organic eggs have larger and creamier yolks than nonpastured eggs. They're worth it when the eggs are the star, like here. And if you can afford duck eggs, even better!

Heat the oil in a medium nonstick skillet over high heat. Give it about 10 seconds, then carefully crack in the eggs. The eggs will start to bubble in the hot oil, so be careful of the oil splatter.

When you see the edges of the eggs start to crisp, about 20 seconds, flip them over to set the yolk, then turn off heat. And that's it! Drizzle some seasoning sauce all over, serve with rice, and enjoy.

ពងទាក្រឡុក
POUNG MU-ANH JIEN KA-LOK
EGG RIBBONS

Serves 2 to 4

A little fish sauce makes these egg ribbons a little savory, and they end up perfect as an extra treat to finish a lot of dishes. Use it to garnish porridge (see pages 53 and 148) or even just a simple bowl of steamed rice (see page 52).

- 4 eggs
- 1 green onion stalk, very thinly sliced
- 1 teaspoon sugar
- ½ teaspoon fish sauce
- 1 teaspoon kosher salt
- ½ teaspoon freshly ground black pepper
- 1 tablespoon grapeseed or other neutral oil

Note: You can use a smaller skillet, but to avoid making the ribbons too thick, first cook half the mixture, remove it from the pan, then cook the other half.

Crack the eggs into a medium bowl and use a fork or whisk to break up the yolks. Add the green onion, sugar, fish sauce, salt, and pepper and mix thoroughly.

Heat the oil in a large nonstick skillet over medium-high heat (see Note). When the oil begins to shimmer, pour in the eggs. Leave them undisturbed. Once they begin to set, cover the skillet with a lid to cook the top of the eggs. After about 20 seconds, turn off the heat and uncover. Transfer the whole thing to a cutting board, roll it up, and slice into ¼-inch strips. It's ready to go!

RICE IS LIFE

Nyum bai! In practice, that loosely translates to a hug, a greeting, a "Hello, have you eaten yet?" But the literal translation of the phrase is "Have you eaten rice yet?," as in "Let's catch up over a meal with rice!" And that tells you everything about the role of rice in Khmer food and culture.

For more than 2,000 years, rice has been cultivated in Cambodia. It has long had symbolic power and is considered sacred: Ceremonies celebrate the beginning and end of the rice harvesting season, and rice is offered to monks for their alms and used to honor ancestors. It's also incorporated into holidays and religious rituals. (A shaman whom my mom took me to visit once in high school had me lie on a bed of rice to ward off evil spirits—including death.) And, of course, rice has been a big part of Cambodia's economy. In fact, it was rice that was the backbone of the towering Angkor Empire that ruled over Southeast Asia between the ninth and fifteenth centuries. The Khmer Empire located its capital city of Angkor at the northern end of Tonlé Sap, the largest freshwater lake in Southeast Asia, and built a sophisticated hydraulic system that could water its vast rice fields even during the dry seasons. This was crucial: Before, farmers would harvest rice once or twice a year. With irrigation and strategic water controls, it was possible to harvest three or four times a year. This abundance of rice fueled the empire's economic and geographic power. Angkor became a vital trading post, and the empire expanded its boundaries beyond Cambodia and through modern-day Vietnam, Laos, and Thailand.

Today, rice is still a central part of Cambodia's agricultural production, and it's a staple of our diet. Planting, crossbreeding, and other cultivation techniques have been passed down from generation to generation, and there are now more than 2,000 varieties of rice indigenous to Cambodia. Jasmine rice—long, slender, sweet, and fragrant like the Malis flower—is the preferred grain; one variety in particular, called Phka Rumduol, is considered among the very best in the world.

Because of this history, I find cooking rice to be a special, special thing to do. The first time I made rice for the family, I was eight or nine years old. It was a big deal, and the pressure was on, because if I burned the rice, no one could eat until another pot was properly made. My mom gave me a quick tutorial. I'm sure I heard those instructions, but I didn't really follow them. Instead, I cooked the rice on instinct, doing what I had seen my mom do a million times: Rinse, add water, level the grains, cover the pot. Bring it to a boil, uncover, wait, put the lid back on, wait. Then wait some more. When I was done and removed the lid, the top layer of rice had a bit of a crust, and the grains underneath were plump and fluffy. It was perfect.

As it turns out, making rice was ingrained in my DNA.

Being able to make rice for my family was a real proud moment for me, one of my favorite moments of being Khmer. And now, whenever I create a dish, I always think about it in relation to the rice: How will the flavors of the dish taste with rice? How will their flavors balance? And I always think about how these grains link up and connect the past with the present. Rice is life.

THE RULES OF RICE

Rice is a must with every meal.

Rice is the star of the table. Everything else—the soups, the curries, the stir-fries, the salads—are the side dishes that support the rice.

Use your fork to fill your spoon with rice.

Soups should be spooned over rice.

A bowl of rice will balance a stir-fry.

Rice should never be drenched in sauce.

To enjoy dried fish, use your hands to pick up a little ball of rice and wrap it around the fish. That's exactly how my mom fed my brothers and me. Rinse your hands in a bowl of water on the table and repeat.

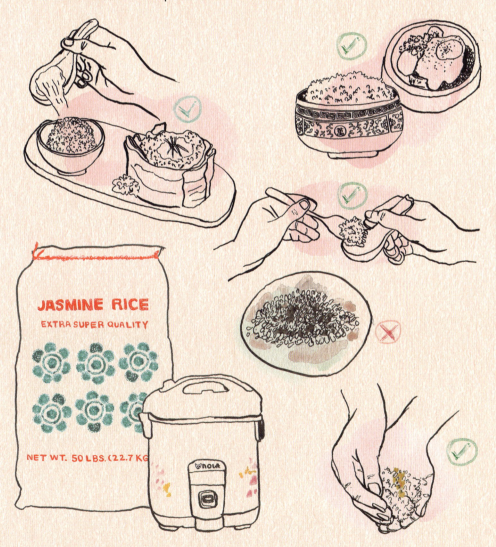

HOW TO MAKE A PERFECT POT OF WHITE JASMINE RICE

I usually cook rice in a rice cooker, because it's nearly foolproof, saves time, and if your machine has a warm setting, it can keep the rice hot and fluffy throughout the meal. But if you don't have a rice cooker, you definitely can achieve perfect rice on the stovetop (see page 52). A few general tips on making rice:

Don't forget to rinse. The rice needs to be rinsed several times to remove its excess starch. That will help keep the grains separated from each other, rather than stuck together, as they cook.

Add the right amount of water. Add too little water, and the rice will be undercooked. Add too much, and the rice will turn mushy. And since rice is a crop, the amount of water you need to add to cook it perfectly could vary slightly with each bag. Generally, though, if you use a rice cooker, follow the manufacturer's instructions for cooking the rice. On the stovetop, I use a ratio of two parts rice to three parts water. Depending on how the rice turns out, use more or less water the next time you cook it. And be extra mindful when cooking new-crop rice.

New-crop rice. When newly harvested rice lands in the market, word spreads fast! For good reason: Fresh from the harvest, the rice is aromatic, with a lovely, soft texture. Newly harvested rice has a higher moisture content than other rice, so if you add as much water to this rice as you otherwise would, it will become mushy. Instead, when cooking new-crop rice, use less water. How much less depends on how fresh the rice is and how much moisture it loses over time as you store it, so you may need to experiment a little bit and adjust as you go through the bag. Newly harvested rice is always labeled so you know what you're buying.

Rest the rice. After the rice has finished cooking, it isn't done yet. The rice needs a few minutes to rest, covered and undisturbed. During that time, the rice will absorb the moisture in the pot and finish cooking.

Fluff the rice. After it's rested, gently fluff the rice to help separate the grains, redistribute the moisture, and release any remaining steam. It's ideal to fluff the rice using a rice paddle, but a fork works, too. (If you use a rice cooker, take care not to scratch the pot with the fork.)

Rest the rice one final time. After fluffing, I like to replace the lid and let the rice rest one final time before serving.

ទាយ

BAI

STEAMED JASMINE RICE

Makes 4 cups / Serves 4 to 6

At home, we usually made rice with a rice cooker, but before I hit Start, my mom would demand that I bring the rice pot to her just so she could check that the exterior of the pot was completely dry. That's because any water there can interfere with the rice cooker's internal thermostat, resulting in undercooked or overcooked rice. So even though the rice cooker is the easiest way to make rice, it needs a little attention, too! And it's still important to rest the rice in the cooker: When the rice is done, fluff it, breathe in deeply to take in the lovely aroma of jasmine, then cover and rest for about 5 minutes before serving. If you don't have a rice cooker, you can easily cook the rice on the stovetop. Be sure to use a pot with a tight-fitting lid so the steam doesn't escape.

2 cups uncooked jasmine rice

3 cups water (a little less if using new-crop rice; see page 50)

1 cup Love

In a medium pot, rinse and drain the rice two or three times, rubbing the grains against one another each time. The water will be milky white the first time you rinse it; the last time, it should run mostly clear.

Add the water to the pot. Use the palm of your hand to even out the top of the rice so it's nice and flat.

Cover the pot and turn the heat to medium. When the water comes to a boil, remove the lid and cook the rice until the water has evaporated, about 6 minutes. Place the lid back on the pot and reduce the heat to as low as you can go. Cook for another 10 minutes, then turn off the heat. Let the rice sit, undisturbed, for 5 minutes. Then, with a rice paddle, rake the top portion of the rice and start fluffing the rest of the rice. Put the lid back on and let it sit for another 5 minutes. It's ready to serve. How did it turn out?

RICE FOR A PARTY

You can easily make more rice by remembering the ratio of rice to water and adjusting the timing slightly. For every two parts rice, add three parts water (or a little bit less if using new-crop rice; see page 50). Cook as directed for the first 6 minutes, then cover, lower the heat, and cook for 10 minutes *plus* 1 to 1½ minutes for each cup you've added beyond the original 2 cups in the recipe.

បបរ

BOR BOR
PLAIN PORRIDGE

Serves 2 to 4

Sometimes when my mom made bor bor, she would show us a small empty can of condensed milk. *This was all the rice they gave us*, she'd say. She was talking about the labor camps and the amount of rice she and others in the camp were given, and how they had to make a very, very watery porridge so that can of rice could stretch as far as it could go. *So*, she'd say as we ate, *finish your bowl, because we had less than that to feed everyone.* That memory is forever attached to bor bor; every time I eat or make it, I think of my parents and what they went through and how they survived what they survived. Oddly enough, though, I've found comfort in bor bor, too, because there are other, more nurturing memories attached to it: how my mom always had a pot going for us on cold days or when we were sick and how it never failed to soothe and nourish. To this day, I think you should get bonus points whenever you make this for someone who's not feeling well, because it's a true gift of comfort, an act of love. And while it definitely can be eaten all on its own with nothing more than egg ribbons and a little soy seasoning, it's also great as part of a meal. I like to have it with a Sa-Om Poung Mu-anh Jien / Sa-Om Omelet (page 71), Kho / Caramelized Pork Belly (page 221), Kho Trey / Caramelized Fish with Tomatoes (page 179), and Trey Prama / Pork + Salted Cod Loaf (page 120).

½ cup uncooked white jasmine rice

6 cups water

1 teaspoon kosher salt

Poung Mu-anh Jien Ka-Lok / Egg Ribbons (page 47; optional)

Chrouk Khtoem / Pickled Garlic (page 41; optional), for serving

Thai seasoning soy sauce or Maggi Seasoning, for serving

In a medium stockpot or saucepot, rinse and drain the rice several times under cold water until the water runs mostly clear.

Add the water and the salt to the pot and place it over medium heat. Using a wooden spoon, stir the rice into the water so the grains won't stick to the bottom. Once the water comes to a boil, reduce the heat to low and simmer, uncovered, until the grains expand and soften, about 1 hour. Every once in a while, stir the rice to loosen any grains stuck to the pot. Top with the egg ribbons (if using) and serve immediately with the pickled garlic (if using) and seasoning sauce on the table.

បាយក្តាំង
BAI KADANG
RICE CRACKERS

Serves 4

Often made with the rice remaining at the bottom of the pan after cooking, these rice crackers are a great way to use leftover rice. In Cambodia, you'll even see locals drying the rice outside under the sun as the first step to make bai kadang. Here you can dry out the rice in the fridge or in a food dehydrator; note that it will take at least a day to completely dry out before you can fry up the crackers. Once made, enjoy them as a snack all on their own, or serve them with a dip like Prahok Ktiss / Prahok Coconut Pork Dip (page 195), Natang / Coconut, Pork + Dried Shrimp Dip (page 117), or Kapeek Pow / Smoked Fish + Shrimp Tapenade (page 163).

3 cups leftover cooked rice

Grapeseed or other neutral oil, for frying

Place the rice on a sheet pan. Flatten and spread out the rice evenly, making sure not to separate the rice kernels. Refrigerate the rice until it's completely dried out, very hard, and crispy, 2 to 3 days. Alternatively, transfer it to a food dehydrator set on low until it's dried out, about 1 day.

When the rice is ready, in a large Dutch oven or other heavy pot, heat 2 inches of oil to 325°F. If you don't have a thermometer, break off a small piece of rice and drop it into the oil. If it sizzles and immediately floats to the top, the oil is ready. But if the oil begins to smoke, lower the temperature and wait a minute before testing again. While the oil heats, set a wire rack on a sheet pan or line a sheet pan with a few layers of paper towels. Break the rice into smaller 3 by 3-inch pieces.

When the oil is hot, drop in the rice, working in batches to avoid overcrowding the pot. Fry for about 5 minutes, flipping halfway through, or until the rice pieces puff and float. Transfer the rice to the wire rack or paper towels to drain. It's best enjoyed immediately, but it'll keep in an airtight container for up to 2 days.

PART I

STOCKTON

Dishes I grew up with that are forever connected to my hometown

ខ្ញុំមានបេះដូងស្មោះសម្រាប់អ្នក
សុំកុំខូចចិត្ត (ខូចចិត្ត)

I have a loyal heart for you
Please don't break my heart
(break my heart)

FROM ROS SEREYSOTHEA'S
"ONE GLASS OF WINE"

The Central Valley of California runs 450 miles north to south across the entire middle of the state. It's an exceptionally rich and fertile region; farmers here are responsible for more than a third of the United States' vegetables and nearly three-quarters of our fruits and nuts. If you take a road trip from San Francisco to Los Angeles, you'll drive right through it and glimpse its bounty: fields of onions waiting to be harvested, rows of green heads of cabbage and lettuce, so many nut trees.

About two hours after leaving San Francisco, you'd come across my hometown, Stockton. It's an incredibly diverse city and is home to the fifth-largest Cambodian population in America. The community began to grow significantly after 1975, when the United States authorized the admission and resettlement of tens of thousands of refugees displaced by the wars in Southeast Asia and the Khmer Rouge's rule in Cambodia. Between 1975 and 1994, the United States accepted 150,000 Cambodian refugees. The refugees were then dispersed throughout the country, in part because of logistics and resources and in part because the government believed separation would force assimilation. But that didn't quite work: Khmers found one another and began forming enclaves. In addition to Stockton, the community settled in large numbers in Long Beach in Southern California; Lowell in Massachusetts; and Seattle in Washington.

We were one of the 150,000 refugees accepted into the United States during that time. I was two years old when we were sponsored out of the refugee camp in Thailand where I was born and where my parents fled to after escaping the Khmer Rouge's charom.[1] We landed in Dallas in 1984. My parents, though, were already thinking of moving to a place called Stockton. They heard there was already a growing community of Khmers there—but that wasn't the only reason they were interested in Stockton.

They also heard that Stockton had a lot of fertile land. A lot of bright sun. Some humidity. My parents wanted to move to Stockton, in other words, because the climate was perfect for a garden.

Between 1980 and 1990, around 10,000 Cambodians settled in Stockton. When we moved there in 1984, we were surrounded by Khmer and other Southeast Asian families. We moved a few times within Stockton, but always to neighborhoods with other Khmers, eventually settling down in a faded gray duplex at the end of a cul-de-sac. My parents even reconnected with some folks they'd met in the camp. And they got their garden: No matter where we lived, my mom always managed to find room to grow a few things, like lemongrass, pumpkins, watermelons, cucumbers, chile peppers, and holy basil.

The community was established enough that grocers, like our family shop Arun Market, stocked ingredients for Cambodian cooking. That, combined with a lack of economic opportunities, led to the creation of an informal food economy in the city. There was, for instance, an incredible

[1] Forced labor camps.

food scene at Angel Cruz Park. It started with maybe three Khmer families who set up at the park and cooked up delicious snacks. It grew to include Laotian families, Hmong families, Vietnamese families, all serving some of the best street food you've ever had. Someone sold beef jerky; someone else grilled up sausages. You could never leave without picking up a few sach ko ang.[2] To this day, there are vendors at the park, some of whom have been there for decades, others who are just getting started.

There also was the psa kroum spen, a very unofficial farmers' market tucked under the freeway overpass. What my mom couldn't grow, or grow enough of, we got at the psa kroum spen. Every week, local Southeast Asian farmers assembled there to sell their fruits and vegetables; a few poultry farmers set up shop, too. We'd lug everything home, and I'd spread out on the kitchen floor and help my mom prep: smashing lemongrass, peeling garlic. My mom usually turned those market vegetables into salads, stir-fries like cha tra koun,[3] and soups like somlaw koko.[4] Of course there was rice—always there was rice. We sat on the floor of what generously would be called a living room, but honestly, it was just the carpeted space right next to where we prepped, with newspapers unfolded and tiled over to protect the carpet and for easy cleanup. We arranged everything atop the newspapers, helped ourselves, ate with our hands and rinsed them in a big bowl of water as needed. During dinner, my dad often popped in a tape he picked up from the Khmer market, and we ate to the beats of 1960s Khmer rock 'n' roll.

Of all my childhood memories, these—family dinners on the floor, Khmer rock on the stereo—were the best ones. These were the good times.

For a while, the good times weren't so overshadowed by the harder times to come. When my parents moved to Stockton, they immediately found work picking apples, onions, and cherries. From there, they took whatever jobs they could find to make ends meet, especially my mom. She spent countless sleepless hours putting zippers on pants, hemming, and sewing her way through pile after pile of clothes for ten cents apiece. My older brother and I helped, ripping hems and trimming short threads.

Right about the time I started high school, our place became *the* place for nightly card games. My mother arranged everything. Players spread out in the living room and played cards under our flickering, buzzing fluorescent lights. My mother was organized, charming, witty, funny, accommodating, hospitable, respected, trusted—the perfect host. A woman everyone knew as the Papaya Lady stopped by during these game nights to keep the players fed as hands were dealt; she had ripped out the back seats in her van so she could set up her salad-making station right there, with all the toppings displayed so you could pick what you wanted. We were on the Fried Chicken Lady's route, too. Because it wasn't just my mom who was running a game; at night, the entire neighborhood transformed into a business district, with

2 Beef skewers marinated in kroeung (page 66).
3 Stir-Fried Water Spinach (page 205).
4 Stirring Soup (page 133).

living rooms and kitchens stringing the underground economy together. Other living rooms had other games, and a kitchen nearby had some kuy teav Phnom Penh simmering on a stove, a few bucks a bowl. If you needed to see a shaman or monk, you knew which door to knock on.

Between the games and the piecework and other odd jobs, my mom was constantly working. But no matter how busy she was, she somehow always made sure there was delicious food on the table, even when she wasn't home. Every day, my brothers and I came home from school to find something going on the stove; rice warming in the rice cooker; and a dish, like pork ribs marinating in oyster sauce, fish sauce, and black pepper, in the fridge, ready for us to reheat in the oven. On the weekends, she made a big pot of kuy teav for my friends. She sewed, she hosted, she hustled, she got us to school. She lived for us.

I often wonder how my parents met, because they are complete opposites, and not in the opposites-attract sort of way. In some ways, that disconnect was symbolic of much of their experience in the States. As comforting as it was to be surrounded by other Khmers, it didn't erase their trauma. I knew something terrible happened to them in Cambodia. But they never talked about any of it. It was all Top Secret. If I asked, they didn't answer, or they murmured the question away. Or my mom would look away and cry.

Day to day, though, my mom did everything she could to make sure we survived here. We had very little money, but what we did have, she lent out to folks who needed it more. Sometimes they took off with it, but she didn't hold a grudge. *There are people that need more help*, she'd say. I like to think that she passed her good karma down to us.

Meanwhile, my father, so cool in Cambodia, the guy who fixed motorbikes at the local Japanese shop, wore bell-bottoms, and listened to Sinn Sisamouth, the King of Cambodian rock and pop music, loved to drive around town, exploring. He found wonderful food gems: which tacos to get at the flea market. Where to find the best Italian sandwich shops. The best place in Chinatown that had the best roast duck. We didn't talk much at home, but I loved tagging along with him, and those little road trips are one of the few good memories I have of him.

But unlike my mom, he never learned English. He couldn't hold on to a job for too long. While my mom ran the games at home, he escaped to gamble, too, somewhere else. Our family dinners became less and less frequent. In its place, a cold cloud settled and hung heavy over everything. Physically, he was in Stockton, but mentally and spiritually, he was stuck in Cambodia. Every night he would pray at the altar, wishing he were back home.

There wasn't a day when my parents didn't fight.

And on top of all that chaos, there was Stockton. I saw darkness swallowing the city as it stumbled into a harsh economic decline. Being in

Playlist

"Glass of Wine,"
ROS SEREYSOTHEA

"Kal Oun Rom Moneys,"
SINN SISAMOUTH

"Bong Khoch Tae Mort,"
SINN SISAMOUTH AND
HAY SOKHOM

"Shave Your Beard,"
ROS SEREYSOTHEA

"One More Month,"
ROS SEREYSOTHEA

"Cold Sky,"
ROS SEREYSOTHEA

"Kolap Khmer Akasajor,"
SINN SISAMOUTH AND
ROS SEREYSOTHEA

---

the midst of it in the 1990s was rough. The violence around the walls of our community just became part of life. So was the meth. It wasn't uncommon to wake up to news that so-and-so's son died in a drive-by, or there was (another) overdose a few doors down.

Everything felt like it was disintegrating. As kids, we had a nickname for Stockton: Stuck Town. Because it always felt like people just sort of... got stuck there. And I was feeling it. I felt stuck in Stuck Town and badly needed to escape. I dreamed of moving to San Francisco, where I visited on a school field trip once. From the big bus windows, I saw the big buildings and people going about their day. It was like a movie. I wanted this energy! I was amazed something like this existed—could exist—outside Stockton. I started collecting a shoebox full of San Francisco–related knickknacks. As soon as I was old enough, I promised myself, I'd get to San Francisco.

And as soon as I was old enough, I did. I spent a year and a half at junior college, then moved to San Francisco to finish out my college degree.

I finally did it. I unstuck myself from Stuck Town.

I was in San Francisco, living my dream. But oddly, something felt... off. There was still a void. Ironically, Stockton was on my mind. At the time, there were several great old-school Cambodian restaurants in the Bay Area, though unless you knew to specifically ask for it, many didn't use prahok at all, a crucial ingredient in Khmer cooking. I imagine they understandably feared scaring off potential customers unfamiliar with fermented fish paste.

How I longed for my mom's kuy teav, her somlaw machoo kroeung, her marinated pork ribs. I drove back home every weekend for her cooking, and in the days between I often thought of her. Away from home and in the quiet of my own thoughts, I realized I wasn't just longing for her cooking, I was also longing to know her past. I felt lost, sad, confused. And I couldn't shake the guilt of knowing that while I was exploring the city and going to underground rave parties, my family was cursed in Stockton.

College wasn't for me. I dropped out. About a week after that, a credit card came in the mail. I knew exactly what to do.

I booked a flight to Cambodia.

RECIPES FROM HOME

Even though times became tough, Stockton is forever part of me, and many of my fondest food memories are connected to my hometown: my mom's soups, noodles, salads, and crispy fish. My dad's love for all things ginger. The snacks we lined up for at Angel Cruz Park. The Fried Chicken Lady's fried chicken in a bag. This chapter is full of my versions of childhood favorites.

សាច់មាន់ចៀន
SACH MU-ANH JIEN
FRIED CHICKEN WINGS

Serves 2 to 4

In Stockton, a woman came by our apartment complex and sold fried chicken tucked into brown paper bags. Hers were the best wings, juicy with a touch of sweetness, and somehow still extra crispy even after sitting in the bag. My fried chicken here is very much inspired by hers, with an overnight brine that seasons the chicken inside out while helping the wings retain their juices during the fry. To achieve that shattering crisp, I dredge the wings in a rice flour batter. The Fried Chicken Lady always offered ketchup on the side, but I always loved pulling the chicken out of the bag and eating it with steamed rice and Chrouk / Pickles (page 38).

2 pounds chicken wings, drumettes and wingettes separated

BRINE
5 cups water
2 tablespoons fish sauce
1½ teaspoons sugar
1 teaspoon chile flakes, or 1 jalapeño, Fresno chile, or bird's eye chile, sliced
1 teaspoon kosher salt

BATTER
1 cup rice flour (preferably Bob's Red Mill)
1 teaspoon kosher salt
1 cup cold water

Grapeseed or other neutral oil, for frying
Kosher salt
Freshly ground black peppercorns (preferably Kampot peppercorns), to finish

Wash the wings with cold water and set aside.

MAKE THE BRINE

Pour the water in a container large enough to fit the chicken, then add the fish sauce, sugar, chile flakes, and salt. Mix well, then add the chicken, making sure each wing is completely submerged. Transfer the container (uncovered) to the fridge for an overnight brine.

THE NEXT DAY, MAKE THE BATTER

Whisk together the flour and salt in a large bowl; then add the cold water. Stir until it's the consistency of pancake batter. Set it aside next to your stove.

Place a wire rack on a sheet pan. In a large Dutch oven or other heavy pot over medium-low heat, warm 3 inches of oil to 375°F on a cooking thermometer, about 20 minutes. If you don't have a thermometer, drop a bit of batter into the oil. The oil should immediately bubble and sizzle around the batter. If the oil begins to smoke, though, it's too hot; lower the heat and wait a minute before testing again.

Working in batches to avoid overcrowding the pot, dip the wings in the batter and drop them carefully into the hot oil. Fry for about 4 minutes, then flip and fry until the chicken is golden brown, crispy, and cooked through (the internal temperature of the thickest part of each piece should be at least 165°F), about another 4 minutes. Transfer the chicken to the wire rack, sprinkle both sides with salt and pepper, and cool. Repeat with the remaining chicken and serve.

សាច់គោអាំង

SACH KO ANG

KROEUNG BEEF SKEWERS

Makes about 40 skewers

Sach ko ang means one thing: party time!! For some, a party might mean pizza or wings; for me, I see these grilled skewers and immediately think of a big, fun gathering. When I was a kid in Stockton, you couldn't leave the informal street food market at Angel Cruz Park without snacking on a few pairs of beef skewers. Everyone makes theirs differently; mine is marinated overnight in kroeung so you can really taste the lemongrass and galangal, and it's great with Chrouk / Pickles (page 38) on the side. This makes plenty to feed a big crowd, with any delicious leftovers stuffed into a baguette the next day.

5 pounds beef tri-tip

1 cup Master Kroeung (page 27)

¾ cup lightly packed light brown sugar

¼ cup + 1 tablespoon Shaoxing rice wine

¼ cup fish sauce

¼ cup grapeseed or other neutral oil

2 tablespoons honey

1 tablespoon kosher salt

Chrouk / Pickles (page 38), for serving

Chrouk Khtoem / Pickled Garlic (page 41), for serving (optional)

Pat dry the tri-tip and remove any silverskin or sinew. Cut the beef against the grain into ⅛-inch slices that are about 2 inches in length. Set aside.

In a large bowl, mix together the kroeung, sugar, wine, fish sauce, oil, honey, and salt until well combined. Add the beef and submerge the slices in the marinade. Cover and refrigerate overnight.

The next day, preheat your grill or broiler on high, depending on how you'd like to cook the skewers. While it preheats, pull the marinated tri-tip out of the fridge and set it on the counter to bring it to room temperature, about 1 hour. Meanwhile, soak 40 (6-inch) bamboo skewers in water.

When you're ready to cook, thread three to four pieces of beef onto each skewer (don't shake off the marinade as you do so). You can bunch them on the skewer if necessary; just be sure to leave about 2 inches at the end of each skewer so you'll have room to hold it.

To grill: Grill the skewers until nicely browned and charred, about 1 minute on each side.

To broil: Place the skewers on a sheet pan and cover with foil to prevent burning. Broil until the beef is nicely browned and you can smell the kroeung, 1 to 2 minutes, then flip and broil for another 1 to 2 minutes.

Once all the skewers are on the grill or under the broiler, discard any remaining marinade. Pile the cooked skewers on a platter and serve with pickles and pickled garlic! Wrap leftovers in foil and refrigerate for up to 2 days.

NOM POW
STEAMED PORK BUNS

Makes 8 buns, plus a few bonus mini-buns

Along with dishes like Mee Ka-tung / Stir-Fried Egg Noodles with Gravy (page 94), these steamed buns are influenced by Chinese cooking in Cambodia. Similar to many bao, nom pow are stuffed with a savory pork or chicken mixture, though honestly, I always loved eating the outer sweet bread more than the filling. In Stockton, we often bought these at the local Asian markets, but if you have the time (and a few friends and family to pitch in), it's rewarding to make these hefty ones from scratch, and you can freeze the leftovers for future snacking. You can even make the meat filling up to a day ahead to break up the work. Before starting, double-check your package of instant yeast to make sure it hasn't expired; if it has, pick up a fresh pack. Then turn on some Khmer rock 'n' roll and start kneading!

DOUGH

1¼ cups whole milk

1½ tablespoons sugar

2¼ teaspoons (1 packet) instant yeast

3¼ cups all-purpose flour, plus more for dusting

1 teaspoon baking powder

½ teaspoon kosher salt

1 tablespoon grapeseed or other neutral oil

FILLING

1 ounce dried shiitake mushrooms (¼ cup)

8 ounces ground pork or chicken

1 tablespoon oyster sauce

1 tablespoon Thai seasoning soy sauce

¼ tablespoon sugar

¼ tablespoon freshly ground black pepper

Kosher salt

8 ounces green cabbage, sliced into ½-inch strips (3 cups)

½ small yellow onion, minced (½ cup)

1 green onion stalk, sliced

1½ teaspoons minced garlic

2 eggs

2 Chinese sausage links (about 3 ounces), thinly sliced into 32 coins

MAKE THE DOUGH

In a small microwave-safe bowl, heat the milk on low for 2 minutes. Alternatively, warm the milk in a small pot on the stovetop over low heat. When the milk is about 100°F, or slightly warmer than body temperature, turn off the heat and pour the milk into a small bowl. Add the sugar and yeast, gently stir, then cover and let sit until the yeast is bubbling in the milk, 10 to 15 minutes.

To knead the dough, you can either use a stand mixer or mix it together by hand.

To use a mixer: In the bowl of a mixer, stir together the flour, baking powder, and salt.

Add the milk mixture and use a spoon or your hands to combine it with the dry ingredients. Attach the dough hook and begin kneading on the lowest speed. Add the oil and continue kneading to incorporate. Increase the speed by one notch and mix, occasionally scraping down the sides of the bowl with a rubber spatula as needed, until you don't see any more dry flour and a soft ball of dough forms, 5 to 8 minutes.

To mix by hand: In a large bowl, mix together the flour, baking powder, and salt, then add the milk. Combine the dry and wet ingredients with your hands, then drizzle the oil on top and slowly work

Note: If you have any dough left over after portioning, shape and steam a few bonus mini buns! How long they'll take to cook depends on how mini the mini buns are. But when they're done, they should be puffy and 20 percent larger than their original size.

it in as you knead the dough. When the dough forms a shaggy ball, lightly dust the counter or work surface with flour and place the dough on the counter. Continue to knead until it forms a nice soft ball, 15 to 20 minutes. Return the dough to the bowl.

Cover the bowl with a clean, damp towel or plastic wrap and leave on the counter until it doubles in size, about 50 minutes if the temperature in your kitchen is around 70°F. (If your kitchen is warmer, it'll proof faster. If it's colder, it'll take longer.)

AS THE DOUGH PROOFS, MAKE THE FILLING

Soak the mushrooms in warm water until softened, about 15 minutes. Drain, then squeeze them to remove the excess water. Mince and set aside.

As the mushrooms rehydrate, in a large bowl, combine the pork, oyster sauce, seasoning soy sauce, sugar, and pepper. Mix together well, then set aside.

Fill a medium pot with water, add a pinch of salt, and turn the heat to high. When the water comes to a boil, submerge the cabbage in the water and boil for about 2 minutes, then immediately drain and rinse. When the cabbage is cool enough to handle, squeeze out as much water as you can from it. Otherwise, the moisture in the cabbage will make the buns soggy when steamed. When the cabbage is as dry as possible, place the strips in the bowl with the pork. Add the onion, mushrooms, green onion, and garlic to the bowl, and mix everything together.

Shape the pork mixture into meatballs ¼ cup (packed) in size or 2 ounces in weight, placing each meatball on a sheet pan as you form them. Transfer the sheet pan to the fridge.

Place the eggs in a small pot and add enough water to cover. Bring the water to a boil over medium heat, then set a timer for 7 minutes. While the eggs cook, fill a large bowl with ice and water. When the timer rings, immediately transfer the eggs to the ice bath. Once the eggs are cool, peel them, then quarter them lengthwise (they should be jammy inside). Set aside.

ASSEMBLE AND STEAM THE NOM POW

When the dough has doubled in size, you're in for some fun: Poke it, watch it deflate, and then punch it down. Transfer the dough to a lightly floured counter. Portion the dough into 3-ounce pieces (see Note), or gently knead it into a log, then cut it into eight equal-size pieces. Shape the pieces into small balls, cover with a damp towel, and rest for 10 minutes.

Meanwhile, cut a sheet of wax paper into eight 3 by 3-inch squares. Stack them near the work surface. Remove the pork mixture from the fridge and place it, the eggs, and the sausage on the counter, too.

After the dough has rested, roll out each ball into a disk about 5 inches in diameter, doing your best to roll out the edges so they're thinner than the center (this will make it easier to pleat the dough). Place a meatball right in the center. Top it off with 4 sausage coins and a quartered egg.

Pull up a bit of the dough and overlap it with an adjacent piece of dough to form a pleat. Continue pulling and pleating around the meatball, then gather all the pleats together at the top and twist to close the bun. Place the bun on a square of wax paper and repeat with the remaining dough.

Fill a pot fitted with a steamer basket halfway with water (make sure the bottom of the basket does not touch the water). Bring the water to a simmer over medium-low heat. Working in batches to avoid overcrowding, place the buns about 1½ inches apart in the basket, cover, and steam until they puff up and are 20 percent larger than their original size, 15 minutes. Cool a few minutes, then serve. But be careful: The meat will still be hot!

To freeze, cool the buns completely, then wrap them tightly in plastic wrap and store in the freezer for up to 2 weeks. To reheat, microwave on high for 1 minute, or resteam for 5 minutes.

ពងជាស្អុម
SA-OM POUNG MU-ANH JIEN
SA-OM OMELET

Serves 2 to 4

One of my favorite ways to enjoy sa-om is one of the simplest ways to prepare it: folded into beaten eggs and cooked into an omelet. If you're not familiar with it, sa-om is a shrub that grows in abundance throughout Southeast Asia, all year long. Because of its accessibility and versatility, you'll find it used everywhere in Cambodia, from homes to roadside stalls. Sa-om has a uniquely pungent—I'd say fishy—smell when raw; once cooked, that smell disappears and it takes on a nutty, complex bitterness with a chewy, creamy, almost meaty texture unusual for an herb. If you're fortunate to know local farmers who grow Southeast Asian herbs, there's a good chance they'll have sa-om. Otherwise, find it fresh or frozen (usually in 4-ounce packages) at Southeast Asian markets, where it also may be labeled "cha-om," "climbing wattle," "stinky leaf," or "acacia leaf." Eat this with rice or porridge any time of the day for a meal, or split it between friends as part of a spread of dishes.

- 2 cups fresh sa-om, or 2 ounces frozen
- 4 eggs
- 1 teaspoon fish sauce
- 1 teaspoon sugar
- ½ teaspoon kosher salt
- 3 tablespoons grapeseed or other neutral oil

Note: You can use a smaller pan if that's what you have. Cook the eggs in two batches to make two thin omelets rather than one thick one.

For fresh sa-om, gently pull off a stem from the main stalk and hold it by its tip. With your other hand, run your fingers down the stem to strip the leaves, being careful to avoid the thorns. Repeat with additional stems until you have 1 cup of leaves. Alternatively, pinch the leaves off the stem until you have 1 cup. Wash the leaves and pat them dry. If using frozen, rinse the sa-om and dry well. Remove any thick fibrous stems.

In a large bowl, beat the eggs, then add the fish sauce, sugar, and salt. Mix well. Gently fold the sa-om into the eggs until well incorporated.

Place a 10- or 12-inch nonstick frying pan over medium heat and add the oil (see Note). Warm the oil a bit, 20 to 30 seconds, then pour in the egg mixture. Swirl the pan around so the eggs completely coat the surface. Cook the eggs, undisturbed, until the bottom is set and the edges are golden brown, about 1 minute. Then, using a spatula, flip the egg. If it breaks, that's okay! Cook just until this side sets, 15 to 20 seconds, then slide it onto a large plate or platter and serve.

TUK KROEUNG

TINNED MACKEREL WITH PRAHOK

Serves 4

The *kroeung* in this dish's name refers not to the spice paste (see page 27) but to its literal translation as "ingredients." And *tuk* means "water," so the dish's name essentially means a bunch of ingredients in water—which is what this is! The specific ingredients are a protein-packed combination of prahok, fish, fish sauce, and chiles. Eaten with raw vegetables and rice, it's all portable, so you can imagine a rice farmer bundling everything up and taking it with her for a quick lunch in the fields. My mom made tuk kroeung a lot, although it would often disappear before any of us had very much of it. I think she made it for herself when she dearly missed classic Khmer flavors. She made it even more often once she started using tinned fish, which is much faster and more convenient than breaking down and cooking a whole fish the way it's commonly done in Cambodia. I've adopted the use of tinned fish, too, so this version of tuk kroeung is a little more Khmer American than Khmer.

2 tablespoons prahok

4 garlic cloves

2 shallots

2 bird's eye chiles

2 (4-ounce) tins mackerel, packed in oil or water, drained

1 cup water

1½ teaspoons sugar

1½ teaspoons fish sauce

¼ teaspoon kosher salt

2 limes, juiced

4 small wedges of cabbage, for serving

1 to 2 cucumbers, unpeeled, sliced, for serving

Your choice of any other sliced seasonal veggies, for serving

Bai / Steamed Jasmine Rice (page 52), for serving

Place the prahok on a small piece of aluminum foil and wrap it up like a package. Place it, along with the garlic, shallots, and chiles, in a medium cast-iron skillet over medium-high heat. Cook the prahok until it's aromatic, about 4 minutes, making sure to char the garlic, shallots, and chiles, stirring frequently so they char evenly on all sides. Remove the prahok and set it aside. Continue to stir the garlic, shallots, and chiles until they're evenly charred on all sides, a few minutes longer.

Transfer the garlic, shallots, and chiles to a mortar and use a pestle to pound them together into a paste. Add the drained mackerel to the mortar. Pound a few times until the paste becomes chunky, then place everything in a medium bowl. Set aside.

In a small pot, bring the water to a boil. Unwrap the prahok and add it to the water, breaking it up as you go. Add the sugar, fish sauce, and salt. Bring to a boil once more, then pour it over the mackerel. Stir until the fish is submerged in the water. Add the lime juice, give it all another stir, and now it's ready to serve with the crunchy vegetables and rice alongside.

ដីកប្រហុក

TUK PRAHOK

PRAHOK DIPPING SAUCE WITH SEARED RIB EYE

Serves 2 to 4

My dad loved this steak dish. Actually, we all loved it, and we ate it a lot. That's one reason I get so excited about it; the other is because it's such a great way to showcase the versatility of prahok and the range of Khmer food. We do love our curries and noodles . . . and we also love a good steak with a great sauce! The sauce has many points of flavor: Prahok that's been cooked briefly to deepen its complexity and umami. Charred garlic, shallot, and chiles to bring in some smokiness. Aromatic lemongrass, makrut lime leaves, galangal, lime juice, plus a shower of fresh herbs, for brightness. There are slivers of Thai eggplant, too, that absorb the sauce and go well with the steak. I use rib eye, but you can use a New York strip, too. Once you dig in, everything around you will disappear, the world will suddenly go silent, and you won't be able to pay attention to anything else. It's that good!

14 ounces rib eye steak

Grapeseed or other neutral oil

Kosher salt

Crushed black peppercorns (preferably Kampot peppercorns)

PRAHOK SAUCE

3 tablespoons prahok

4 garlic cloves

2 bird's eye chiles

1 small shallot

3 Thai eggplants, cut into ¼-inch matchsticks

3 makrut lime leaves, center veins removed, thinly sliced

1½-inch piece galangal, cut into matchsticks (¼ cup) (see page 22)

2 lemongrass stalks, trimmed (see page 23) and thinly sliced (¼ cup)

1 cup water

1 tablespoon sugar

1 teaspoon kosher salt

3 tablespoons fresh lime juice

1 cup packed mix of thinly sliced Thai basil, cilantro, and mint

2 tablespoons unsalted butter

Preheat the oven to 375°F.

Pat the steak dry, then lightly coat it with oil. Generously season both sides of the steak with salt and peppercorns. Set aside.

MAKE THE PRAHOK SAUCE

Place the prahok on a small sheet of aluminum foil. Wrap it up like a packet and place it on a sheet pan. Bake for 10 minutes.

Place a medium or large cast-iron skillet over medium-high heat. Add the garlic, chiles, and shallot and turn frequently until all sides are nice and charred, about 10 minutes. Remove them from the skillet, mince all three, then place them in a medium bowl. Add the eggplants, lime leaves, galangal, and lemongrass.

In a small pot or saucepan, bring the water to a boil. Break up the prahok with a spoon and add it to the water, then add the sugar and salt. Stir until the sugar melts, then strain the liquid over the bowl with the eggplants. Discard the solids from the strainer.

PRAHOK DIPPING SAUCE WITH SEARED RIB EYE, CONTINUED

Add the lime juice a little bit at a time until it tastes good to you. Lastly, add the herbs and stir. Let this sit while cooking the steak.

Wipe the skillet clean and place it over medium-high heat. Heat for about 1 minute, then add the steak and sear until it develops a crust and is well browned, 2 to 3 minutes if you like your steaks cooked medium-rare. Flip and repeat on the other side, another 2 to 3 minutes for medium-rare.

Pull the pan off the burner, lower the heat to medium, and wait for 1 minute. Place the pan back over the heat and add the butter. Once it melts, tilt the pan toward you and, using a spoon, baste the steak with the butter about eight times.

Transfer the steak to a cooling rack and let it rest for 5 minutes. Then place the steak on a cutting board, slice it against the grain into thick strips, and place on a serving platter. If you'd like, pour what's left of the pan's butter and steak juices over the eggplants and stir.

Dress the steak with the sauce, or serve the sauce on the side. OMG, bomb! Store leftover steak and sauce, if any, in an airtight container and refrigerate for up to 2 days.

ប៉ុកល្ហុង
BOK LA HONG
GREEN PAPAYA SALAD

Serves 4 to 6

Grab your tissues, because this salad is spicy! And it's so good it might make you cry. This salad takes me back to the Papaya Lady in Stockton. Her van was basically a salad bar; my brothers and I would point to various ingredients—including a few extra chiles, because we constantly dared each other to eat the spiciest salad possible—and she'd pound it all together and pack it up in a resealable bag to take home. Take a cue from the Papaya Lady and use a mortar and pestle if you can; smashing the papaya is the best way to break it down and combine it with the other ingredients. If you are serving just the salad, a wedge of cabbage alongside will help tame the spice and cool down the mouth as you eat it. The cabbage isn't necessary if you serve the salad with other dishes; I especially like bok la hong with dishes that benefit from its acidity, like Sach Ko Ang / Kroeung Beef Skewers (page 66) and other grilled meats, or fried foods like Sach Mu-anh Jien / Fried Chicken Wings (page 65).

- 5 garlic cloves
- 6 to 8 bird's eye chiles, depending on your preferred spice level
- 2 teaspoons shrimp paste
- 2½ cups lightly packed shredded green papaya (from 1 small papaya; see page 23 for shredding tips)
- 2 limes, juiced
- 2 teaspoons palm sugar or granulated sugar
- 1 teaspoon fish sauce
- 8 cherry tomatoes, halved
- 2 tablespoons crushed salted peanuts, toasted (optional)
- Wedge of cabbage (optional)

You can make the salad with a mortar and pestle, or in a medium bowl.

To make the salad with a mortar and pestle: Place the garlic and chiles in the mortar and use the pestle to smash them together into a paste. Add the shrimp paste and smash several times to break up the paste and combine it with the garlic and chiles. Once it's smooth, add half of the papaya and smash it for about 40 seconds. Use a spoon to scrape any bits of papaya that may have climbed up the sides of the mortar. Repeat with the remaining papaya.

Add the lime juice, sugar, and fish sauce. Smash everything together for about another 20 seconds, then give it all one final mix. Taste and adjust the seasoning if necessary. Throw in the tomatoes and toss gently.

To make the salad in a bowl: With your knife, smash the garlic cloves and mince the chiles. Place them in a large bowl and add the shrimp paste, lime juice, sugar, and fish sauce. Whisk them together, being sure to break up the shrimp paste. Once smooth, add the papaya. Use your hands to massage the papaya with the rest of the ingredients until the papaya is soft, 1 to 2 minutes. Add the tomatoes and give it a good toss.

Transfer the salad to a serving bowl to share. Garnish with the peanuts (if using). Serve it along with other dishes you've prepared for the meal, or if it's the only dish on the table, serve it with a wedge of cabbage on the side.

ភ្លាសាច់គោ

PLEA SACH KO
BEEF CARPACCIO SALAD

Serves 4 to 6

My dad loved making this salad. He loved beef and he loved anything that goes well with beer, and plea sach ko checks both those boxes. It's easy to make, too: I use cabbage, Thai basil, and mint, but feel free to use any other lettuce or leafy green and experiment with the herbs. The beef is "cooked" just in lime juice but otherwise served raw (for that reason, use the highest-quality meat you can afford). Everything is tossed in a quick prahok dressing that adds deep umami to the salad. That combination of refreshing and savory makes this a very satisfying drinking snack, but if you want to turn this salad into a meal, serve it with some rice.

- 8 ounces sirloin steak, thinly sliced
- 2 limes
- 3½-inch piece galangal, minced (3 tablespoons) (see page 22)
- 4 garlic cloves
- 1 bird's eye chile
- ½ cup water
- 1 tablespoon prahok
- 1½ teaspoons fish sauce
- 1½ teaspoons sugar
- ½ teaspoon kosher salt
- 2 radishes, thinly sliced
- 2 lemongrass stalks, trimmed (see page 23) and thinly sliced (about ½ cup)
- 2½ ounces green cabbage, thinly shredded (1 cup)
- 1 small shallot, thinly sliced (¼ cup)
- 1 cup Thai basil or mint leaves, or a combination of both
- 2 tablespoons crushed salted peanuts, toasted

Place the steak in a large bowl and add the juice of 1 lime. Massage the juice lightly into the steak for about 15 seconds, then cover and place the bowl in the fridge.

Use a mortar and pestle to pound the galangal into a paste. Remove the beef from the fridge and add the galangal. Gently coat the beef with the galangal, cover, and return the bowl to the fridge.

In the same mortar, add the garlic and chile. Smash them together to form a paste, then set aside.

In a small saucepan over high heat, bring the water, prahok, fish sauce, sugar, and salt to a boil, then lower the heat and simmer for 5 minutes.

If you prefer the beef cooked medium-rare: Remove the beef from the fridge and immediately add the hot sauce from the pan. The residual heat from the sauce will cook the beef.

If you prefer the beef rare: Completely cool the prahok sauce first, then add it to the beef.

Once you add the prahok sauce, give it all a toss, squeeze the juice from the remaining lime into the bowl and toss again. Add the radishes, lemongrass, cabbage, and shallot. Toss once more, then transfer to a serving plate. Garnish with the herbs and peanuts and serve.

PLEAY TREY
KHMER CEVICHE

Serves 4

Full of aromatics and fresh herbs, this is a wonderful, refreshing fish salad that's especially good on hot summer days. I think of my dad when I make this dish; he loved raw fish, and he made pleay trey often for friends. Like ceviche, the fish here is "cooked" in a bath of lime juice; unlike ceviche, we throw in some galangal, too. The marinade becomes the basis for dressing the salad. I use halibut here, but sea bass, cod, or any other firm whitefish would be great. Poached shrimp or sliced squid is nice, too.

- ½ cup fresh lime juice (4 to 5 limes)
- 3 garlic cloves, thinly sliced
- 2 galangal slices (¼-inch), smashed
- Kosher salt
- 14 ounces halibut fillet, cut into ¼-inch slices
- 1¼ teaspoons sugar
- 1 cup packed mix of Thai basil, cilantro, and mint leaves, roughly chopped
- 2 bird's eye chiles, minced
- 1 red bell pepper, sliced into matchsticks
- 1 lemongrass stalk, trimmed (see page 23) and thinly sliced (about 2 tablespoons)
- 1 cup mung bean sprouts
- ¼ cup salted peanuts, crushed, plus more for garnish
- Scant ¼ cup thinly sliced shallots

In a large bowl, mix together the lime juice, garlic, galangal, and a pinch of salt. Gently fold in the fish. Cover and refrigerate for about 20 minutes.

Remove the bowl from the fridge. Pick up the slices of fish with your hands, and over a small saucepan, squeeze them gently to collect the marinade (you should collect about ¼ cup of the marinade). Return the fish to its original bowl.

Set the saucepan with the reserved marinade over low heat. Add the sugar and 2 pinches of salt. Simmer for 5 minutes, then cool completely.

Remove the galangal from the bowl with the fish mixture and discard. Add the cooled marinade to the bowl along with the remaining herbs, the chiles, bell pepper, lemongrass, bean sprouts, peanuts, and shallots. Toss gently. Plate the fish salad, garnish with some more peanuts, and serve.

សម្លរគ្រឿងឆ្នុក

SOMLAW KRAUNG CHNUK
SOUP OUTSIDE THE POT

Serves 4

When we were kids, my mom had a repertoire of soups that she regularly made for us, and by the time I was in high school, I thought I had tried them all. Then one day, she busted this one out. I thought she made it up, because there was barely any cooking involved. It was just smoked fish, boiled eggs, sliced vegetables and fruit, lime juice, some seasoning, and a quick broth made of prahok and fish sauce, all thrown into a bowl rather than set to simmer in a pot (hence the dish's name—the soup is made outside the pot!). As it turns out, growing up, my mom loved this cold soup. It's perfect for a hot, humid environment and could be made when they didn't have time to start a fire. I really love this, too, especially during the summer when tomatoes and mangoes are at the markets. That said, I encourage you to change it up throughout the year and use whatever vegetables are in season. It will make all the difference.

3 eggs

1½ cups water

1 tablespoon prahok

1 teaspoon sugar

1 teaspoon fish sauce

½ teaspoon kosher salt

1 (4-ounce) hot-smoked salmon, mackerel, or any whitefish fillet

4 garlic cloves, minced

1 medium or 2 small green tomatoes, or 2 Roma tomatoes, sliced into small wedges

2 green onion stalks, thinly sliced

1 shallot, thinly sliced

½ cup thinly sliced unpeeled cucumbers

½ cup shredded green mango (from 1 mango; see page 23 for shredding tips)

¼ cup thinly sliced Thai basil

2 limes, juiced

Preheat the oven to 375°F.

Place the eggs in a small pot and add enough water to cover. Bring the water to a boil over medium heat, then set a timer for 8 minutes. While the eggs cook, fill a large bowl with ice and water. When the timer rings, immediately transfer the eggs to the ice bath. Once the eggs are cool, peel them, halve them lengthwise, then cut each half into thirds. Set aside.

Discard the cooking water. Pour 1½ cups fresh water into the pot and set over medium heat. When the water begins to boil, add the prahok, sugar, fish sauce, and salt. Stir until the sugar dissolves, then strain over a small bowl. Discard the solids and set the broth aside.

Remove and discard the skin from the smoked fish. Cut the fish into 4-inch pieces, then place the pieces on a sheet pan. Bake for 5 minutes, then flip and bake until the fish has dehydrated a bit and has a consistency similar to jerky, 5 to 10 more minutes. Let cool, then shred the fish into 1-inch pieces. You should have about ½ cup.

Now the fun part: Place the garlic, tomatoes, green onions, shallot, cucumbers, mango, and Thai basil in a medium serving bowl. Pour in the prahok broth and gently mix everything together. Add the lime juice, shredded fish, and eggs. Mix once more. Serve. How refreshing!

SOMLAW MACHOO KROEUNG
TAMARIND KROEUNG SOUP

Serves 4 to 6

Somlaw machoo kroeung is a sour, tangy, umami-filled soup that's a staple throughout Cambodia and is the soup I missed the most when I started living on my own. When I opened my restaurant Nyum Bai, I was surprised I wasn't the only one who yearned for it: This was one of our most requested soups, especially among Khmers and Khmer Americans. The broth is made with beef or pork, and some, like my mom, like to add pork ribs, too. Others use tripe. I like tender tri-tip because the cut gives the broth body and a rich, luscious quality (for similar reasons, boneless short ribs are lovely, too). Most versions include water spinach and eggplants, though I've also seen it filled with papaya, chayote, Japanese eggplants, and watercress, so feel free to experiment. Whatever you use, be sure to also include jalapeños, as the soup benefits from that kick of heat. In Cambodia, vendors add a sour apple called kra-suing for tartness, which unfortunately is not available in the States. We do have tamarind, though, and that works. Serve with rice, always.

1 pound tri-tip, sliced into ¼-inch-thick pieces

Kosher salt

1 cup packed fresh curry leaves (see Note)

2 jalapeños

1 pound water spinach (also called morning glory, tra koun, ong choy, and rau muống), leaves picked and discarded

¼ cup grapeseed or other neutral oil

1 cup Yellow Kroeung (page 28)

2 tablespoons prahok

1 tablespoon palm sugar

1½ cups Tuk Ampil / Tamarind Water (page 30)

3 cups beef broth or water

1½ tablespoons fish sauce

8 Thai eggplants, quartered

Bai / Steamed Jasmine Rice (page 52), for serving

Place the tri-tip in a large bowl and season with big pinches of salt on all sides. Set aside while you prepare the other ingredients.

If the curry leaves are still on the stem, turn the stovetop heat to low and pass the leaves over the burner a few times until fragrant, then pick the leaves and discard the stems. Otherwise, preheat the oven to 375°F. Place the leaves on a sheet pan and dry roast them until fragrant, about 8 minutes, giving them a good toss once or twice. Set aside.

You can leave the jalapeños raw or char them to add a smoky flavor to the soup. To char, place the jalapeños either directly over an open flame or in a small cast-iron or nonstick skillet over medium heat. Using tongs, turn the jalapeños frequently until they're charred on all sides. Alternatively, broil the peppers for 5 minutes, rotating them a few times so they char evenly.

Note: Fresh curry leaves can be found at Indian and other South Asian grocers. If you can't source them, they can be omitted.

TAMARIND KROEUNG SOUP, CONTINUED

Prepare the water spinach. The bottom 2 inches or so of the stems tend to be fibrous and tough; trim those parts and discard or compost. If the remaining part of the stems are a little tough, give them a squeeze to soften. Slice the stems into 4 to 5 segments, each about 2 inches long. Set aside.

In a medium Dutch oven or other heavy pot over medium-high heat, heat the oil. When the oil begins to shimmer, add the kroeung, prahok, and palm sugar and stir until fragrant, 5 minutes.

Add the tri-tip and sauté until the slices are seared on all sides, another 5 minutes. Add the tamarind water, lower the heat to medium, and cover. Simmer for another 10 minutes.

Add the broth, fish sauce, and 1 teaspoon salt, then increase the heat to high. Once the broth is at a boil, add the jalapeños, water spinach, and eggplants. Cover, turn off the heat, and let the soup sit for 15 minutes. Ladle the soup into bowls, add a handful of curry leaves to each bowl . . . and it's ready to serve with rice! Store leftovers in an airtight container and refrigerate for up to 2 days.

SOMLAW CHAP CHAI
CELEBRATION SOUP

Serves 4

This Khmer Chinese soup filled with meatballs and vegetables is usually made for weddings and anytime there's something to celebrate, but it's also so satisfying when the weather turns crisp. Usually, the soup begins with a roasted pig and sautéed vegetables, which are then added to simmering chicken broth. But back when I was a broke college student learning this recipe, I could never justify buying an expensive piece of roast pork just for myself. Instead, I picked up more affordable ground pork and turned those into meatballs, then threw in some crunchy pork rinds for texture. If you already made some Prahut / Pork Meatballs (page 222), you can use those instead of the ones I make here. To save time, I also add the vegetables directly to the soup instead of sautéing them first.

MEATBALLS

- 8 ounces ground pork
- 1 garlic clove, minced
- 1 tablespoon Thai seasoning soy sauce
- 1 tablespoon fish sauce
- ½ teaspoon crushed or freshly ground black pepper
- ½ teaspoon kosher salt
- ¼ teaspoon sugar

SOUP

- 7 dried wood ear mushrooms or dried black fungus
- 1 cup dried shiitake mushrooms
- 2 ounces dried yuba (also called soy or tofu skin) (about 2 cups or 5 sticks)
- 2 tablespoons dried shrimp
- 2½ quarts Somlaw Mu-anh / Chicken Broth (page 32), or store-bought
- 6 garlic cloves, smashed
- 1½ cups unflavored pork rinds or chicharrones, cut into 2-inch pieces (see Note 1)
- 4 carrots, peeled, cut on the oblique into 1-inch pieces (about 2 cups) (see Note 2)
- 1 small napa cabbage, or 2 bunches bok choy, cut into 3-inch chunks (about 6 cups)
- ½ small daikon, cut on the oblique into 1-inch pieces, about 1 cup (see Note 2)
- 1 tablespoon oyster sauce
- 1 tablespoon fish sauce
- 1 teaspoon kosher salt
- 1 teaspoon sugar
- Sliced green onion stalks, for garnish
- Garlic oil (see page 42), for garnish
- Freshly crushed black pepper, for garnish
- Bai / Steamed Jasmine Rice (page 52), for serving

MAKE THE MEATBALLS

In a large bowl, combine the pork, garlic, seasoning soy sauce, fish sauce, pepper, salt, and sugar. Have some fun and use your hands to mix it all up until well combined. Scoop out about 1 tablespoon, shape it into a meatball, and place it on a large dish or sheet pan. Repeat with the remaining mixture. It should make about 12 meatballs.

MAKE THE SOUP

Wash your hands well and start on the broth. Place the wood ear mushrooms, shiitake mushrooms, dried yuba, and dried shrimp in separate medium bowls and add about 1 cup of warm water to each. Soak for 15 minutes to rehydrate, then drain. Quarter the wood ear mushrooms, slice the shiitakes into half-inch strips, then slice the yuba into 1-inch squares. Set these three ingredients aside.

Pour the broth into a large pot over high heat. Once it begins to boil, add the meatballs, garlic, and dried shrimp. Cover and lower the heat to medium. Cook until the meatballs float to the top and are cooked through, about 8 minutes.

CELEBRATION SOUP, CONTINUED

Add the wood ear mushrooms, shiitake mushrooms, yuba, pork rinds, carrots, cabbage, daikon, oyster sauce, fish sauce, salt, and sugar. Increase the heat to high to bring the soup back to a boil, then cover, lower the heat to medium, and cook until the carrots are tender, about another 10 minutes.

Ladle the soup into four bowls, then garnish each with some green onions, a drizzle of garlic oil, and a dash of pepper. Serve with rice. Store leftover soup in an airtight container and refrigerate for up to 2 days.

Note 1: Pork rinds (or fried pork skin) intended for use in soups and hot pots are available at Asian markets.

Note 2: Oblique cuts of long vegetables like carrots are great for soups because they cook evenly while maintaining their shape. To make the cut, position the vegetable horizontally at the center of the cutting board. Starting at the tip, cut it on a diagonal, then roll it a quarter turn toward you. Make another cut at the same angle about 1½ inches away from your previous cut. Repeat for the rest of the vegetable. That's it!

Vegetarian variation: Swap out the meatballs for store-bought fried tofu (also called tofu puffs; cut them into similar-size pieces before adding them to the broth). Instead of chicken broth, combine the water used to soak the mushrooms with 4 cups of water or vegetable broth. When cooking the broth, omit the shrimp, pork rinds, and fish sauce and add another cup of napa cabbage and an additional teaspoon of salt, or to taste.

ការីសាច់មាន់

CURI SACH MU-ANH
CHICKEN CURRY

Serves 4 to 6

Curi sach mu-anh was a big hit at Nyum Bai from day one. But while it was a regular item at the restaurant, the curry traditionally is more of a holiday or special-occasion food; my brothers and I usually ate it only when my mom made it as an offering to take to the temple. And when she made it, that meant a fun trip with my dad to pick up a crusty baguette from Giovanni's, an Italian deli he discovered during one of his many food jaunts around Stockton. As for the curry itself, my mom added all sorts of things to it, like pork blood and bamboo shoots. My version is simpler, but feel free to experiment with adding your favorite seasonal vegetables. Note that like most Cambodian curries (and unlike, say, many Thai curries), this is pretty mild and a bit soupy, with prahok and kroeung providing layers of flavor and a silky texture. If you can plan ahead, I highly suggest making the curry the night before serving, as the flavors will develop and deepen very nicely overnight.

3 tablespoons grapeseed or other neutral oil

Kosher salt

2 pounds skin-on chicken parts (preferably 2 bone-in thighs and 2 drumsticks)

3 tablespoons Master Kroeung (page 27)

3 tablespoons Bok Mtes / Chile Paste (page 31)

2 tablespoons palm sugar

1 tablespoon prahok

1 tablespoon + 2 teaspoons Madras curry powder

2 (13.5-ounce) cans coconut milk

2 large russet potatoes, peeled, cut into 1½-inch chunks

1 small yellow onion, cut into 1-inch dice

1 teaspoon fish sauce

Khtoem Krahm Jien / Crispy Shallots (page 44), or store-bought, for garnish (optional)

Toasted baguette, Bai / Steamed Jasmine Rice (page 52), or vermicelli noodles, for serving

In a medium pot over high heat, heat the oil. Quickly sprinkle a few pinches of salt all over the chicken. When the oil begins to shimmer, add the chicken skin side down. Once the pieces have a nice sear, about 4 minutes, flip and sear the other side, about another 4 minutes. Transfer the chicken to a plate.

Lower the heat to medium and add the kroeung, chile paste, palm sugar, and prahok. Stir until nice and fragrant, about 3 minutes, then lower the heat to medium-low. Return the chicken to the pot and add the curry powder and 3 teaspoons salt. Stir, then add one can of coconut milk, potatoes, and onion. Stir again, then cover for 15 minutes (you should see a shiny layer of rendered fat on top of the coconut milk).

Uncover and add the second can of coconut milk. Bring to a simmer. Cover and cook until the potatoes are nearly fork-tender, another 15 minutes. Add the fish sauce, turn off the heat, and let it sit, undisturbed and still covered, for another 10 minutes so the potatoes can finish cooking. Portion the curry into individual bowls, garnish with fried shallots, and serve with the baguette, rice, or noodles. Store leftover curry in an airtight container in the refrigerator for up to 2 days.

Vegetarian variation: Replace the chicken for tofu and/or your choice of vegetables, omit the prahok and fish sauce, and increase the salt in the broth up to 2 teaspoons, or to taste.

ឆាមីសូរ
CHA MEE SOU

PEPPERY STIR-FRIED GLASS NOODLES WITH YUBA

Serves 4

I always looked forward to going to the wat just to eat cha mee sou. The elders at the temple nestled each component—noodles, vegetables, rice—in a beautifully decorated sruak, a silver tiffin carrier, and I'd unlock each tier one by one like a treasure box. At home, my mom made this during holidays and other special occasions. Not because it's difficult to make, but because prepping all the ingredients takes some time (fortunately, everything can be found at an Asian market). And like many special-occasion dishes, cha mee sou is imbued with symbolism and luck: As the story goes, the long, sturdy strands of the glass noodles represent longevity and strength. Indeed, unlike rice noodles, which become mushy when cooked too long, glass noodles are more forgiving and will hold their shape and nice, springy texture in a hot wok. I love the interplay of all the different textures in the bowl, finished with a bit of extra black pepper at the end.

- 8 ounces glass noodles
- 2 ounces dried yuba (also called soy or tofu skin) (about 2 cups or 5 sticks)
- 1 dried calamari (about 2 ounces)
- 1 cup dried wood ear mushrooms or dried black fungus
- ¼ cup dried shrimp
- ¼ cup dried lily buds (also called dried lily flowers) (about 24 buds)
- 2 tablespoons oyster sauce
- 1 tablespoon fish sauce
- 1 tablespoon Maggi Seasoning
- 1 tablespoon sugar
- 1 teaspoon kosher salt
- Freshly ground black pepper
- 1 tablespoon grapeseed or other neutral oil
- 6 garlic cloves, minced
- 8 ounces ground pork or thinly sliced skinless pork belly
- 1 small yellow onion, cut into ¼-inch slices (2 cups)
- 2 cups Somlaw Mu-anh / Chicken Broth (page 32), or store-bought, or water
- 2 green onion stalks, cut into ½-inch strips

Submerge the noodles in room-temperature water and soak until softened, about 10 minutes. Drain, then cut the noodles in half.

Place the yuba, calamari, mushrooms, dried shrimp, and lily buds in separate medium bowls. Cover each with warm water and soak until they've softened, about 15 minutes, then drain. Cut the yuba, calamari, and mushrooms into ¼-inch wide strips. Set aside.

In a small bowl, stir together the oyster sauce, fish sauce, Maggi Seasoning, sugar, salt, and 1 teaspoon of pepper. Set this sauce aside.

In a wok or very large skillet over medium-high heat, heat the oil. When the oil begins to shimmer, add the garlic and sauté until fragrant, about 30 seconds or so. Add the pork and stir until browned but not yet fully cooked, about 5 minutes. Then add the yuba, calamari, mushrooms, dried shrimp, lily buds, and the sauce. Stir for a good 5 minutes, then lower the heat to medium and cover for 5 minutes.

Add the noodles and onion and stir-fry for about 5 minutes. Add the broth, stirring until the liquid has evaporated and the noodles are soft, 5 to 7 minutes. Turn off the heat, garnish with the green onions and some more pepper if you'd like, and serve. Store leftovers in an airtight container and refrigerate for up 2 days.

មីកាតាំង

MEE KA-TUNG

STIR-FRIED EGG NOODLES WITH GRAVY

Serves 4 to 6

You often see mee ka-tung at old-school Cambodian restaurants. It's a nostalgic dish for a lot of us and one my nieces and nephews always ask my mom to make. The name translates to "Chinese noodles," reflecting the Chinese influence on Cambodian cooking: There have been Chinese settlements in Cambodia at least since the thirteenth century, when diplomat Zhou Daguan wrote about Chinese traders in Angkor. With Chinese migration to the kingdom came soy sauce, noodles, steaming, stir-frying, and other ingredients and techniques, many of which were incorporated into Khmer cooking. Mee ka-tung is similar to chow fun, even using the same wide, flat rice noodles. The biggest difference is the addition of a gravy sauce that turns the dish into a slurpy stir-fry. I toss the noodles with tri-tip and gai lan, but you can use any other cut of beef, or chicken, pork, tofu, seafood, or even seasonal vegetables. Some like to top the noodles with a fried egg, but my mom cracked the eggs right in, so that's what I do, too. Black pepper completes the dish, and it's worth using Kampot peppercorns if you have them.

3 tablespoons oyster sauce

1 tablespoon palm sugar

1 tablespoon Thai seasoning soy sauce

Kosher salt

2 cups Somlaw Mu-anh / Chicken Broth (page 32), or store-bought, or water

1 tablespoon cornstarch, tapioca starch, or arrowroot flour

12 ounces tri-tip, thinly sliced

1 pound gai lan (Chinese broccoli) (about 1 bunch)

3 tablespoons grapeseed or other neutral oil

5 garlic cloves, minced

2 tablespoons Shaoxing wine or sake

14 ounces fresh or dried flat, wide rice noodles (see Note)

2 tablespoons Maggi Seasoning

2 eggs

Freshly ground black pepper (preferably Kampot peppercorns), for garnish

Chrouk Mtes Khtoem / Pickled Garlic Chile (page 35) or your favorite hot sauce, for serving

Let's start with the gravy. In a medium bowl, combine the oyster sauce, palm sugar, seasoning soy sauce, and 1 teaspoon of salt. In another medium bowl, combine the broth and cornstarch and mix well to make a slurry. Set both aside.

Place the beef in a medium bowl with a big pinch of salt. Toss, then set aside to marinate.

Trim and discard the tough ends of the gai lan stems. Peel the thick outer layer of the stems and discard. Separate the leaves from the stems, then slice the leaves into thirds and thinly slice the stems. Set the stems and leaves aside, keeping them separate.

Let's cook the beef and broccoli! In a large wok over high heat, heat 1 tablespoon of the oil. When the oil begins to shimmer, add the garlic and stir just until the garlic is light brown and smells nice, about 15 seconds. Add the sliced beef and sauté for about 5 minutes, until the slices are no longer pink. Add the Shaoxing wine and stir until evaporated, another 5 minutes.

Note: If using dried noodles, soak them in lukewarm water for 30 minutes, then strain before using.

Add the oyster sauce mixture and stir until all the slices of beef are nicely coated. Give the chicken stock slurry one last stir and pour it into the wok. Lower the heat to medium. When the sauce begins to bubble, add the gai lan stalks and cover. Steam for 5 minutes, then turn off the heat and add the leaves. The leaves may overflow and seem like they won't fit, but push them down and they'll settle in as they wilt. Cover and let sit until the stalks are easily pierced with a fork, about 10 minutes.

As the beef and broccoli cook, separate the noodle strands and place them in a large bowl. Add the Maggi Seasoning and toss.

Transfer everything from the wok to a large plate or bowl, then wipe the wok clean with a paper towel (or you can use another wok). Over high heat, add the remaining 2 tablespoons of oil and the noodles. Stir until the noodles have softened, then crack the eggs right on top. Break the yolks and stir the eggs with the noodles. Once the eggs are cooked, immediately turn off the heat.

To serve, divide the noodles among plates, then place the sauce, beef, and gai lan right on top. Garnish with pepper–it's a must!–and have pickled chiles or hot sauce on the table for anyone who'd like to add it. Store leftovers in an airtight container and refrigerate for up to 2 days.

TREY JIEN JUEN

WHOLE FISH WITH GINGER + SALTED BEANS

Serves 2 to 4

A whole fish on a plate almost always catches everyone's attention, but the real star of this dish is the ginger and salted bean sauce. It was a favorite of my dad's, because he loved all things ginger, and this is super gingery. Combining that ginger with salted soybeans (found in jars at Asian markets) might seem a little unexpected if you've never had trey jien juen before, but trust me, it's delicious. The heat and warmth from the ginger mixes with the saltiness from the beans, and then the fish comes in with its sweetness.

1 (1- to 1½-pound) whole red snapper, branzino, or tilapia, scaled and cleaned

Kosher salt

½ cup Somlaw Mu-anh / Chicken Broth (page 32), or store-bought, or water

¼ cup salted soybeans (preferably Yeo's brand), drained

2 tablespoons unsweetened rice vinegar

1½ teaspoons sugar

1 teaspoon fish sauce

6 tablespoons grapeseed or other neutral oil

8 ounces ginger, peeled and thinly sliced into matchsticks (2 cups)

4 garlic cloves, minced

3 green onion stalks, thinly sliced, for garnish

Pat the fish dry. Make three or four slits on each side and season both sides and the inside cavity with a few pinches of salt. Set aside.

In a small bowl, prepare the sauce by mixing together the broth, salted soybeans, rice vinegar, sugar, and fish sauce.

In a large frying pan over medium-high heat, heat 2 tablespoons of the oil. Add the ginger and sauté until fragrant, about 6 minutes. Then add the garlic and stir until that's lovely and fragrant, too, about 2 minutes. Pour in the sauce and cook, stirring constantly, for about 3 minutes so the flavors get to know one another. The liquid will almost completely absorb into the ginger. Transfer everything, including any remaining sauce, to a bowl. Wipe the pan clean with a paper towel, or grab another frying pan, and place it on the burner.

Lower the heat to medium and add the remaining 4 tablespoons of oil. When the oil begins to shimmer, add the fish. Cook for 5 to 7 minutes per side, until the fish is cooked through, flakes easily, and is no longer translucent.

Transfer the fish to a plate. Add the ginger, garlic, and sauce on top and garnish with the green onions. Serve.

ឆាសាច់មាន់ខ្ញី
CHA SACH MU-ANH KYAI
CHICKEN + CARAMELIZED GINGER

Serves 4

Oul is a Khmer word that translates roughly to that special experience of enjoying something so delicious that you inhale it so fast you nearly choke on it. And that's exactly what happens whenever I have cha kyai. It's that good! The stir-fry part of the dish is rooted in Chinese cooking, but the generous use of ginger is very Cambodian. Ginger is, in fact, the main ingredient, and you'll very slowly caramelize it to crisp it up and bring out its sweetness. For that reason, it's worth sourcing the freshest ginger you can find: You'll know it's good to go if its flesh is vibrant yellow and it's still juicy when you cut into it (see page 23 for additional shopping tips). Caramelizing the ginger does take some time, but it's worth it! You'll often find this stir-fried with frog legs, but I love it with chicken, which is what I do here.

1 pound boneless, skinless chicken thighs, cut into bite-size pieces

Kosher salt

1 pound ginger (about 3 big pieces the size of the palm of your hand), peeled

STIR-FRY SAUCE

1 tablespoon oyster sauce

1 tablespoon palm sugar

1 tablespoon Thai seasoning soy sauce

1 teaspoon kosher salt

4 tablespoons grapeseed or other neutral oil

5 garlic cloves, minced (3 tablespoons)

2 green onion stalks, thinly sliced

½ teaspoon freshly ground black pepper

Bai / Steamed Jasmine Rice (page 52), for serving

Place the chicken in a large bowl. Add a big pinch of salt and toss to coat. Cover and refrigerate while you prepare the ginger and sauce.

Thinly slice the ginger into ⅛-inch matchsticks, about the width of a mung bean sprout. (I like to first cut the pieces into large planks, then stack and slice them into matchsticks.) Keep going until you have 4 cups. Set aside.

MAKE THE STIR-FRY SAUCE

In a small bowl, make the sauce by combining the oyster sauce, palm sugar, seasoning soy sauce, and salt. Stir well (but it's okay if the palm sugar is still lumpy).

You'll need some patience for this next step: Grab a large wok or deep skillet. Set it over medium-high heat and add 3 tablespoons of the oil. When the oil begins to shimmer, add the ginger and cook, stirring constantly. This is where you'll need a bit of patience, because it will take 15 to 20 minutes to bring out the ginger's sweetness, and you'll need to keep stirring the whole time so the ginger doesn't burn. When done, the ginger should be

CHICKEN + CARAMELIZED GINGER, CONTINUED

crispy, lightly browned, and resemble hash browns. Carefully taste a piece, too: It'll be gingery but should be a bit sweet, too.

Turn off the heat and use a slotted spoon to remove the ginger to a bowl. Leave the oil in the wok. It's now infused with a lovely ginger flavor!

Lower the heat to medium. Add the remaining 1 tablespoon of oil to the wok. When the oil begins to shimmer, add the garlic and sauté until fragrant, about 30 seconds, then add the chicken. Sauté until the chicken is about halfway cooked, 3 minutes or so. Then add the sauce. Stir for 3 to 5 minutes, until the chicken pieces are cooked through and glossy from being coated in the sauce. Stir in the crispy ginger, then turn off the heat. Let everything sit together for about 5 minutes, then transfer to a large serving bowl. Sprinkle the green onions and pepper over the top.

You can serve immediately . . . or, if you can wait a few minutes before digging in, this is an extra step, but it's the best step: Take all the cooked rice and throw it in the hot wok set over high heat. Give it all a really good toss. Once the rice crisps up a bit, about 2 minutes, you will have a bonus of delicious ginger rice to eat with your cha kyai! Store leftovers in an airtight container and refrigerate for up to 2 days.

សាច់មាន់អាំង

SACH CHROUK ANG
GARLIC + PEPPER PORK RIBS

Serves 2 to 4

These pork ribs were a huge time-saver for my mom. She'd put the ribs in the marinade right before bed or first thing in the morning, then pop them into the fridge. Then when my brothers and I came home from school, all we needed to do was put them the oven, steam some rice, bring out the chrouk, and we had a meal. I made this a lot when I was on my own for the first time, because it is just so quick and easy to do. An overnight soak in the marinade is ideal for maximum flavor, but if you didn't plan ahead, the ribs can marinate for as little as an hour and they'll still be delicious.

- 4 garlic cloves, minced
- 2 tablespoons grapeseed or other neutral oil
- 1 tablespoon oyster sauce
- 1 tablespoon Thai seasoning soy sauce
- 1 tablespoon sugar
- 2 teaspoons freshly ground black pepper (preferably Kampot peppercorns)
- ½ teaspoon kosher salt
- 1½ to 2 pounds pork baby back ribs
- Bai / Steamed Jasmine Rice (page 52), for serving
- Chrouk / Pickles (page 38), for serving

In a large bowl, combine the garlic, oil, oyster sauce, seasoning soy sauce, sugar, pepper, and salt.

Place the ribs on a cutting board, meaty side down. Check if the silvery membrane that stretches across the bones has been removed. If not, use a small knife or your fingers to pull it off and discard (if left on, it'll become very tough and chewy once cooked).

Slice the ribs into individual pieces and place them in the bowl. Coat each piece generously with the sauce, then cover and marinate for at least 1 hour (overnight is best!). If cooking within 2 hours, marinate the ribs at room temperature. If marinating for longer, refrigerate immediately.

When you're ready to cook, preheat the oven to 425°F. If the ribs are in the fridge, take them out so they can come to room temperature before cooking. Set a wire rack on a sheet pan.

Right before cooking, pick up the ribs, shake off the excess sauce, and transfer them from the bowl to the wire rack. Place the ribs in the oven and cook for 25 minutes, then flip and cook until the ribs are cooked through, 25 to 30 more minutes. Transfer the ribs to a serving platter and serve with rice and chrouk on the side! Store leftover ribs in an airtight container and refrigerate for up to 2 days.

CAMBODIA

Dishes inspired by my visits to Cambodia

ឱ!បាត់ដំបងខ្ញុំប៉ងឃ្យូរហើយ តើ
ថ្ងៃណាឯ្យើយ បានឃល់ក្បា

Oh, Battambang!
Long have I desired
but when will I see your face?

FROM SINN SISAMOUTH'S
"CHAMPA BATTAMBANG"

I was home. The second I landed in Phnom Penh and got off the plane, I felt like I was home. It was 2009, and it was my first trip back. That doesn't make any sense, I know: I never had been to Cambodia. But everything just felt so familiar: the orange and purple hue of the sky, the sounds, the smells, the food, the language, the culture, the people. Phnom Penh had come a long way over the last few decades. By the time I arrived, high-rises were as much a part of the cityscape as the temples on every block, which functioned both as places for worship and public spaces for gathering. As I walked around, there were puffs of smoke around every corner—locals burning their trash—that gave the streets a mysterious air. But with everyone speaking Khmer and the aroma of sach ko ang[1] and kuy teav Phnom Penh[2] from the street food stalls, it didn't feel unknown. In fact, everything felt so strikingly familiar. I was inspired.

I knew I belonged there the day I dropped acid and rode my bike to a quiet corner at the Angkor Wat. That was the most beautiful experience I had ever had. As I sat on the sacred land and watched the carvings of the Angkor Wat come to life, I heard a voice whisper to me: *This is where dreams come true. Follow your heart. That's where the truth lies.* Behind me, I heard a rustle: a woman, no taller than four feet, her teeth stained purple from chewing betel nuts. She grabbed my hand and said I looked familiar. She read my palm and told me Cambodia would give me my life's purpose. That same night, I dreamed I was a boy during the Angkorian era. I was to swim down a moat to retrieve a sapphire gem—but I'd be able to grasp the gem only if it was meant to belong to me. I swam down the moat. I saw the glimmer of the sapphire. I reached out to grab it . . .

I woke up when the gem was in my hand. I knew I was home.

I was supposed to be there for a week. I stayed for a month. After that, I went back every year. At one point, I stayed and traveled throughout Southeast Asia for nine months. I stayed with my maternal grandmother in Battambang. I visited my mother's childhood home, a beautiful colonial-style house built on stilts, surrounded by nothing but green. Through these trips, I began to piece together who my mom was. I learned her mother was a formidable woman who commanded respect everywhere she went. I learned my mother was "one of the strongest women" my relatives knew; I think they were referencing the strength she must have had in order to endure what she endured in the camp, but what exactly she experienced, I still don't know. There's still a lot to learn.

I learned about my dad's side, too. I learned his side of the family was known for their food. His parents made moonshine for fishermen back then, and his mother was known for making the lightly fermented rice noodles that go into nom pachok, a fish chowder scented with lemongrass.

Being in their villages, I also couldn't help but picture them back when they were younger. Cambodia became a protectorate of France in 1863; almost a century later, in 1953, Cambodia gained its independence. What followed was the Golden Era, an amazing period between the 1960s and

[1] Kroeung Beef Skewers (page 66).
[2] Pork Noodle Soup (page 213).

early 1970s when Khmer rock, film, architecture, fashion—everything—flourished. I imagined my parents in those less complicated times, celebrating and partying with the rest of the country. I woke up to the crow of the rooster and hopped on my bike, setting off through the morning mist on the same path I imagined that my mother once took to the market. Were monks chanting nearby then, too? Did she also breathe in the strong scent of incense in the air? At the market, I channeled her as a young woman, picking and choosing vegetables and herbs, just as I was doing. I listened to Sinn Sisamouth crooning songs about young love and pictured my dad putting the record on as he tinkered with a motorcycle. I imagined them both happy.

It was on my third trip back to Cambodia in 2012 that the idea came to me. I was in Phnom Penh, at a stall, chopsticks and soup spoon in hand, at complete peace, devouring a bowl of kuy teav, slurping the rice noodles, sipping the pork broth, squeezing in a lime. It was at this moment that something burst in me. And what came tumbling out was an epiphany.

I had been searching for so long to find the right words to talk to my parents about what they went through. Maybe food could be our shared language, the way I could learn more about them: who they were before, who they are now. And if I understood my parents, maybe I would understand myself more. And I could honor my mom especially and show her: *I understand your sacrifices*.

And if I shared what I knew, maybe it could help other Khmer kids, too. I imagined creating a space for us, where younger Khmers could connect with their elders over bowls of rice, pots of somlaw, and platters of whole fish served with green mango salad. From there, the conversations could flow and together we could celebrate all things Khmer.

That was it. I was going to learn how to cook this food—and share it with as many people as I possibly could.

Playlist

"Champa Battambang,"
SINN SISAMOUTH

"Chorl Mseat,"
PEN RAN

"Khlach Brapon,"
SINN SISAMOUTH AND PEN RAN

"Phat Cheay Bondal Chat,"
SINN SISAMOUTH

"Onn Chhou Moat Nas,"
DRAKKAR

"Reatrey Ngor Ngit,"
DRAKKAR

"Chong Bondue Bdey,"
KOY SARIM

RECIPES INSPIRED BY CAMBODIA

The recipes here are all rooted in Cambodia in some way: the lessons I learned, the flavors I first tasted, the food I ate, the people I met. There was the woman who welcomed me into her home to show me how she made prahok kop.[3] There was the moment I watched villagers pounding dough to make nom pachok noodles[4] and learned why one must taste nom pachok in Cambodia. And there were the soups, rice plates, and snacks from skilled food vendors all over the country. My trips to Cambodia were life changing. Every one of the recipes in this chapter reflects something I learned on each visit.

[3] Buried Prahok (page 115).
[4] Fermented rice noodles (see page 131).

ឆាពោត

CHA PORT
STIR-FRIED CORN

Serves 2 to 4

Corn is one of Cambodia's biggest crops, and this popular savory-sweet street snack, found all across Cambodia, makes good use of that abundance. You can hear the sizzle of the kernels as vendors stir-fry the cha port to order. I wonder how something so simple can be this delicious!

- 2 ears corn, shucked
- 3 tablespoons grapeseed or other neutral oil, or unsalted butter
- 3 tablespoons dried shrimp
- 1 tablespoon fish sauce
- ¼ teaspoon chile powder
- ¼ teaspoon kosher salt
- 2 tablespoons condensed milk
- ½ cup chopped green onions

Bring a large pot of water to a boil. Add the corn and cook until the kernels are darker yellow in color, shiny, and plump, about 15 minutes. Drain and cool completely. With a sharp knife, carefully shave the corn kernels off the cobs.

Place a large saucepan over high heat and add the oil or butter. When the oil is hot (or the butter has melted and has stopped foaming), carefully add the dried shrimp (the oil might splash) and sauté for about 2 minutes, looking for the color of the oil (or butter) to turn pinkish red.

Add the corn kernels and sauté for another 5 minutes until the kernels become sticky. Add the fish sauce, chile powder, and salt. Stir, then add the condensed milk and stir again. Lastly, add the green onions and stir one more time. Serve hot, wiping the drool from your mouth!

ប្រហិតត្រី
PRAHUT TREY
LEMONGRASS FISH CAKES

Serves 4 / Makes 20 fish cakes

These fish cakes look fancy, as if they were time-consuming to make, but once you have the kroeung, it comes together quickly and easily. Commonly served as drinking snacks, they also make great appetizers or can be part of a light meal with, say, Chrouk / Pickles (page 38) and steamed rice. Add chiles to the mix for some heat if you'd like; you also can make the fish cakes as thick or thin as you want (just remember that the thicker they are, the longer they'll take to cook). And if you like your fish cakes with a bit of texture, try adding some crushed unsalted peanuts into the mixture.

- 1 pound cod fillet or other firm whitefish, skin removed, sliced into large chunks
- ¼ cup Yellow Kroeung (page 28)
- 1 tablespoon chopped pickled fingerroot
- 1 tablespoon oyster sauce
- 2 teaspoons fish sauce
- 1½ teaspoons sugar
- 1 teaspoon kosher salt
- ½ cup thinly sliced snake bean coins (also called yardlong beans)
- 2 bird's eyes chiles, thinly sliced (optional)
- Grapeseed or other neutral oil, for frying

Place the cod, kroeung, fingerroot, oyster sauce, fish sauce, sugar, and salt in the bowl of a food processor and pulse about ten times, or just until the mixture turns into a thick paste that pulls away from the sides of the bowl (if you pulse too much, the mixture will become mushy). Transfer the fish paste to a large bowl and mix in the beans and (if using) the chiles with a spoon or your hands.

Before cooking all the fish cakes, first check the seasoning with a little test patty: In a medium frying pan over medium heat, heat a little bit of oil. When the oil begins to shimmer, drop a small spoonful of the mixture into the pan, flatten it slightly with the back of the spoon, and cook until it's browned and crisped. Flip and cook the other side. Carefully taste and add a pinch of salt to the mixture if you think it needs it.

When the mixture is where you want it to be, turn off the heat. Scoop out 1½ tablespoons (or use a #50 cookie scoop) of the fish mixture and roll it into a small ball. Place it on a sheet pan and repeat with the remaining paste. Oil your hands and flatten the balls into a disk about 3 inches in diameter.

Line a sheet pan or large plate with a few layers of paper towels and place it next to the stove. Heat 1 inch of oil in the same frying pan you used for the test patty over medium heat. When the oil begins to shimmer, gently add the fish patties, working in batches to avoid overcrowding the pan. Fry until the cakes are nicely browned and crisped, about 1 minute. Then flip and fry until the other sides are also browned and crispy and the fish is cooked through, 1 to 2 more minutes. Transfer the fish cakes to the paper towel–lined sheet pan to soak up the oil, then serve!

បង្គាដុតទឹកសាបទឹកជ្រលក់កំពតប្រហុក
BANGKEA DOT TUK KAMPOT
GRILLED FRESHWATER PRAWNS IN KAMPOT SAUCE

Serves 4

This savory, bright sauce is popular in the Kampot province along the coast, where seafood is in abundance. I pair it here with prawns—which are extra delicious if grilled over charcoal, though cooking them on the stovetop also works well—but it goes with all sorts of seafood, whether grilled, poached, or fried. I use a mortar and pestle to make the sauce because smashing the garlic and chiles is a very effective way to break down their fibers and release their flavors, but if you don't have one, you can use a food processor. If you want, you can even make the sauce ahead of time. It'll keep, refrigerated in an airtight container, for up to 2 days.

KAMPOT SAUCE

8 garlic cloves

3 bird's eye chiles, or more if more spice is desired

½ cup loosely packed palm sugar, light brown sugar, or date sugar

½ cup fresh lime juice (4 to 5 limes)

½ cup fish sauce

PRAWNS

Kosher salt

8 prawns, head- and shell-on, deveined

Grapeseed or other neutral oil, for greasing

2 heads Little Gem lettuce, leaves separated

2 cucumbers, unpeeled, cut into matchsticks

MAKE THE SAUCE

Using a mortar and pestle, smash together the garlic, chiles, and sugar to bring the flavors together. You can smash them as finely or coarsely as you'd like, but I suggest smashing them into smaller pieces to make the sauce easier to dip into. Stir in the lime juice and set aside for 15 minutes.

MAKE THE PRAWNS

The prawns can be grilled or prepared on the stovetop.

To grill: Preheat the grill to high. Lightly oil the prawns, then sprinkle a pinch of salt on each side. Oil the grill, then add the prawns. Cook until the prawns are opaque and bright pink, 4 to 5 minutes, flipping them over halfway through.

To cook on the stovetop: In a large skillet or frying pan over medium heat, heat 2 tablespoons of oil. When the oil begins to shimmer, add the prawns in a single layer and cook until both sides are pink, 2 to 3 minutes per side.

To serve, place the cooked prawns on a large plate or tray and pile the lettuce on the side. Add the fish sauce to the kampot sauce, stir, and portion the sauce into four individual bowls. Bring everything out to the table, wrap a prawn and cucumber stick in lettuce, and dunk!

Cambodia

PRAHOK KOP
BURIED PRAHOK

Makes 8 packets

Fishermen and farmers would often pack rice with these little parcels of prahok kop and eat them for lunch using their hands. I loved this growing up, but my mom didn't make it very often. I learned how to cook it from a woman I met in a village in Cambodia (who, in turn, learned how to make it from her mother). She gently combined mushrooms, pork, and holy basil with kroeung and prahok (sort of "burying" the prahok in the mix, hence the name), wrapped the mixture neatly in banana leaves that she clipped from a tree in her garden, and placed the packets over a wood fire. The banana's grassy fragrance hung in the air as it cooked. Once the packet was unwrapped, you could so clearly taste a smoky depth to the prahok and mushrooms. That magic can come only from the grill, but if it's not grilling season, you can bake or steam the packages instead and they'll still be delicious.

3 cups mixed oyster, maitake, and enoki mushrooms

4 ounces ground pork

¼ cup Yellow Kroeung (page 28)

1½ tablespoons prahok

1½ tablespoons sugar

2 cups packed holy basil (see Note)

2½ tablespoons Tuk Ampil / Tamarind Water (page 30)

8 banana leaves, cut into 6 by 6-inch squares

8 bird's eye chiles

4 radishes, thinly sliced

1 cucumber, unpeeled, sliced into ½-inch coins

¼ head green cabbage, leaves separated

Bai / Steamed Jasmine Rice (page 52)

Note: Holy basil has a savory aroma and a floral, lemon-pepper flavor that turns almost meaty when cooked. It's worth using here, as it does make a difference. If you can't source it from a Southeast Asian market, lemon basil or Thai basil can be substituted, though the flavor of the dish will be different.

Tear the oyster and maitake mushrooms into thick strips. For the enoki, trim off and discard the bottoms.

Combine the pork, kroeung, prahok, and sugar in the bowl of a food processor and process until creamy. Alternatively, you can use a heavy cleaver on a cutting board. Transfer the mixture to a large bowl and gently fold in the mushrooms, holy basil, and tamarind water. Set aside.

Wipe both sides of the banana leaves clean with a damp cloth. Turn the stovetop heat to low and hold the leaves right above the burner for a few seconds, flipping and rotating them a few times, just until they're soft and pliable. Alternatively, place them in a 200°F oven for about 3 minutes to soften. (If you skip this step, the leaves will tear rather than fold when you work with them.) Scoop ⅓ cup of the mixture into the center of each leaf. Using the back of a spoon, flatten it so it's about 3½ inches long and 2½ inches wide. Place a chile right on top. Fold the bottom of the leaf up and over the mixture, then fold in the left and right sides. Finally, fold the top of the leaf down to finish the wrapping. Repeat with the rest of the mixture and banana leaves.

BURIED PRAHOK, CONTINUED

To grill (which I prefer over the other methods): Preheat the grill to high. Place the banana leaf packets on the grill and grill until the pork is cooked through, about 5 minutes per side.

To bake: Preheat the oven to 375°F. Place the banana leaves on a sheet pan and bake until the pork is cooked through, about 15 minutes.

To steam: Fill a pot fitted with a steamer basket halfway with water (make sure the bottom of the basket does not touch the water). Bring the water to a simmer over medium-low heat. Place the banana leaf packets in the steamer—it's okay to stack them so they all fit—cover, and steam until the pork is cooked through, about 15 minutes.

Place the banana leaves on a large platter and arrange the radishes, cucumber, cabbage, and rice on the side. Use the fresh veggies to scoop up some of the pork mixture, or add the pork to a spoonful of rice and enjoy!

ណាតាំង

NATANG

COCONUT, PORK + DRIED SHRIMP DIP

Serves 2 to 4

Originally a royal family recipe, natang is a dish that I tried for the first time at Kravanh, a restaurant located in a colonial-era building in Phnom Penh. It was unlike any Khmer dish I'd ever had. The dip had a sweet aroma of coconut, an almost creamy texture, and distinctly savory, peanutty flavors. And to be enjoying it in a building that, like this recipe, survived the war—well, it meant a lot. Some add a bit of turmeric or saffron to give the dip a yellowish hue; Kravanh's version was a brilliant reddish color due to their addition of chile paste, which I incorporate into my version, too. Served with Bai Kadang / Rice Crackers (page 55), it's very shareable, making it a great appetizer or snack.

- 1 cup + 1 tablespoon coconut cream
- 2 tablespoons grapeseed or other neutral oil
- 1 tablespoon Bok Mtes / Chile Paste (page 31)
- 1 tablespoon palm sugar
- 1 shallot, minced
- ¼ cup dried shrimp, minced
- 6 garlic cloves, minced
- 2 teaspoons fish sauce
- ½ teaspoon kosher salt
- 8 ounces ground pork
- 4 ounces medium shrimp, without tails, peeled, deveined, and minced
- 2 tablespoons unsalted roasted peanuts
- Bai Kadang / Rice Crackers (page 55), or store-bought, for serving

In a medium saucepan over medium heat, stir together the coconut cream, oil, chile paste, and palm sugar until the sugar melts, about 3 minutes. Add the shallot, dried shrimp, and garlic. Stir for another 2 minutes to release their flavors, then add the fish sauce and salt. Give it all a good stir, then add the ground pork and shrimp, breaking up the pork as you do so to avoid big clumps. Drop the heat to low and continue cooking until the pork is cooked through, 8 to 10 minutes. Transfer to a large bowl and garnish with the peanuts. Serve with plenty of rice crackers. Store leftovers in an airtight container and refrigerate for up to 3 days.

NOM PUNG JIEN
CRISPY TOAST WITH PORK + JICAMA

Serves 8 to 12 as an appetizer

Ground pork spread on slices of baguette and pan-fried in loads of butter is found all over Cambodia, but especially in Phnom Penh, where butter and bread are more prevalent than the rest of the country. The pork itself is quite savory, with bits of jicama and onion in the mix for a little sweetness and crunch. It's great as a substantial snack, or treat it like an open-faced sandwich and make a meal of it. A day-old baguette works best for pan-frying, though you also can use fresh bread if you really can't wait.

- 1½ pounds ground pork shoulder
- ¼ small jicama, finely chopped (½ cup)
- ½ small yellow onion, finely chopped (½ cup)
- 2 green onions, finely chopped
- 1 shallot, finely chopped (¼ cup)
- 4 garlic cloves, chopped
- 1 tablespoon sugar
- 1 scant tablespoon Thai seasoning soy sauce or Maggi Seasoning
- 1 tablespoon freshly ground black pepper
- 1½ teaspoons kosher salt
- 1 baguette (preferably day-old)
- 8 tablespoons (1 stick) unsalted butter
- ½ bunch chives, sliced (optional)

In a large bowl, mix together the pork, jicama, yellow onion, green onions, shallot, garlic, sugar, seasoning soy sauce, pepper, and salt. Cover and refrigerate for at least 1 hour or at most overnight.

Cut the baguette on a bias into ½-inch slices. Spread a thin layer of the pork mixture on one side of each slice.

In a medium skillet on medium heat, melt 1 tablespoon of the butter. Add a slice or two of the baguette bread side down (or however many you can fit in your pan without overcrowding) and fry the toast until it's golden brown, about 2 minutes. Then flip and cook the pork until it's golden brown, too, 2 to 3 more minutes. Repeat with the remaining toasts, buttering the pan between slices as necessary. Garnish with the chives (if using). That's it. Enjoy hot!

ត្រីប្រម៉ា
TREY PRAMA
PORK + SALTED COD LOAF

Serves 4

This steamed pork and fish loaf is traditionally made with prama, a croaker fish found in Cambodia's great lake, Tonlé Sap. Locals will catch and gut the prama, then stuff them with salt before hanging them to dry in the sun. Once dried and preserved, prama becomes quite pungent and is used as an omelet filling or combined with pork to make this, trey prama. Here in the United States, sourcing prama can be difficult; if you ever come across it fresh or frozen at an Asian market, try it with this recipe! Otherwise, I use salted cod, especially those from Portugal (bacalhau) or Italy (baccalà). You'll end up with a ramekin full of briny, salty, umami flavors with a bit of funk mixed in. To balance those strong flavors, serve it with plenty of steamed rice and cool, refreshing raw vegetables.

- 8 ounces ground pork belly
- 2 ounces salted cod, washed well, deboned
- 2 eggs
- 2 garlic cloves, minced
- ½ teaspoon sugar
- 1 teaspoon minced shallot
- 1 teaspoon kosher salt
- 1 teaspoon fish sauce
- 1 egg yolk
- 3 radishes, thinly sliced, for serving
- 1 small cucumber, unpeeled, sliced into ½-inch coins, for serving
- Wedge of cabbage, for serving
- Bai / Steamed Jasmine Rice (page 52), for serving

Using a cleaver, mince and mix together the pork and cod on a cutting board until they're thoroughly combined. Alternatively, place the two in the bowl of a food processor and pulse about twenty times until combined.

Transfer the pork and cod mixture to a medium bowl. Crack in the eggs, then add the garlic, sugar, shallot, salt, and fish sauce. Mix everything until thoroughly combined and transfer to a large ramekin. Flatten the top with the back of a spoon, being careful not to compact the mixture.

Fill a pot fitted with a steamer basket halfway with water (make sure the bottom of the basket does not touch the water). Bring the water to a simmer over medium-low heat. Place the ramekin in the basket, cover, and steam until the pork and fish are nearly cooked through, about 20 minutes. Lightly scramble the egg yolk and pour it right on top of the ramekin. Cover and steam until the egg sets, about 5 minutes. The center of the filling should be just barely firm to the touch.

Arrange the radishes, cucumber slices, cabbage, and rice on a small serving platter and bring to the table with the ramekin. To eat, scoop out some of the loaf and place it right on top of the rice, and enjoy it with a bite of a crunchy fresh veggie! Store the leftover loaf in an airtight container and refrigerate for up to 3 days.

JIEN BAWNKWANG
CRISPY SHRIMP FRITTERS

Makes 7 fritters

Roadside vendors across Cambodia fry up rafts of shrimp fritters in shallow pans set over wood fires. And every time I watch them cook, I'm so, so impressed. It takes real skill to tend to the fire and maintain the oil at the right temperature so the fritters don't overcook or burn. That said, even if you're not a master fryer, you can definitely make these fritters at home! The batter I make here is pretty thin, resulting in fritters that are extra crispy and extra delicious, just like the ones the vendors make. The fritters do fry up pretty quickly, so cook only as many as you feel comfortable handling. You'll want to eat these almost as soon as they come out of the fryer, but they are so good dipped into the Tuk Krauch Chhma + Ambel + Mrech / Lime + Salt + Pepper Sauce (page 36) and with Chrouk / Pickles (page 38), if you have some. Or serve them with Kuy Teav Phnom Penh / Pork Noodle Soup (page 213) and either dip it into the broth or drop it into the soup to soak a bit before enjoying.

4 ounces baby shrimp (see Note)

½ teaspoon kosher salt, plus more as needed

½ teaspoon garlic powder

½ teaspoon onion powder

5 ounces water (a generous ½ cup)

⅔ cup Thai rice flour

½ teaspoon paprika (any type; optional)

Grapeseed or other neutral oil, for frying

½ cup Tuk Krauch Chhma + Ambel + Mrech / Lime + Salt + Pepper Sauce (page 36)

Note: Instead of baby shrimp, you also can use large peeled and deveined shrimp (without tails) cut into 1-inch-long by ¼-inch-wide pieces.

Pat the shrimp very dry and place them in a large bowl. Add the salt, garlic powder, and onion powder and give it a good toss. Set aside.

In a large cup with a spout or a medium bowl, make the batter by mixing together the water, flour, and paprika.

Place a wire rack on a sheet pan. In a wok or large cast-iron skillet over medium-high heat, heat 2 inches of oil to 375°F. If you don't have a thermometer, drop a bit of batter into the oil. If it sizzles and floats, the oil is ready. If it sinks, the oil's not yet hot enough.

Pour about ¼ cup of the batter into a wok spatula or a shallow soup spoon and place 1 shrimp in the middle. Place the spatula in the hot oil until the fritter releases. Fry for 1 minute, then flip and cook until the shrimp is opaque and the fritter is golden brown, 1 to 2 more minutes, then use the spatula to lift the fritter from the oil and transfer it to the rack. Sprinkle it with salt. Repeat with the remaining batter and shrimp, frying in batches to avoid overcrowding the pot. Serve with the sauce. Dip, eat, enjoy!

TREY JIEN SVAY

GREEN MANGO SALAD WITH A CRISPY FISH FILLET

Serves 2 to 4

Khmers love mangoes in all of their stages, from the time they're green, unripe, and tart to when they soften, turn sweet, and ripen into the color of the sunset. This dish, like my other green mango salad (see page 124), showcases how unripe mangoes can be used in a savory way. It also happens to be one of my mom's favorite dishes, because she loves anything sour and spicy. When I was younger, I so enjoyed watching her pick through the fish, then take a bite of the mango. The mango was so tart, she'd immediately squint her eyes and laugh.

2 garlic cloves, minced

1 small shallot, thinly sliced

2 tablespoons fresh lime juice

2 tablespoons fish sauce

1 tablespoon sugar

1 bird's eye chile, minced (optional)

1 green mango

1½ pounds catfish or cod fillet, skin removed

Kosher salt

½ cup cold water

¼ cup rice flour (preferably Bob's Red Mill)

1 cup grapeseed or other neutral oil

Bai / Steamed Jasmine Rice (page 52), for serving

Let's start with the salad dressing. In a medium bowl, stir together the garlic, shallot, lime juice, fish sauce, and sugar until the sugar dissolves. Add the chile (if using), then refrigerate until you're ready to cook the fish.

Peel and shred the mango until you have about 2 packed cups (see page 23 for shredding tips). Set aside on the counter.

Now prepare the fish. Pat the fish dry and season both sides with a pinch of salt.

In a large bowl, mix together the water and rice flour until it's the consistency of pancake batter. Set a wire rack on a sheet pan and layer a large plate with a few paper towels. Set both next to the stove.

In a medium frying pan or cast-iron skillet over medium-high heat, heat the oil to 375°F, about 10 minutes. If you don't have a thermometer, drop a bit of batter into the oil. If it puffs up, the oil is ready. If not, wait another minute and try again. If the oil begins to smoke, though, it's too hot. Lower the temperature, wait a minute, and test again.

Once the oil is at the right temperature, dip the fish into the batter. Shake off any excess and carefully slide the fish into the oil. Fry until the fish is cooked through, firm, and opaque, about 10 minutes, flipping it halfway through. Scoop it out and place it on the wire rack. Sprinkle the fish with a little bit of salt. Cool slightly for 2 minutes, then transfer it to the paper towel–lined plate to soak up the oil.

Remove the dressing from the fridge and add the mango. Toss to combine. Place the fish on a large plate or serving platter. You can either place the salad right on top of the fish, or if you want to make sure the fish stays crispy, transfer the salad to a serving bowl instead. Serve bowls of rice to everyone. Then give it a try: Pull off a piece of the fish with your hands. Dip the fish into the dressing (try to get some mango, too) and place it on top of the rice. Scoop up that bit of rice, give it a slight squeeze, and take a bite! The fish is the crispiest and the best the day it's made, but you can store leftover fish and dressing in separate airtight containers and refrigerate. The fish will keep for up to 1 more day, and the salad for 2 days.

ញាំស្វាយ
NGYOM SVAY

GREEN MANGO SALAD WITH DRIED SMOKED SALTED FISH

Serves 2 to 3

This is a super satisfying salad, especially if you're into sour and tart flavors and crunchy textures. It's also a special salad, because you can make it only when green mangoes are in season in the early spring, before they turn ripe and they go from crunchy to soft, from tart to sweet. The other component of this salad is fish, usually snakehead, that's been skewered on bamboo, dried in the sun, then laid flat over a wood fire for a smoky flavor. In Cambodia, locals in floating villages around Tonlé Sap have been passing on the tradition of catching, salting, drying, and smoking fish for thousands of years. Here, you can find smoked salted fish at Asian markets with the other dried fish. If you can't find it, you can use salted salmon instead: Just dehydrate and crisp it up slowly in a 250°F oven for about 30 minutes, or until it has the texture of jerky. Then shred the dried salmon into smaller pieces.

2 tablespoons dried shrimp

1 green mango, shredded (about 2 packed cups; see page 23 for shredding tips)

1 cup smoked salted fish

1 cup Thai basil, cilantro, or mint leaves, or any combination of the three

¼ cup sliced shallot

¼ cup Tuk Trey Piam / Fish Sauce Dressing (page 37)

1½ teaspoons fresh lime juice

Kosher salt

1 to 2 bird's eye chiles, depending on desired spice level, thinly sliced

Crushed salted peanuts, toasted, for garnish (optional)

Khtoem Krahm Jien / Crispy Shallots (page 44), or store-bought, for garnish (optional)

In a small bowl, submerge the dried shrimp in warm water and soak until softened, about 15 minutes, then drain.

While the shrimp soaks, place the shredded mango in a large bowl. Remove the head of the fish and discard. Pick off the meat and skin and place them in a mortar. Using the pestle, lightly pound the fish to break it into smaller pieces. Transfer the fish to the bowl with the mango.

Place the shrimp in the mortar and smash it into small pieces. Transfer the shrimp to the bowl.

Add the herbs, shallot, dressing, lime juice, a pinch of salt, and the chiles to the bowl. Toss to combine. Garnish with some crushed peanuts and fried shallots (if using). Serve immediately. Store leftovers in an airtight container and refrigerate for up to 1 day, though note that the fish may get soggy.

ញាំមីស៊ូរ
NGYOM MEE SOU
POTLUCK GLASS NOODLE SALAD

Serves 2 to 4

The parts of this salad—glass noodles, pork belly, shrimp, crunchy vegetables, fresh herbs, and a fish sauce dressing—are all delicious on their own, but put them together and the sum is greater than the parts. I like the fattiness of the pork belly and how it almost melts as you eat the noodles, but if you prefer, you can sauté the same amount of ground pork instead. You'll often see this salad at potlucks and at the temple, because with so many textures and colors, it looks so festive, and it has the added advantage of being able to sit for a bit without becoming mushy. At home, I like to serve it with Sach Ko Ang / Kroeung Beef Skewers (page 66), Jien Cho-Yah / Crispy Pork Egg Rolls (page 196), and, of course, Bai / Steamed Jasmine Rice (page 52)!

- 4 ounces glass noodles
- ¼ pound skinless pork belly
- Kosher salt
- 6 medium shrimp (about 3 ounces), without tails, peeled, and deveined
- 1 cup Tuk Trey Piam / Fish Sauce Dressing (page 37)
- ¼ small red or green (or a combination of both!) cabbage, thinly shredded (1 cup)
- 1 small carrot, thinly shredded (¼ cup)
- ½ small bell pepper (any color), thinly sliced (¼ cup)
- 1 Persian cucumber, or ¼ English cucumber, unpeeled, sliced into ¼-inch coins (½ cup)
- 1 cup loosely packed mix of Thai basil, cilantro, and mint leaves
- 2 tablespoons chopped salted peanuts

Bring a medium pot of water to a boil. Drop in the noodles, boil for 20 seconds, then immediately drain and rinse well with cold water. Cut the noodles into 3-inch strands.

Refill the pot halfway with water and bring to a boil. Add the pork belly and 2 teaspoons salt. Boil until the water turns cloudy and a fork easily pierces the pork, about 15 minutes, then transfer the pork to a cutting board. Once cool, thinly slice the pork.

As the pork cools, rinse out the pot, fill it halfway with water again, and turn the heat to high. Separately, fill a large bowl with water and ice.

Once the water in the pot begins to boil, turn off the heat and add the shrimp and 1 teaspoon salt. Poach the shrimp by letting them sit in the water until they turn pink and are no longer translucent, about 5 minutes, then transfer them to the ice bath. Cool, then drain and pat the shrimp dry. Cut them in half, or into bite-size pieces.

In a large bowl, stir together the sliced pork belly, shrimp, and dressing. Let the pork and shrimp soak up the dressing for about 10 seconds, then mix in the noodles. Add the cabbage, carrot, bell pepper, and cucumber and mix again. Top with the herbs and peanuts and serve.

ដំបញ្កសម្លខ្មែរ
NOM PACHOK SOMLAR KHMER

RICE VERMICELLI WITH FISH CHOWDER

Serves 4

If I had to pick one dish that defines Khmer cooking, nom pachok would be the one. Complex yet delicate, sophisticated and rustic, this is an ancient dish that goes back centuries. Every household has their own version, but generally the broth incorporates the Khmer duo of prahok and kroeung. I prefer using green kroeung, as that's how it's prepared in Cambodia, but if you don't have the lemongrass leaves needed to make it, yellow kroeung works. I also add coconut milk to the broth; not every nom pachok includes it, but I love how it carries the flavors of the kroeung and prahok and thickens the soup.

The other major component of the chowder is, of course, what the soup is named after: the fermented rice noodles called nom pachok. Making these noodles is an art; my dad's parents were well known for theirs. There are villages in Siem Reap that have been making and fermenting rice noodles using techniques more than 300 years old, passing down knowledge from one generation to the next—knowledge that has improbably survived war, colonization, and time. Unfortunately, freshly made nom pachok noodles aren't available in the United States, so we use rice vermicelli instead. It's not the same, but it's still a lovely dish.

1 pound cod fillet

¼ cup + 1½ teaspoons grapeseed or other neutral oil

1 cup Green Kroeung (page 29) or Yellow Kroeung (page 28)

2 tablespoons prahok

2 (13.5-ounce) cans coconut milk

1 quart Somlaw Mu-anh / Chicken Broth (page 32), or store-bought

¼ cup fish sauce, plus more as needed

¼ cup sugar

1 pound uncooked rice vermicelli

ASSEMBLY + SERVING

1 cup mung bean sprouts

1 cup Thai basil leaves

2 cups sliced banana blossoms (from 1 blossom) (see How to Slice Banana Blossoms, page 202)

1 small cucumber, unpeeled, sliced

Lime wedges

Chile flakes

Preheat the oven to 375°F.

Lightly coat the cod with 1½ teaspoons of oil, place it on a sheet pan, and bake for 10 minutes. Once it's cool enough to handle, pull the fish apart into small pieces. Place the fish and kroeung in a mortar and smash them together with a pestle until roughly combined.

Pour the remaining ¼ cup of oil in a medium pot over medium heat and add the prahok. Sauté until aromatic, about 5 minutes. Add the coconut milk, bring to a boil, then lower the heat and simmer until the milk reduces by about ¼ inch. Add the fish and kroeung mixture and continue to simmer until the milk turns pale green or yellow in color, depending on which type of kroeung you added, 10 to 15 minutes. Add the broth and stir, then add

RICE VERMICELLI WITH FISH CHOWDER, CONTINUED

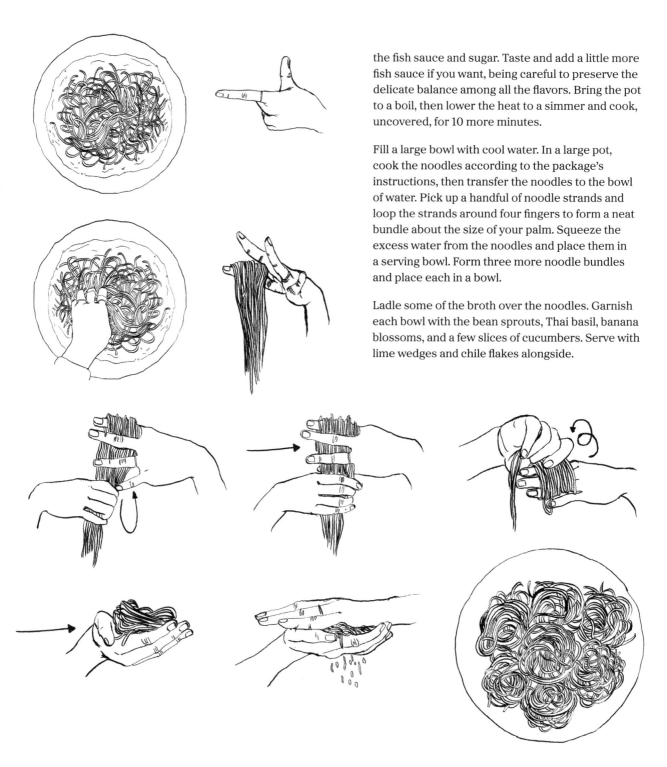

the fish sauce and sugar. Taste and add a little more fish sauce if you want, being careful to preserve the delicate balance among all the flavors. Bring the pot to a boil, then lower the heat to a simmer and cook, uncovered, for 10 more minutes.

Fill a large bowl with cool water. In a large pot, cook the noodles according to the package's instructions, then transfer the noodles to the bowl of water. Pick up a handful of noodle strands and loop the strands around four fingers to form a neat bundle about the size of your palm. Squeeze the excess water from the noodles and place them in a serving bowl. Form three more noodle bundles and place each in a bowl.

Ladle some of the broth over the noodles. Garnish each bowl with the bean sprouts, Thai basil, banana blossoms, and a few slices of cucumbers. Serve with lime wedges and chile flakes alongside.

NOM PACHOK NOODLES

A woman I met in a village in Cambodia made her nom pachok noodles with a very specific variety of rice that she sourced from a specific farmer. Which is to say, nom pachok noodles are a point of pride for Khmers.

Making the noodles is a true craft, and a laborious one. After the rice is ground by hand in a stone mill, the rice flour is soaked in water and fermented for several hours. It's this fermentation process that makes nom pachok noodles so distinctive and so difficult to replicate outside Cambodia. Fermenting the noodles also gives them a slight tartness that goes well with the fish broth.

After fermentation, it's time to knead the dough. Kneading the tough dough requires two people and a wooden contraption that connects a large pedal to a large mallet. During my visit, I watched as one person stepped on the pedal, raising and lowering the mallet to pound the dough. Every few seconds, before the mallet came down, another person was there to quickly but carefully rotate the dough so it could be evenly kneaded. The softened dough was then passed to a woman on a nearby bench, who pressed it through an extruder to form the noodles. The noodles were dropped into a bowl of water, and then she'd lift a handful, squeeze out the excess water, and coil the strands into lovely spiral bundles called ja vai. She laid the ja vai in a basket and covered them with lotus leaves. The noodles finally were ready for use or sale.

Back in the day, street vendors would sell nom pachok on a carrying pole over their shoulders, one basket filled with the fresh noodles tucked under lotus leaves, the other with the broth. I think about this a lot whenever I have a bowl of nom pachok: My ancestors ate this, too! It's a beautiful thing to know.

សម្លកកូរ
SOMLAW KOKO
STIRRING SOUP

Serves 4

Somlaw koko gets its name from the way it's in constant motion: Each time you add an ingredient, you stir. And each time you add an ingredient, you have to be mindful of time so everything will be cooked just right by the time it's ready to serve. I actually hated this soup when I was younger, because its many fillings meant a lengthy prep time, and I didn't enjoy the slight bitterness from the toasted rice powder. But I've come to appreciate it so much more, become proud of it, even, because it's one of the oldest and most quintessential Khmer dishes, one that reflects the wisdom of our ancestors who understood the nutritional and medicinal benefits of edible plants. And so while the soup does have some pork (which can be substituted for catfish, or a combination of both), this soup really is a showcase of the abundance and variety of fruits, vegetables, and edible flowers in the Khmer diet. The exact fillings can change from season to season; I like to make it in the fall and winter, when pumpkin and moringa leaves are available and the weather calls for a big bowl of hearty comfort. Serve with a big helping of rice.

- 8 ounces pork shoulder, sliced into ½-inch cubes
- 3 teaspoons kosher salt
- 1 tablespoon grapeseed or other neutral oil
- ¼ cup Green Kroeung (page 29)
- 2 tablespoons prahok
- ½ tablespoon palm sugar
- 1 tablespoon fish sauce
- ½ kabocha, peeled, seeded, and cut into 1-inch cubes (2 cups)
- 4 cups water
- 1 small (1½-pound) green papaya, cut into ¼-inch cubes (2 cups)
- 12 ounces baby eggplants, quartered (2 cups)
- 5 ounces long beans, trimmed and sliced into 2-inch pieces
- 2 tablespoons Toasted Rice Powder (recipe follows)
- 1 cup packed moringa or pumpkin leaves (optional)
- Bai / Steamed Jasmine Rice (page 52), for serving

Place the pork in a medium bowl and season it with 1 teaspoon of the salt. Toss and set aside.

In a heavy 4- to 6-quart pot over medium heat, heat the oil. When the oil begins to shimmer, add the kroeung and prahok and stir until fragrant, about 3 minutes. Add the palm sugar, stir until it melts, 1 minute, then add the pork. Sauté for another 3 minutes and cover the pot with its lid. Cook for 5 minutes—you should smell the lovely prahok and kroeung—then uncover, add the fish sauce and stir, and cover again. Let it cook for 1 minute for the flavors to meld.

Add the kabocha and water. Increase the heat to high and bring the pot to a boil, then lower the heat to medium. Add the papaya, eggplants, long beans, rice powder, and the remaining 2 teaspoons of salt and stir once more. Once it boils, reduce the heat to medium-low, cover, and simmer until the long beans turn pale green and are tender, about 8 minutes. Turn off the heat, uncover, and add the leaves. Serve with rice. Store leftovers in an airtight container and refrigerate for up to 2 days.

TOASTED RICE POWDER

Makes almost 1 cup

The first step to making this rice powder is to toast the rice, which takes about 30 minutes of constant stirring so the grains don't burn. You also can toast the rice in the oven, which won't require as much stirring, though it will take more time. Aside from adding this rice powder to somlaw koko, add it for a little crunch in a salad, like Plea Sach Ko / Beef Carpaccio Salad (page 77) or Pleay Trey / Khmer Ceviche (page 79).

1 cup uncooked white jasmine rice

Soak the rice in water for 30 minutes, then drain completely.

In a wok or medium skillet over medium heat, toast the rice until golden brown, about 30 minutes, constantly stirring. It feels like a long time to be standing and stirring, but if you leave the rice unattended, it may burn!

Alternatively, toast the rice in the oven. Preheat the oven to 300°F. Over high heat, toast the rice in an ovenproof wok or skillet until the grains start to turn light brown in color, about 5 minutes. Then transfer the wok to the oven and toast until the rice is golden brown, about 1½ hours, stirring every 15 minutes so they toast evenly.

Once the rice is toasted, set the wok aside to cool the rice. Once it cools, place the rice in a mortar or in a spice grinder. Grind into a coarse powder. Store the rice powder in an airtight container in the pantry or other cool, dark place for up to 1 month.

សម្លប្រហើរ

SOMLAW PRAHOR
COUNTRYSIDE SOUP

Serves 2 to 4

This hearty soup is very popular in Cambodia, especially in the countryside. It was the first soup my mom learned to make; Grandma would send her out to gather the vegetables and buy the fish, and then they would make the soup together. It's very vegetable forward, and I appreciate how healthy it is and how the ingredients highlight the way Khmers have foraged and lived off the land and water. I use kabocha, taro, and spinach here, all of which are available year-round, but if you want to keep to the spirit of the soup, add seasonal vegetables and edible flowers, too. Also, I use canned straw mushrooms for nostalgic reasons—my mom added them—but if you prefer another type of mushroom, feel free to use that instead. Just be sure to tear them into small pieces before tossing them into the pot.

2 tablespoons grapeseed or other neutral oil

2 (2-inch) pieces fingerroot, smashed

2 tablespoons Master Kroeung (page 27)

1-inch piece galangal, sliced into ¼-inch coins (1 tablespoon) (see page 22)

1 tablespoon prahok

1 small kabocha, peeled, seeded, and cut into 1½-inch cubes (2½ cups)

1 pound taro, cut into 1½-inch cubes (2½ cups)

5 cups Somlaw Mu-anh / Chicken Broth (page 32), or store-bought

12 ounces cod, salmon, catfish, or any firm whitefish fillet, cut into 2-inch pieces

1 teaspoon kosher salt

1 teaspoon fish sauce

1 bunch spinach or pea tendrils

2 cups straw mushrooms, drained and rinsed if using canned

Bai / Steamed Jasmine Rice (page 52), for serving

In a small pot, heat the oil over medium heat. When the oil begins to shimmer, about 1 minute, add the fingerroot, kroeung, galangal, and prahok. Stir until fragrant, about 5 minutes. Add the kabocha and taro, stir, then add the broth. Once it begins to boil, drop the heat to low, cover, and simmer for 10 minutes, or until the kabocha and taro are almost tender.

Add the fish, salt, and fish sauce. Cover and simmer until the fish is halfway cooked, about another 10 minutes. Add the spinach and mushrooms, re-cover, and turn off the heat. Let the soup sit for 10 more minutes, until the spinach has wilted and the fish is cooked through. Now it's ready! And, of course, serve with plenty of rice. Store leftovers in an airtight container and refrigerate for up to 2 days.

ការីសាច់មាន់

CURI SARAMAN
SARAMAN CURRY

Serves 2 to 4

Curi saraman is rooted in the Cham Muslim community, a group of people who migrated to Cambodia from Vietnam starting in the late nineteenth century and today represent about 2 percent of the country's population. The curry makes good use of beef and cardamom, two ingredients not used very often in Khmer cooking. The first time I tasted the curry in Cambodia, I was taken with its tender beef and luscious broth, so fragrant with the cardamom and other spices. Over time, the Cambodian influence on the curry came with the addition of shrimp paste and, in some versions, a bit of kroeung, too. I combine both using my red kroeung. It helps to have the kroeung ready before making the curry, as the curry itself takes a bit of time to build the flavors layer by layer. It might sound daunting, but it won't be. In fact, seeing how it all comes together is a big part of the satisfaction of this dish. That, and dipping into it with a crusty toasted baguette.

1 pound beef chuck or short ribs, cut into 1-inch cubes

2 teaspoons kosher salt

2-inch piece ginger, smashed

CURRY SPICE BLEND

6 green cardamom pods

1 star anise pod

1 cinnamon stick

1 teaspoon coriander seeds

2 shallots, halved

1 garlic bulb, cloves separated and peeled

3 tablespoons grapeseed or other neutral oil

3 tablespoons Bok Mtes / Chile Paste (page 31)

½ cup Red Kroeung (page 28)

2 cups coconut milk

1 yellow onion, quartered

½ cup water

3 tablespoons fish sauce

1 tablespoon sugar

1 cup coconut cream

2 tablespoons unsalted peanuts, toasted, for garnish

Bai / Steamed Jasmine Rice (page 52) or toasted baguette, for serving

Preheat the oven to 300°F.

As the oven preheats, place the beef in a medium bowl and toss the pieces with 1 teaspoon of the salt and the smashed ginger. Set aside.

MAKE THE SPICE BLEND

Spread the cardamom pods, star anise, cinnamon, and coriander seeds on a sheet pan and place in the oven. Stir every 2 minutes, then check on them at 7 minutes: They should be toasted and fragrant. If they're not yet toasted, continue to toast, checking on them every minute until they're done. It shouldn't take much longer than 10 minutes in total (you want to avoid burning them, as they'll become bitter). Slide them onto a plate to cool, then use a mortar or spice grinder to crush and blend them together.

Now open your windows and have the fan on blast, because it's going to get smoky! Turn the oven to broil.

CONTINUED

SARAMAN CURRY, CONTINUED

Place the shallots and garlic cloves on the same sheet pan you used to toast the spices and broil until they're thoroughly charred, about 5 minutes. Alternatively, you can char the shallots and garlic in a cast-iron skillet over high heat for about 5 minutes, using tongs to turn them frequently. But don't walk away—if you don't keep flipping, they'll burn instead of char. Let cool, then chop the shallots and set them aside with the garlic.

Transfer the cooled garlic and shallots to the bowl of a food processor. Pulse just a few times until roughly combined; the texture should be a coarse rather than a smooth puree. Place the mixture in a small bowl and add the crushed spices. Stir to combine. Set aside.

In a medium Dutch oven or other heavy pot over high heat, heat the oil. When the oil begins to shimmer, add the beef and sear the cubes on all sides until they're nicely caramelized and dark brown, about 2 minutes. Remove the beef from the pot and set aside.

Lower the heat to medium-high and add the garlic-shallot-spice mix, chile paste, and kroeung. Sauté until fragrant, about 5 minutes, then add the coconut milk and onion. Once it's gently simmering, drop the heat to low, cover, and simmer for 5 minutes. (Be sure it's at a simmer so the fats will slowly release from the milk and give the curry a nice, velvety texture. If you rush and boil it, the curry will be thick and heavy.)

Increase the heat to medium-high. Uncover and return the beef to the pot. Stir, then add the water, fish sauce, sugar, and the remaining 1 teaspoon of salt. When the mixture comes to a boil, cover, reduce the heat to low, and simmer until the broth is bright red in color, about 30 minutes. Add the coconut cream and increase the heat to high. When the cream begins to boil, drop the heat to low, cover, and simmer until the beef is tender, about 40 minutes.

Garnish with peanuts and serve with rice or a baguette. Phew, that's it! But definitely worth it!

KUY TEAV KHO KO
CARAMELIZED BEEF STEW

Serves 6

Don't let the long list of ingredients discourage you from making this stew. Once everything is prepped, it comes together very fast, and it's perfect for a blustery fall or winter evening. I love the combination of star anise and other warming spices and how a bit of palm sugar and condensed milk give the broth a luscious thickness. As the stew simmers, the meat will become so tender it'll practically melt in your mouth (and if you're feeling fancy, use short ribs!). Serve it with noodles to turn it into a saucy noodle stew or with a crisped baguette for dipping. Either way, bliss.

- 2 pounds well-marbled chuck or short ribs, cut into 1½-inch chunks
- 5 teaspoons kosher salt
- 4 star anise pods
- 2 (4-inch) cinnamon sticks
- 2 tablespoons grapeseed or other neutral oil
- ⅓ cup Bok Mtes / Chile Paste (page 31)
- 2 tablespoons palm sugar
- 8 garlic cloves, smashed
- 5 lemongrass stalks, trimmed (see page 23) and smashed
- 5 makrut lime leaves
- Thumb-size piece ginger, peeled and smashed (1½ tablespoons)
- 1-inch piece galangal, sliced into ¼-inch coins (1 tablespoon)
- 1 tablespoon fish sauce
- 2 tablespoons Maggi Seasoning
- 1 tablespoon condensed milk
- 4½ cups Somlaw Mu-anh / Chicken Broth (page 32), or store-bought
- 6 to 8 carrots, peeled and cut on the oblique (3 cups) (see Note 2, page 88)
- 13 ounces daikon, peeled and sliced into ½-inch coins (2 cups)
- 1 yellow onion, cut into 1-inch chunks

ASSEMBLY + SERVING

- 1 pound rice noodles or egg noodles, or 2 toasted baguettes
- 1½ cups mung bean sprouts
- 6 teaspoons garlic oil (see page 42)
- Freshly ground black pepper
- Freshly ground white pepper
- ½ bunch cilantro, leaves only
- ½ bunch green onions, sliced
- 2 limes, quartered

In a large bowl, season the beef with 3 teaspoons of the salt, then set aside.

In a Dutch oven or other heavy bottom pot over low heat, toast the star anise and cinnamon, stirring frequently to avoid burning, until fragrant, about 10 minutes. Alternatively, toast the spices in the oven at 300°F for 10 minutes. Remove the spices and set aside. Increase the heat to high and add the oil. When the oil begins to shimmer, add the beef and sear the pieces until all sides are nicely browned, about 10 minutes.

Lower the heat to medium. Return the toasted spices to the pot and leave them undisturbed to bloom for 1 to 2 minutes. Add the chile paste and palm sugar and stir to mix everything together. Add the garlic, lemongrass, lime leaves, ginger, galangal, fish sauce, Maggi Seasoning, condensed milk, and the remaining 2 teaspoons of salt. Stir for about 5 minutes to release the aromatics, then drop the heat to low, cover, and simmer for 15 minutes.

Add the broth and increase the heat to medium. Once it comes to a boil, lower the heat to medium-low and simmer, uncovered, for 1½ hours. Remove the star anise, cinnamon, lime leaves, lemongrass, ginger, and galangal. Add the carrots, daikon, and onion and cook uncovered until they're tender, about another 30 minutes. Now it's ready to assemble!

CARAMELIZED BEEF STEW, CONTINUED

If serving with noodles: Cook the noodles according to the package's instructions. To assemble, place about ¼ cup of bean sprouts in each bowl, then the cooked noodles on top. Add 1 teaspoon garlic oil and a bit of black and white pepper. Ladle 2 to 3 cups of the stew into the bowls and top with a sprinkling of cilantro and sliced green onions. Squeeze lime juice over the top (don't leave the lime rind in the broth, as it'll make the broth bitter).

If serving with a baguette: Ladle the stew into bowls and garnish with the bean sprouts, garlic oil, black and white pepper, cilantro, and green onions. Squeeze a bit of lime over the bowl, and serve with the toasted baguettes on the side to dip into the stew.

Store leftover broth, noodles or baguette, and garnishes separately in their own airtight containers and refrigerate for up to 2 days.

ដំបញុកកំពត
NOM PACHOK KAMPOT

KAMPOT NOODLES WITH COCONUT FISH SAUCE DRESSING

Serves 4

This dish is usually made with nom pachok noodles (see page 131), but the rice noodles, more widely available in the States, are a great substitute. Outfitted in a unique dressing of coconut milk and fish sauce, this can be found all over the Kampot province in the southwestern part of Cambodia. Feel free to customize the toppings; the most important thing is to have plenty of the dressing to go around. Served cold, this is a great summer dish.

- 1 pound tri-tip or flank steak, cut into pieces ⅛ inch thick and 2 inches long
- 4 garlic cloves, minced
- 2 tablespoons oyster sauce
- ½ teaspoon kosher salt
- 1 cup dried shrimp
- 3 tablespoons grapeseed or other neutral oil
- 1 yellow onion, thinly sliced

COCONUT FISH SAUCE DRESSING

- 1 cup coconut milk
- 1 cup Tuk Trey Piam / Fish Sauce Dressing (page 37)
- 4 green onion stalks, sliced
- 14 ounces uncooked rice vermicelli
- 2 tablespoons garlic oil (see page 42)
- 1 small cucumber, unpeeled, cut into matchsticks
- ½ cup crushed salted peanuts
- Chrouk Mtes Khtoem / Pickled Garlic Chile (page 35; optional)

In a medium bowl, mix together the beef, garlic, oyster sauce, and salt. Marinate for 15 minutes, or cover and marinate in the refrigerator overnight.

In a small bowl, submerge the dried shrimp in warm water and soak until softened, about 15 minutes.

Heat the oil in a wok over high heat. When the oil begins to shimmer, add the beef (without the garlic and marinade) and onion and sauté until the beef is slightly charred and the onion has caramelized, 5 to 7 minutes. Turn off the heat and cover to keep it warm.

MAKE THE DRESSING

In a small pot over low heat, stir together the coconut milk and fish sauce dressing. Bring it to a simmer, being careful not to let it boil over, just until the ingredients have nicely emulsified into a sauce, about 4 minutes. Add the green onions and turn off the heat.

Drain the shrimp and place them in a mortar. Smash several times with the pestle, just until the shrimp is crumbly—it should still have texture. Alternatively, pulse the shrimp a few times in the bowl of a food processor. Set aside.

Cook the noodles according to the package's instructions (but be sure to give them some TLC and stir them a few times while they cook; otherwise, they'll stick together and clump). Drain and rinse the noodles and transfer them to a large bowl. Add the garlic oil and stir.

Divide the noodles into bowls. Everyone can add their preferred fixings; I like to eat mine with a few slices of beef, some onion, dried shrimp, cucumber, peanuts, and (if using) pickled garlic chile. However you make the bowl, be sure to drizzle a generous amount of the dressing over the top—enough to coat the noodles—and to give it a good mix before digging in. The noodles are the best the day they're cooked, but you can store leftovers in an airtight container and refrigerate for up to 3 days. To reheat, microwave the noodles on low for a few seconds just to soften them. Store all other leftovers in separate airtight containers and refrigerate for up to 3 days.

នាម៉ឹកាម្រេចបៃតង

CHA MOUK MRECH BAITANG

STIR-FRIED SQUID WITH GREEN PEPPERCORNS

Serves 2

The coastal town of Kampot in Cambodia has an abundance of peppercorns and seafood, and I love this dish because of the way it highlights both. Green peppercorns are unripe peppercorns; unlike black peppercorns, they're a bit nutty, mild, and fruity. They're also fun to eat whole because they'll burst with flavor when you bite into them, and that flavor will linger. If you can't find them fresh, many spice shops offer them pickled or preserved in brine. The flavors of the peppercorns pair so nicely with the sweetness of the squid. I suggest sourcing fresh squid if you can (and asking the fishmonger to clean it for you, too), but if that's not possible, frozen squid will do, though note its flavors will be more muted. Or, if you don't mind picking the meat from the shell as you eat, crab is a delicious and great alternative to squid.

1 pound whole squid

2 tablespoons grapeseed or other neutral oil

4 garlic cloves, minced

1 tablespoon oyster sauce

1½ teaspoons sugar

1 teaspoon fish sauce

½ teaspoon kosher salt

¼ cup whole green peppercorns

Bai / Steamed Jasmine Rice (page 52), for serving

If the squid hasn't already been cleaned, start by pulling the head from the body. Using scissors, cut the body open. Remove and discard the innards and cartilage, then snip off the head (keep the tentacles). Scrape across the squid body with a knife to remove the membrane and any other remaining innards. Rinse and pat dry. Set aside.

In a wok over medium-high heat, heat the oil. When the oil begins to shimmer, add the garlic and sauté until fragrant, less than 1 minute, then add the oyster sauce, sugar, fish sauce, and salt. Simmer together for 10 seconds, then add the squid and sauté for 5 minutes. Add the peppercorns, stir for another 30 seconds, then turn off the heat. Let it sit for 1 minute before serving with rice. This dish is best eaten the day it's made.

KAMPOT PEPPERCORNS

The use of Kampot peppercorns is one way Khmer cooking differs from the cooking of other Southeast Asian countries. Where our neighbors may add chiles to add heat and spice to a dish, we often reach for these peppercorns instead. Distinctly floral and earthy, with some sweetness and a warm, lingering spice, Kampot peppercorns truly are special.

These peppercorns are grown in the Kampot and Kep provinces of southwestern Cambodia, where the Gulf of Thailand laps at the shores and the Dâmrei Mountains are in full view (Kep was part of Kampot until it became its own province in 2008). The region's environment and climate are ideal for cultivating peppercorns: The vines are planted on porous, fertile hillside soils rich in quartz and other minerals. It's also humid and warm throughout the year, with a long, heavy rainy season perfect for thirsty peppercorns.

Two types of peppercorns are grown in the area, the small-leaf Kamchay variety and the big-leaf Lampong variety. Some sources suggest that peppercorns have been cultivated in Cambodia as early as the tenth century. Certainly by the thirteenth century, they were established enough that a Chinese envoy named Zhou Daguan observed peppercorns "twisted round the stems of the rattan, fastening on like a hop vine" during his visit to the Angkor Empire. When Cambodia became a protectorate of France in 1863, the French greatly expanded the pepper production for their own use. By the 1920s, much of the pepper used in French kitchens could be traced back to a farm in Cambodia. It's worth noting what was happening in some of those French kitchens: As France extracted this bounty of peppercorns, along with other spices and raw ingredients, from Cambodia and other Southeast Asian countries, seminal chefs like Auguste Escoffier were revolutionizing French cuisine.

When the Khmer Rouge came to power in 1975, pepper farms were considered remnants of French colonial rule, and they were forcibly converted into rice fields. It was only in the 1990s that the industry slowly began to recover, thanks to families who moved back to the country and began replanting with support from the government and private investors. Today, Kampot peppercorns have Protected Geographical Indication (PGI) status, which recognizes the connection between the peppercorns and their unique growing regions, in Cambodia and the European Union. Similar to other products with PGI status (like Gruyère cheese and Parma ham), peppercorns can be labeled "Kampot peppercorns" only if they're grown in Kampot or Kep and only if farmers follow specific growing and harvesting practices to ensure their quality, including using only natural or organic fertilizers and harvesting by hand.

Here in the United States, you can find Kampot peppercorns at spice shops, some specialty markets, and reputable online vendors who work directly with Kampot farmers. Because of the smaller supply, as well as high demand, they're more expensive than those conventionally grown. If you're on a budget, I suggest saving the Kampot peppercorns for dishes where their floral flavor and tingling heat will have the most impact.

GREEN, BLACK, RED, AND WHITE: THE COLORS OF KAMPOT PEPPERCORNS

Peppercorns grow in long, thin bundles that resemble bunches of grapes. Their color and flavor varies depending on the timing of the harvest:

COLOR	RIPENESS	FLAVOR	USE IN...
Green	Unripe	Mild, nutty, fruity	Cha Mouk Mrech Baitang / Stir-Fried Squid with Green Peppercorns (page 144) and other seafood stir-fries
Black	Nearly ripe, harvested just before the peppercorns ripen. They turn black when dried.	Floral, warm, spicy, earthy	Any dish with a strong peppery flavor, like Kho / Caramelized Pork Belly (page 221), Kho Trey / Caramelized Fish with Tomatoes (page 179), Loc Lak / Stir-Fried Beef Cubes (page 223), and Tuk Prahok / Prahok Dipping Sauce with Seared Rib Eye (page 73)
Red	Fully ripe	Fruity, floral, sweet	Breakfast dishes as garnish, or in desserts
White	Fully ripe. Red peppercorns are soaked in boiling water. Then their outer red husks are removed. They turn white when dried.	Herbal, woodsy	Meat marinades or as garnish in dishes that use white peppercorns, like Kho Trey / Caramelized Fish with Tomatoes (page 179) and Kuy Teav Kho Ko / Caramelized Beef Stew (page 139)

បបរសាច់មាន់

BOR BOR SACH MU-ANH
CHICKEN PORRIDGE

Serves 2 to 4

Whenever I was in Cambodia and spent a long night partying, the breakfast I craved the most the next morning was a restorative bowl of chicken porridge with a side of cha kwai (crispy crullers). The porridge wraps you up in a big, warm hug, so it's also an absolute comfort on any day when you're feeling down or a little lonely. I include shredded chicken in my version, but you can have it with fish, sliced pork belly, or seafood instead. The best things are the fun toppings, so you can customize your bowl exactly how you'd like. If you want to serve cha kwai sticks, pick up freshly fried ones from your favorite dim sum spot, or find them refrigerated or frozen at Asian markets. It may be labeled "youtiao," "dầu cháo quẩy," "Chinese cruller," or "Chinese donut."

½ cup uncooked jasmine rice

5 cups Somlaw Mu-anh / Chicken Broth (page 32), or store-bought

1 tablespoon dried shrimp

½ tablespoon fish sauce

1 cup shredded cooked chicken

ASSEMBLY + SERVING

Khtoem Jien / Crispy Garlic Oil (page 42)

Freshly ground black pepper

Mung bean sprouts

Roughly chopped cilantro

Green onions, thinly sliced

Salted soybeans (preferably Yeo's brand), drained

Lime wedges

Chrouk Mtes Khtoem / Pickled Garlic Chile (page 35)

Chrouk Khtoem / Pickled Garlic (page 41; optional)

Cha kwai sticks (optional)

Rinse the rice several times until the water runs clear. In a medium pot over medium-high heat, stir the rice until all the grains are dry, about 5 minutes. Then stir in the broth, dried shrimp, and fish sauce. Increase the heat to high to bring it to a boil; then drop to low and simmer, uncovered, until the rice expands by about 20 percent, about 15 minutes. Add the shredded chicken, stir, and simmer, still uncovered, for 10 minutes. Give it one final stir to loosen any rice that may be stuck to the pot, then simmer for another 5 minutes or so, until the rice expands a little more and you have a nice, thick porridge.

To serve, ladle the porridge into bowls. Add a bit of crispy garlic and its oil and a dash of pepper. Top with bean sprouts, cilantro, green onions, and salted soybeans. Squeeze a wedge of lime over each bowl (discard the rind). Bring the bowls to the table along with the pickled garlic chile, pickled garlic, and cha kwai sticks and enjoy. And try to finish the pot—the porridge won't be the same the next day.

ាយមាន់

BAI MU-ANH

POACHED CHICKEN + GINGER RICE WITH SPICY, LIMEY FISH SAUCE

Serves 4

I could eat bai mu-anh every day—and I did when I lived in Cambodia. Every day, I stopped by a hann bai (rice stall) for a plate of bai mu-anh. The honks of motorcycles, the clatter of street noise, the chatter from conversations all faded away as I entered a zen state, fluffing the delicate ginger rice and dipping the poached chicken into the spicy, limey fish sauce. On the side waiting, always, was delicious chicken broth for sipping and fresh cucumbers to balance the whole meal. It's a different experience when you make bai mu-anh at home of course, but it is just as comforting. To start, you'll want to first make my chicken broth (see page 32) so you'll have both the broth and poached chicken you need for this recipe. You'll also use the chicken skin to render some fat, but if you prefer, you can skip that step by buying chicken fat from your local butcher.

1 poached chicken (page 32), cut into 8 pieces

Kosher salt

2 cups uncooked jasmine rice

7 cups Somlaw Mu-anh / Chicken Broth (page 32)

3 garlic cloves, smashed

2-inch piece ginger, peeled and smashed

½ teaspoon sugar

ASSEMBLY + SERVING

1 small cucumber, unpeeled, sliced into ¼-inch coins

Chrouk Mtes Khtoem / Pickled Garlic Chile (page 35)

Tuk Trey Piam / Fish Sauce Dressing (page 37)

Garlic oil (see page 42) (optional)

Freshly ground black pepper

Tuk Trey Mtes / Fish Sauce + Chile (page 33; optional)

Remove the skin from the poached chicken, lay it in a skillet or frying pan as evenly as you can, and turn the heat to medium. Refrigerate the chicken pieces.

Leave the skin undisturbed so the heat can do its magic and render the fat. Watch it carefully and lower the heat if necessary to avoid burning the skin. After about 10 minutes, you should have 2 tablespoons of fat. Turn off the heat and season the skin with a sprinkle of salt and enjoy as a treat while you cook.

Rinse and drain the rice under cold water about three times, until the water is almost clear. After rinsing for the last time, drain well.

In a small pot over low heat, warm 3 cups of the broth. You'll use this broth as the liquid to cook the rice.

Transfer the chicken fat to a medium heavy pot over medium-high heat and add the garlic and ginger. Sauté for 2 minutes, then add the rice. Sauté until the grains of rice are completely dry, about 5 minutes.

Pour the hot broth over the rice, then add the fish sauce, ½ teaspoon salt, and the sugar. Bring it to a boil, then immediately lower the heat to the lowest setting. Cover and cook undisturbed for 15 minutes, then remove from the heat. Transfer the chicken from the refrigerator to the top of the rice, re-cover, and cook for 5 more minutes.

When you're ready to serve, warm the remaining 4 cups of broth in the small pot over medium-low heat. Meanwhile, remove the chicken from the rice pot. It should be warm and its delicious juices will have flavored the rice! Slice the chicken, then fluff the rice. Scoop some rice onto four plates. Top each with a few chicken slices, cucumber, some pickled garlic chile, and a spoonful of dressing. Separately, divide the warm broth among four bowls and add a drizzle of garlic oil (if using) and a dash of pepper. Serve the broth and Tuk Trey Mtes / Fish Sauce + Chile (if using) alongside each rice plate. Store leftover broth, chicken, and rice in separate airtight containers and refrigerate for up to 2 days.

មាន់ដុតកូកា
MU-ANH DOAT COLA
COCA-COLA CHICKEN

Serves 4

On a trip to Cambodia in 2019, I had the chance to shadow Chef Sothea Seng at his contemporary Khmer restaurant, Lum Orng, in Siem Reap. At one point, I followed the sweet aroma of lemongrass to a pot on the stove, where a cook named Lim was making a meal for the staff. Lim let me take a peek inside the pot: a whole chicken resting on a bed of lemongrass. There was a dark sauce swirling at the bottom of the pot, which Lim said was Coca-Cola! When I got back home, I did the same for my staff, and it became part of our rotation. Note the chicken needs to be marinated overnight before cooking.

3½- to 4-pound whole chicken

2 tablespoons oyster sauce

2 teaspoons kosher salt

½ teaspoon freshly ground black pepper

½ teaspoon sugar

1 garlic bulb, cloves separated and peeled

1 shallot, halved

SAUCE

12 ounces Coca-Cola

1 teaspoon fish sauce

1 teaspoon unsweetened rice vinegar

½ teaspoon kosher salt

5 stalks lemongrass, trimmed (see page 23) and smashed

Bai / Steamed Jasmine Rice (page 52), for serving

Chrouk / Pickles (page 38), for serving

Pat the chicken dry, then set it aside on a plate.

In a small bowl, mix together the oyster sauce, salt, pepper, and sugar. Stuff the bird with the garlic and shallot, then brush the marinade all over the chicken. Make some room in your fridge and refrigerate the chicken overnight, either covered or uncovered. The next day, remove the chicken from the fridge about 30 minutes before you plan to cook.

MAKE THE SAUCE

Pour the soda in a medium Dutch oven or heavy pot and add the fish sauce, rice vinegar, and salt. Stir, then arrange the lemongrass in a single layer at the bottom of the pot. Place the chicken right on top of the lemongrass, cover the pot, and turn the heat to medium-high. Cook for 15 minutes—the chicken skin will tighten a little during that time—then drop the heat to low and simmer until the chicken browns, about 30 minutes. Turn off the heat, uncover, and leave the chicken undisturbed until cooked through (165°F on a thermometer), about another 15 minutes.

Remove the chicken from the pot and place it on a cutting board. Carve the chicken and place the pieces on a large platter. Spoon the sauce from the pot over the chicken. Serve with rice and chrouk alongside! Store leftover chicken and sauce together in an airtight container and refrigerate for up to 3 days.

Variation: If you want crispy skin, roast the bird instead: Marinate the chicken as directed. The next day, preheat the oven to 350°F. Arrange the lemongrass in the smallest baking tray or casserole dish you have that will fit the chicken, and place the chicken right on top. In a small bowl, stir together the soda, fish sauce, vinegar, and salt. Brush the soda sauce all over the chicken and set aside to rest. Pop the chicken into the oven and bake for 30 minutes, basting it with the sauce every 10 minutes. Increase the temperature to 400°F. Continue to roast and baste every 10 minutes until the chicken is cooked through and the internal temperature of the thickest part of the chicken reaches 165°F, about 30 more minutes (the total roast time will be about 1 hour). Rest 15 minutes before slicing.

PART III

SF LOVE

Formative dishes, experiments, and life lessons from my pop-ups

ស្តាប់ផ្គរលាន់ផ្គរលាន់ជាមួយភ្ជៀង
សំឡេងត្រហឹមមួយពេធ
ឱ្យានរឿងអាឡោះអាល័យ

Listen to the thunder harmonizing with the rain
A rhythmic pounding sound sings
Narrating a story of nostalgia

FROM SINN SISAMOUTH'S
"UNDER THE SOUND OF RAIN"

After my epiphany that day at that kuy teav stall in Phnom Penh, I came back home to my apartment in the Mission neighborhood of San Francisco and got started. I began calling my mom with cooking questions. She answered generally at first, but, slowly, bit by bit, she began to open up more. Her instructions became more specific and thorough, and she'd wait until I finished a step before guiding me through the next. She became excited to share her recipes with me.

My dad, too, would tell me about all the dishes he missed. Between those conversations, hands-on cooking lessons, visits to Cambodia, and my own taste memories, I began to master the basics of pounding together lemongrass, galangal, garlic, shallots, and lime leaves to make kroeung. I re-created mee kola, a cold noodle dish, and other favorites from home. I experimented with the Khmer food I missed the most from my trips to Cambodia and made and remade the broth for kuy teav until it was exactly what I remembered it to be.

I didn't go to culinary school, and I didn't know the first thing about opening or running a business. But the combination of naivete and passion for my dream pushed me to go for it. And while learning the recipes was my goal, it was also a means toward reaching an even larger goal: to learn more about my parents.

It didn't happen right away, but somewhere between the phone calls and our time cooking together in the kitchen, my mom started to slip in stories, some heavy, some light, about her life before. Stories like what it was like to grow up in her village. Stories like the one about her dog, Apollo, whom she named after the space flight that landed the first man on the moon. Apollo, whom she had to leave behind, barking and crying, the morning she made a run for it.

Once I felt comfortable enough, I invited friends over for dinner. With Khmer rock in the background, they tasted and offered feedback. From there, it was time to share my cooking with a wider audience. I called my pop-up Nyum Bai, which literally translates to "eat rice." In practice, though, it's more of a greeting, a "Let's eat!!" It's something my mom would say to visitors or when we came home. It seemed like the perfect name.

Soon enough, I booked a few small catering gigs, and that gave me some confidence. In 2014, I catered for an organization called La Cocina, a food business incubator for women, immigrants, and people of color. I had heard about the program, but I was too terrified to apply. But they believed in me, saw the passion behind my story, and accepted me into the program.

La Cocina was the turning point. I had help fine-tuning my brand and creating my business plan. More opportunities came to cater and hone my cooking. For the next few years, I popped up at farmers' markets, bakeries, restaurants, bars, even a donut shop, all over the East Bay. I kept the menu simple: kuy teav Phnom Penh, stir-fried noodles, papaya salads, fried chicken. I figured these dishes would be comforting for those who craved Khmer food, and a good entry point for those who needed the introduction.

But as exciting as all this was, it also was tough. We had a booth at the farmers' market, but on rainy days, few people came. Some pop-ups were excruciatingly slow. It was so demoralizing; all the confidence I built from those early apartment dinners and catering gigs started to drain away. More than once, I almost called it quits.

Yet life kept giving me chances. In 2017, I had a yearlong residency at a food stall in a public market—and it was a hit! People were genuinely curious about what I was doing. It seemed to me that though many were already familiar with Southeast Asian flavors, Khmer cooking was a cuisine they couldn't seem to pinpoint, and that wasn't a bad thing. They were ready to try new flavors. The positive reception was a reminder of the bigger picture, of why I was doing what I was doing. My confidence slowly started to come back. And I was ready to take the next step.

RECIPES FROM SAN FRANCISCO

I did so much cooking, experimentation, and planning for my pop-ups and eventual restaurant in my San Francisco apartment kitchen. This chapter is a compilation of that time: dishes I made for myself, dishes I developed for my pop-ups and restaurant, dishes that I tried to develop for the restaurant but ended up just making for myself and friends. All delicious and comforting whether you're cooking for yourself or looking to impress for a Sunday dinner party.

Playlist

"Kheunh te Mouy,"
SINN SISAMOUTH

"Cyclo,"
YOS OLARANG

"New Generation Youth,"
SINN SISAMOUTH AND ROS SEREYSOTHEA

"Cool Water Falling,"
SINN SISAMOUTH

"ChomNo Palin,"
ROS SEREYSOTHEA

"Full Moon,"
MOL KAMACH AND BAKSEY CHAM KRONG

"Khob Yok Pdey Baib Nah,"
ENG NARY AND PEN RAN

ពោតអាំង

POT ANG

GRILLED CORN WITH COCONUT MILK + GREEN ONION

Serves 4

This street food snack is so delicious and so easy to make at home. The fresh corn here is brushed in a sauce that has a little bit of everything: richness from coconut milk, sweetness from palm sugar, umami from fish sauce, a touch of heat from chile flakes. You can roast the corn in the oven, but it's a thousand times better cooked and charred on a hot grill. It's perfect for the summer: Add Sach Ko Ang / Beef Skewers (page 66) and Chrouk / Pickles (page 38) and it's a party!

Grapeseed or other neutral oil, for greasing

2 cups coconut milk

¼ cup palm sugar

¼ cup fish sauce

½ cup sliced green onions

1 tablespoon chile flakes

4 ears corn, shucked

Oil the grill grates and preheat the grill to medium-high.

As the grill heats, stir together the coconut milk and palm sugar in a small pot over medium heat to melt the palm sugar. Turn off the heat and add the fish sauce. Give the sauce a good stir, then set aside to cool. Add the green onions and chile flakes.

Place the corn on the grill. When the kernels start to get a little bit of shine on them, about 10 minutes, brush the sauce all over the corn and rotate. Grill until you start to see char marks on the kernels, about 10 minutes, then brush more sauce on the corn and rotate again. Continue grilling and rotating, adding more sauce as you do so, until the kernels are tender and cooked through, about 30 minutes in total. Place the corn on a platter or plate, drizzle any remaining sauce all over, and serve.

TO ROAST INSTEAD OF GRILLING

Preheat the oven to 400°F. Place the corn on a wire rack set on a sheet pan. Roast until the kernels are tender, about 30 minutes, brushing the sauce on the corn about every 5 minutes and rotating them each time you do so. Before serving, lather more sauce all over the corn.

CHA DAU FU KH-CHAI

QUICK STIR-FRY WITH FRIED TOFU + CHIVES

Serves 2 to 4

My mom made this the classic way, which is to stir-fry the tofu with sliced pork belly and cubes of pig blood curd. But once on my own, I realized I prefer the stir-fry with just the tofu, plus tons of bean sprouts, garlic chives, and black pepper. And since I almost always have all these ingredients in my fridge and pantry, it's easy to throw together when I want a simple, quick meal after a tiring day. For maximum convenience, I use store-bought fried tofu, which soaks up the sauce and makes each bite a juicy one.

- 2 tablespoons grapeseed or other neutral oil
- 4 garlic cloves, minced
- 3 tablespoons water
- 1 tablespoon oyster sauce
- 1 tablespoon fish sauce
- 1 teaspoon sugar
- 1 teaspoon mushroom powder or MSG
- ½ teaspoon freshly ground black pepper
- 5½ ounces fried tofu (4 cups) (see Note)
- 9 ounces mung bean sprouts (3 cups)
- 5 ounces garlic chives, sliced into 2-inch segments (2 cups)
- 3 tablespoons Khtoem Krahm Jien / Crispy Shallots (page 44), or store-bought
- Bai / Steamed Jasmine Rice (page 52), for serving

Note: Fluffy cubes of fried tofu, sometimes labeled "tofu puffs," can be found in the refrigerated section at Asian markets. Check to make sure it's just fried tofu in the bag, without any marinade or seasoning.

In a large wok over medium-high heat, heat the oil. When the oil begins to shimmer, add the garlic and sauté until fragrant. Add 1 tablespoon of the water, the oyster sauce, fish sauce, sugar, mushroom powder, and pepper. Simmer until it bubbles and you can start to pick up the fragrance of fish sauce, about 1 minute, then add the tofu. Stir to coat the tofu in the sauce.

Now, it will look like a lot, but add all the bean sprouts and chives, plus the remaining 2 tablespoons of water, to the wok. Cover until the sprouts wilt and shrink to half their original size, about 5 minutes. Then uncover and stir.

Plate it up and garnish with the fried shallots. Serve immediately with bai (steamed jasmine rice, that is!). It's best the same day it's made, but if you have leftovers, place them in an airtight container, refrigerate, and finish them as soon as you can.

Vegetarian and vegan variations: Replace the fish sauce and oyster sauce with Thai seasoning soy sauce or Maggi Seasoning and salt to taste.

កាពិកធារ

KAPEEK POW
SMOKED FISH + SHRIMP TAPENADE

Serves 6

A combination of shrimp, chiles, dried fish, garlic, sugar, and tamarind, kapeek pow is funky, sweet, a bit tangy, and perfect for smearing on a toasted baguette like a tapenade or eating with raw veggies. I initially wanted to serve kapeek pow as an appetizer for the restaurant, but while it's not difficult, it took more time than we had in the kitchen to make it. At home, though, it's totally worth the effort. In Cambodia, kapeek pow is made with a fish called trey cheaw, which are skewered through their gills on bamboo poles and smoked over a wood fire. Khmers have preserved fish this way for generations; you can even see it depicted in carvings at Angkor Wat. Unfortunately, dried trey cheaw is a rare find here in the States, so I dehydrate smoked fish in my oven.

½ cup dried shrimp

8 ounces hot-smoked salmon, mackerel, or any whitefish

4 teaspoons shrimp paste

2 tablespoons grapeseed or other neutral oil

6 garlic cloves, minced

1 small shallot, minced

3 tablespoons sugar

1 tablespoon Bok Mtes / Chile Paste (page 31)

3 tablespoons Tuk Ampil / Tamarind Water (page 30)

4 teaspoons kosher salt

1 teaspoon chile flakes or more, depending on how spicy you like things!

4 Thai eggplants, quartered or cut into wedges, for serving

1 to 2 English or Persian cucumbers, unpeeled, sliced into ½-inch coins, for serving

Bai / Steamed Jasmine Rice (page 52), Bai Kadang / Rice Crackers (page 55), or toasted baguette, for serving

Preheat the oven to 375°F. While the oven heats, in a small bowl submerge the dried shrimp in warm water and soak until softened, about 15 minutes, then drain. Transfer the shrimp to a mortar and use a pestle to pound the shrimp into small crumbly pieces. Alternatively, chop the shrimp finely with a knife or pulse in the bowl of a food processor. Set aside.

Place the smoked fish on a sheet pan. Separately, drop the shrimp paste onto a piece of foil and fold it into a packet. Place both in the oven. After 5 minutes, remove the shrimp paste. Continue to bake the fish, about 3 more minutes, then flip and bake until it has the consistency of jerky, about 7 minutes longer (the total bake time for the fish is around 15 minutes). Once the fish is cool enough to handle, shred it into smaller pieces until you have about 2 cups.

In a medium skillet over medium-high heat, heat the oil. Wait about 30 seconds, then drop the heat to low and add the garlic, shallot, and dried shrimp. Sauté until aromatic, about 4 minutes, to really extract their flavors. Add the sugar and chile paste. Cook for about 1 minute, stirring the whole time.

Add the shrimp paste, breaking it up as you drop it into the skillet. Add the fish, tamarind water, salt, and chile flakes. Stir until the mixture becomes a chunky spread, about 4 minutes. Transfer it to a ramekin or bowl and serve with the eggplants, cucumbers, and rice. Refrigerate leftovers in an airtight container for up to 3 months.

TURN LEFTOVERS INTO RICE BALLS!

Mix 1 tablespoon of the kapeek pow with 2 cups of cooked jasmine rice. Then use your hands to form some into Cambodian rice balls!

សាច់មាន់ចោក

SACH MU-ANH BOUNGK
STUFFED CHICKEN WINGS

Serves 4

I often made these wings when I wanted to serve my friends something a little fancy and impressive. That's because these are true labors of love: deboning the chicken wings and stuffing them with a mixture of seasoned ground meat and kroeung take a bit of time and a lot of care. But the results look and taste incredible. The wings are marinated—for best results, marinate them overnight—then grilled to a lovely golden brown, and the stuffing flavors the wings from the inside out (if it's not grilling season, you can bake the wings instead). In Cambodia, you'll see stuffed frog legs instead of wings, so you can do that, too, if you like frog legs. Either way, eat these with a big bowl of Bai / Steamed Jasmine Rice (page 52) and Chrouk / Pickles (page 38) on the side.

4 whole chicken wings (including wing tips)

2 tablespoons oyster sauce

1 tablespoon Thai seasoning soy sauce

Grapeseed or other neutral oil

1 teaspoon kosher salt

1 teaspoon sugar

STUFFING

1½ ounces glass noodles

6 makrut lime leaves, center veins removed, very thinly sliced

½ pound ground pork or chicken

½ cup Yellow Kroeung (page 28)

¼ cup crushed salted peanuts, toasted

1 tablespoon oyster sauce

1 tablespoon fish sauce

1 teaspoon sugar

Chrouk / Pickles (page 38), for serving

Bai / Steamed Jasmine Rice (page 52), for serving

Let's start by deboning the chicken. Start at the drumette. With sharp kitchen shears, snip around the bone and gently tug and scrape the meat down to separate it from the bone. Being careful to not puncture the skin, continue to snip and tug, essentially turning the chicken inside out, as you work your way toward the joint. When you reach the joint, carefully snap and remove the bone from the joint. Continue snipping, tugging, and scraping down the wingette/flat, still being careful to not puncture the skin, until you reach the wing tip. Snap off the bone. Re-form the wing into its original shape and place it in a large bowl. Repeat with the remaining wings.

Add the oyster sauce, seasoning soy sauce, 1 tablespoon oil, the salt, and sugar to the bowl. Coat the wings in the marinade and refrigerate for at least an hour, or overnight.

MAKE THE STUFFING AND GRILL

Oil the grill grates and preheat your grill to high or your oven to 375°F.

Soak the glass noodles in warm water for 10 minutes, then drain and pat dry. Using scissors, cut the noodles into 1-inch pieces and pat dry a few more times. Set aside.

In a medium bowl, combine the lime leaves, pork, kroeung, peanuts, oyster sauce, fish sauce, and sugar. Mix in the glass noodles.

Remove the chicken from the fridge. Stuff each wing with ½ cup of the filling, arranging the filling so it's evenly distributed. To make it easier, you can place the filling in a piping bag (or in a strong resealable plastic bag with a bottom corner snipped off) and pipe the filling into the wings.

To grill: Place the chicken on the grill. Lower the heat to medium and grill the chicken until they're nicely charred, golden brown, and cooked through (the thickest part of the wing should reach an internal temperature of 165°F), about 20 minutes on each side.

To bake: Place the wings on a sheet pan and bake for 15 minutes, then flip and bake until they're cooked through (the internal temperature of the thickest part of the wing should reach 165°F), about 15 more minutes.

Serve the chicken with chrouk and rice on the side. Store leftover wings in an airtight container and refrigerate for up to 2 days.

CHA TREK SAK

STIR-FRIED CUCUMBERS WITH BLACK PEPPER + EGG

Serves 4

This is an easy and quick recipe that's packed with flavor, and it's even good for you! My mom made this stir-fry for us using winter melon, but when I started to cook for myself, I decided to use more manageable cucumbers instead. I tend to use English cucumbers for this, but use any variety you like. Sliced pork belly makes the stir-fry more substantial, but you can omit it, especially if you have other proteins on the table. Whatever you do, the key to the dish is that final bit of ground black pepper right at the end. That warm pop of spice really completes the dish.

2 tablespoons grapeseed or other neutral oil

4 garlic cloves, minced

¼ cup sliced (⅛-inch thin and 1-inch wide) pork belly (optional)

2 tablespoons oyster sauce

1 tablespoon fish sauce

½ tablespoon sugar

Freshly ground black pepper

1½ pounds cucumbers, unpeeled, quartered lengthwise, deseeded, and cut into 2-inch spears (5 cups)

2 eggs

Kosher salt (optional)

2 green onion stalks, sliced

Bai / Steamed Jasmine Rice (page 52), for serving

In a wok or large skillet over high heat, heat the oil. When the oil begins to shimmer, add the garlic and sauté until fragrant, about 30 seconds. If you're adding pork belly, now's the time. Sauté the pork until the slices are nice and browned, about 5 minutes. Add the oyster sauce, fish sauce, sugar, and ½ teaspoon pepper and stir everything all together. Add the cucumbers and sauté until they've softened, 3 to 5 minutes.

Crack the eggs into a small bowl and beat them lightly with a fork or chopsticks. Make a well at the very center of the wok and add the eggs. Scramble them right in the well. Once they've set, about 2 minutes, sauté everything together for about another 5 minutes, or until well combined. Carefully taste. Add a pinch of salt if you think it needs more seasoning. Top with the green onions and some more pepper. Serve with rice. That's it! It's best to eat it up right away, but if you have leftovers, store them in an airtight container and refrigerate for up to 1 day.

Vegetarian and vegan variations: To make this vegetarian, omit the fish sauce and oyster sauce and add salt to taste. To make it vegan, omit the egg, too.

ស្ងោរសាច់មាន់

SGNOR SACH MU-ANH
CHICKEN LIME SOUP

Serves 4

Sgnor! We do love our soups. While a somlaw like Somlaw Machoo Ktiss Ban Kong / Shrimp Tamarind Coconut Soup (page 170) incorporates many components in a thick broth, a sgnor is the opposite: It's simpler, filled with just a few ingredients in a clear, soothing broth. The highlight of this sgnor is the chicken broth, which is aromatic and bright from the lemongrass, galangal, makrut lime leaves, and lime juice. While you can, of course, pick up broth from the market, I recommend you make it yourself. With so few ingredients in the soup, you really will be able to taste the difference.

- 7 cups Somlaw Mu-anh / Chicken Broth (page 32), or store-bought
- 6 makrut lime leaves
- 3 lemongrass stalks, trimmed (see page 23) and smashed
- 2 garlic cloves, smashed
- 2 tablespoons fish sauce
- 1-inch piece galangal, sliced into ¼-inch coins (1 tablespoon)
- 1 tablespoon kosher salt
- 1 teaspoon sugar
- 1½ pounds chicken thighs or breasts, sliced, or 1 Cornish hen, cut into chunks
- 3 limes, juiced (¼ cup)
- Mix of thinly sliced cilantro, green onions, and Thai basil, for garnish
- Tuk Trey Mtes / Fish Sauce + Chile (page 33), for serving
- Bai / Steamed Jasmine Rice (page 52), for serving

In a large pot, bring the broth to a boil. Add the lime leaves, lemongrass, garlic, fish sauce, galangal, salt, and sugar and stir. Bring the broth back to a boil and cook for 2 minutes, then add the chicken. Lower the heat to medium and simmer, uncovered, until the chicken is cooked through, about 20 minutes, occasionally skimming and discarding any foam or scum that rises to the top.

Turn off the heat. Stir in the lime juice; the soup will turn cloudy as you do so. Ladle the soup into individual bowls (the lemongrass, galangal, and lime leaves shouldn't be eaten; you can discard them, or just give a heads-up to your guests) and garnish each with the herbs.

Serve each bowl of soup with fish sauce and chile on the side, plus some steamed rice. To enjoy, spoon some soup over the rice, drizzle in some fish sauce, and yum!

Variation: For a fancier version of this soup, substitute the chicken for mushrooms and lobster, or giant prawns (with their heads and tails on) and mushrooms. The shellfish and mushrooms add more sweetness and umami to the broth, giving it a richer, more complex flavor. Bring 4 cups chicken broth to a boil, then add the lime leaves, lemongrass, garlic, fish sauce, galangal, salt, and sugar and stir. Boil for 5 minutes, then add 1 cup oyster mushrooms and 1 pound lobster or 2 giant prawns. (In many markets, you can ask the butcher to cut up the lobster for you. Be sure to ask for the head, too, because that's where the flavor is!) Simmer until cooked through, about 20 minutes, skimming the broth as necessary. Continue with the recipe for finishing and serving the soup.

ស្ងោរឆ្អឹងគោ
SGNOR CHUONG KHO
COZY OXTAIL SOUP

Serves 6

France colonized Cambodia for nearly a century between 1863 to 1953. During that time, the French brought a number of ingredients and dishes to the country: butter, baguette, pâté, and pot-au-feu, a stew of boiled meat and vegetables. This oxtail soup has its roots in pot-au-feu, but the resulting dish, served with a dipping sauce for the oxtail, is all Khmer. This soup takes time to make, but most of that time is passive once the soup is at a simmer. And while this is enough for a nice cozy dinner with family or friends, I really like making the soup even when it is just me. The leftovers can last all week, and it's so, so comforting on a cold day.

- 3 pounds oxtail or any other braising beef, like short ribs or beef chuck, cut into 2-inch chunks
- 2 tablespoons kosher salt
- 1 large yellow onion, quartered
- 3 tablespoons sugar
- 2 tablespoons fish sauce
- 3 carrots, peeled and cut into 1½-inch segments
- 3 russet potatoes, peeled, washed well, diced into 2-inch cubes
- 2 bunches Swiss chard, or 1 small head green cabbage, cut into large squares
- ½ cup Tuk Krauch Chhma + Ambel + Mrech / Lime + Salt + Pepper Sauce (page 36), for dipping
- Bai / Steamed Jasmine Rice (page 52), for serving

Preheat the broiler.

Wash the oxtails under cold water and pat the pieces dry with a paper towel. Sprinkle all sides with 1 tablespoon of the salt and massage the salt into each piece. Place the oxtails on a sheet pan and broil for about 15 minutes, then flip and broil for about another 15 minutes, or until well browned.

Transfer the oxtail to a large stockpot and cover with water. Bring the water to a medium boil, then immediately lower the heat so that the water simmers—you want small bubbles. Simmer, uncovered, for 1 hour, occasionally skimming and discarding any foam or scum that rises to the top. Add more water as necessary to keep the oxtails submerged.

After 1 hour, add the onion, sugar, fish sauce, and the remaining 1 tablespoon of salt. Gently stir. Simmer the soup for 30 minutes, at which point the broth should be mostly clear. If it's not, skim again.

Add the carrots and potatoes. Cook until the carrots, potatoes, and oxtail are tender and the onion is translucent, about 30 minutes. Continue adding water if necessary to ensure the oxtails stay submerged. Bring the soup to a light boil, add the chard, gently stir, and turn off the heat.

Serve the soup hot with sauce and rice on the side for everyone at the table. Store leftovers in an airtight container and refrigerate for up to 3 days (the soup is so good the day it's made, but it will be even better on the next day, after the flavors have had a day to develop).

សម្លម្ជូរខ្ទិះបង្គង
SOMLAW MACHOO KTISS BAN KONG

SHRIMP TAMARIND COCONUT SOUP

Serves 4

I didn't grow up with somlaw machoo ktiss ban kong. I learned about it only on a trip to Cambodia, when I heard elders talking about it; the idea of combining pineapple's sweet-tart flavor with the tang of tamarind and the creaminess of coconut milk sounded so good! But unfortunately, I didn't get a chance to actually try it. Sometime later, I was back home and had some pineapple left over from a day of recipe testing for my restaurant. I remembered this soup and gave it a try—and it was as delicious as it sounded. You end up with a bowl that's similar to a bisque or a light chowder. If you have the kroeung ready to go, it'll be ready in less than an hour.

5 jumbo shrimp, unpeeled, heads and tails on

2 tablespoons grapeseed or other neutral oil

1 tablespoon Master Kroeung (page 27)

1 tablespoon palm sugar

1 teaspoon prahok

1 teaspoon shrimp paste

4 makrut lime leaves

4 tablespoons Tuk Ampil / Tamarind Water (page 30)

2 tablespoons Bok Mtes / Chile Paste (page 31)

1 tablespoon fish sauce

½ teaspoon kosher salt

1 (13.5-ounce) can coconut milk

1 small pineapple, cut into 1-inch cubes (1½ cups)

1 cup oyster mushrooms

½ cup water

1 cup loosely packed Thai basil

Bai / Steamed Jasmine Rice (page 52), for serving

Snip off the pointy tip on the head of each shrimp, trim their whiskers, then devein. Rinse the shrimp and set them aside.

In a heavy saucepan over medium-low heat, heat the oil. When the oil begins to shimmer, or when you listen close and hear a bit of a crackle, add the kroeung, palm sugar, prahok, and shrimp paste. Stir stir stir! The palm sugar and lemongrass in the kroeung will burn quickly if you don't keep things moving in the pan. Keep stirring until all the ingredients are incorporated and the shrimp paste and prahok dissolve, about 5 minutes.

Add the lime leaves, tamarind water, chile paste, fish sauce, and salt. Stir, then drop the heat to low and cover for 5 minutes. Add the coconut milk and pineapple. Increase the temperature to high to bring the liquid to a boil, then drop the heat to low, cover, and simmer undisturbed for 10 minutes.

Meanwhile, tear the oyster mushrooms into smaller pieces about the width of two fingers. Add them to the pan, along with the shrimp and water. Cover and cook until the shrimp is opaque and cooked through, about another 10 minutes. Stir in the Thai basil until just wilted. Ladle into bowls and serve with rice alongside. Store leftovers in an airtight container and refrigerate for up to 3 days.

RE-CREATING NEARLY LOST DISHES

As a young girl, my mom learned how to cook by observing her aunt and other cooks prepare the day's meals. She prepped ingredients under their watchful eyes, and she was sent to the market to pick out produce and proteins. Historically, this is how Khmer cooking has been taught, with one generation teaching the next. In this oral tradition, recipes were committed to memory. The rare fully documented recipe usually related to the elite cooking of the royal courts.

But during Cambodia's civil war in the 1970s, records were destroyed. The Khmer Rouge carried out its genocidal campaign. In less than a decade, generations of knowledge about Khmer food and culture vanished.

For those who resettled in the United States, often the only way to re-create beloved dishes was to work from memory. Neighbors helped one another fill in the gaps. It's this collective patchwork and profound power of taste memories that have defined much of Cambodian cooking in the United States over the past few decades.

I find this desire and desperate love for familiar, comforting flavors so sad and so beautiful. With all that perished in the war, much of the cuisine could have been forever lost. But that's not what happened: Oceans away from Cambodia, diasporic communities still found ways to cook food from home.

When I set out to learn how to cook Khmer food in 2012, resources were limited. Other than Longteine De Monteiro's *The Elephant Walk Cookbook*—one of the first Khmer cookbooks published in the States—and Sorey Long and Kanika Linden's *Ambarella: Cambodian Cuisine*, there weren't a ton of print resources. Online, one or two YouTube video channels were dedicated to Khmer cooking, though they focused more on showcasing the food than on formal instruction. With so few references, I had to rely on oral histories. I interviewed my parents and extended family about their memories. I cooked with my mom. On every visit to Cambodia, I talked to locals about their food memories. Some, like a woman who taught me how to make prahok kop,[1] generously invited me into their outdoor kitchens.

Still, putting the pieces together wasn't easy. I wanted to connect how the dishes tasted in the past with how I could re-create them in the present while also making them my own. Some dishes, I knew, probably couldn't be exactly replicated; my parents, for instance, always said nom pachok noodles[2] here never tasted the same as they did in Cambodia.

There were others, though, that I wanted to re-create as faithfully as possible. Kuy Teav Phnom Penh[3] was one of those recipes; it was (and still is) one of my favorites. It also was the noodle soup that inspired me to share Khmer food with the world. I grew up helping my mom prep it and watching her cook it.

---

[1] Buried Prahok (page 115).
[2] Fermented rice noodles (see page 131).
[3] Pork Noodle Soup (page 213).

It took almost four months of trial and error until I got it. I realized that though my mom's kuy teav always tasted the same to me, she didn't follow one consistent recipe. Instead, she adjusted the pot based on what she had in the kitchen at the time and tasted and tasted until it tasted right to her. And some things were so natural to her that she didn't feel the need to tell me, like not to overboil the broth or it would be too cloudy. It was very frustrating, but I came to appreciate that I was part of an oral tradition, and my mom was teaching me the way she was taught. Once I did get it, I was so proud, relieved, and excited that I could finally share it.

Things are so different now from when I set out to learn how to cook Khmer food. It's amazing to see so many Khmer Americans create new dishes based on ones that, if not for memory, could have disappeared. I hope we all can continue to preserve and evolve Khmer food—and pass on what we've learned to the next generation, too.

ម៉ីឆា

MEE CHA
STUDENT NOODLES

Serves 1 to 2

These noodles are called student noodles for good reason: They're affordable, easy to prepare, and more than satisfying. I had this a bunch when I was backpacking through Cambodia; because I was on a budget, these seventy-five-cent packages of instant rice noodles were really all I could afford. Before that, my dad liked to make this for us; he'd go really fancy by adding shrimp, squid, and Chinese broccoli. My version here is much more minimal, but feel free to add whatever vegetables and proteins you'd like. As for the noodles, I'm usually driven by nostalgia to pick up the ones from the Wai Wai brand, which is what my dad used, but the Mama brand is also excellent. Of course, your favorite brand of instant rice noodles works, too.

SAUCE

1 tablespoon Maggi Seasoning

1 tablespoon oyster sauce

1 teaspoon granulated sugar or palm sugar

1 teaspoon fish sauce

2 (2-ounce) packages instant rice noodles (any flavor)

2 tablespoons grapeseed or other neutral oil

3 garlic cloves, minced

2 ounces (¼ cup) sliced chicken, pork, or any other protein (optional)

1 small head green cabbage, cut into ½-inch slices (2 cups)

1 small yellow onion, cut into ½-inch slices

1 to 2 Poung Mu-anh Jien / Crispy Fried Eggs (page 45) or Poung Mu-anh Jien Ka-Lok / Egg Ribbons (page 47)

Chrouk Mtes Khtoem / Pickled Garlic Chile (page 35), for serving

Tuk Trey Mtes / Fish Sauce + Chile (page 33; optional), for serving

MAKE THE SAUCE

In a small bowl, whisk together the Maggi Seasoning, oyster sauce, sugar, and fish sauce until the sugar dissolves. Set aside.

To cook the noodles, bring 2 quarts of water to a boil. Add the noodles and their powder mixes. Cook until the noodles are al dente, about 3 minutes. Transfer the noodles to a colander to drain.

In a wok or large skillet over medium-high heat, heat the oil. When the oil begins to shimmer, add the garlic and sauté for about 1 minute. If you're adding any protein, now is the time; sauté the pieces until they're about halfway cooked, 5 to 7 minutes. Add the cabbage, onion, and sauce. Cook for 5 minutes, then add the drained noodles. Give it all a good stir and continue to sauté until the sauce thickens, 5 to 10 minutes. Turn off the heat. Transfer the noodles into one big bowl for yourself or two bowls to share. Top with eggs and serve with the pickled garlic chile and fish sauce and chile on the side.

ម៊ីកូឡា
MEE KOLA

COLD NOODLES WITH CUCUMBER RELISH + DRIED SHRIMP

Serves 4

Mee kola is a cold noodle dish that my mom ate a lot when she was a kid. In turn, she made it for us often, especially in the summer. The roots of the dish go back to the Kola people, who migrated from Burma to the Pailin region of northwestern Cambodia in the eighteenth and nineteenth centuries and mined the mountainous terrain for sapphires and other gems. The original version of these noodles includes soy sauce and pickled cucumbers; the Khmer version adds eggs and dried shrimp. There are several components to this salad, but they're not difficult to prepare; the cucumber relish can even be made a day in advance (and, in fact, the longer it sits, the better!). Once you have everything prepped, assembling each bowl of noodles is super easy.

CUCUMBER RELISH

¼ cup water

½ cup unsweetened rice vinegar

½ cup granulated sugar

1 garlic clove, minced

Kosher salt

2 to 3 Persian cucumbers, unpeeled, very thinly sliced

¼ cup dried shrimp

4 eggs

2 cups mung bean sprouts

1 pound thin, flat rice noodles (see Note)

¼ cup Maggi Seasoning

2 tablespoons garlic oil (see page 42)

ASSEMBLY + SERVING

6 teaspoons Tuk Trey Piam / Fish Sauce Dressing (page 37)

¼ cup roasted salted peanuts, coarsely crushed

6 to 8 green onion stalks, sliced on a bias (1 cup)

1 cup loosely packed Thai basil leaves

1 cup loosely packed cilantro

1 lime, quartered

Note: If using dried noodles, soak them first in cold water for 15 minutes, then drain.

PREPARE THE CUCUMBER RELISH + TOPPINGS

In a small bowl or jar, combine the water with the rice vinegar, sugar, garlic, and a pinch of salt and stir until the sugar dissolves. Place the cucumber slices in the brine and let them sit for at least 15 minutes. If you're making this a day ahead, place the cucumbers and brine in an airtight container, cover, and refrigerate.

Now prepare the toppings. In a small bowl, submerge the dried shrimp in warm water and soak until softened, about 15 minutes, then drain. Place the shrimp in the bowl of a food processor and pulse a few times to coarsely chop it into big chunks. Alternatively, use a mortar and pestle to break up the shrimp.

Bring a medium pot of water to a boil. While it heats, fill a large bowl with ice and water. Set aside.

Gently lower the eggs in the water, then set a timer for 7 minutes. Once the timer rings, use a spider to immediately transfer the eggs to the ice bath.

COLD NOODLES WITH CUCUMBER RELISH + DRIED SHRIMP, CONTINUED

Reserve the cooking water in the pot. You can peel the eggs as soon as they're cool, but they may be easier to peel if you let them sit in the ice bath for 15 to 30 minutes.

Bring the pot of water back to a boil. As the water boils, fill another large bowl with iced water. Once the water is at a boil, add the bean sprouts, stir, then immediately pull them out with the spider and transfer them to the ice bath. Once cool, transfer them into a colander and drain the ice bath.

Drain the water from the pot and refill it with fresh water for the noodles. Refill the large bowl with iced water, too, one last time. Bring the pot of water to a boil, then drop in the noodles and blanch them for about 20 seconds. Immediately pull them out and dunk them into the ice bath. Give the noodles a good stir to loosen them up (otherwise, they will clump), then remove them from the water, shaking to remove as much excess water as possible (if you don't, the seasoning may be diluted). Place the noodles in a large bowl and toss with the Maggi Seasoning and garlic oil.

NOW'S THE TIME TO ASSEMBLE!

Divide the noodles among four bowls. For each bowl, spoon 1½ teaspoons of the fish sauce dressing over the noodles, then 1½ teaspoons of the relish brine. Top with as many sliced cucumbers, dried shrimp, and peanuts as you'd like, then the green onions, Thai basil, and cilantro.

Place an egg in each bowl (you can place it whole or quarter the egg lengthwise). Serve the bowls with lime. To eat, break the yolk, squeeze the lime, give everything a good mix, and slurp! These noodles should be eaten right away, but if you have any leftover cucumber relish, store it in an airtight container and refrigerate for up to 3 days. The color of the cucumbers may pale as the days go by, but the flavor won't be affected.

KHO TREY

CARAMELIZED FISH WITH TOMATOES

Serves 2 to 4

As with any kho, this dish starts with caramelizing sugar just to the edge of burning it before dropping in and braising a protein—in this case, fish! Any firm fish will do, whether it's salmon or catfish or sea bass. Ground white and black peppers give the kho a warm glow, and the addition of tomatoes brings in some brightness to an otherwise deeply savory dish. Because it is so rich, some variations of kho trey also include sliced or shredded green mango on the side. My favorite way of serving kho trey, though, goes back to my most vivid memory of it: my mom making kho after working all day, then serving it with a bowl of hot porridge. Pure comfort.

1½ pounds salmon, sea bass, cod, or catfish fillet, skin on, or steak, cut into 3-inch pieces

1 teaspoon kosher salt

2 tablespoons palm sugar

½ cup water

4 garlic cloves, smashed

2 teaspoons fish sauce

1 teaspoon Thai seasoning soy sauce

1 teaspoon freshly ground black pepper

½ teaspoon freshly ground white pepper

2 ripe tomatoes, quartered

2 green onion stalks, thinly sliced

Sliced or shredded green mango (see page 23 for shredding tips), for serving (optional)

Bor Bor / Plain Porridge (page 53), for serving (optional)

Wash and pat dry the fish, then season both sides with the salt. Set aside.

In a small heavy pot over medium-high heat, heat the palm sugar. Using a wooden spoon, stir until the sugar is caramelized and a reddish, deeply brown color, about 6 minutes. Add the water, garlic, fish sauce, seasoning soy sauce, and black and white peppers. Mix well.

Add the fish, drop the heat to low, and cover. Cook for 10 minutes, then flip the fish over, place the tomatoes on top, and cover. Cook until the fish is opaque and cooked through, about 10 more minutes. Transfer the fish to a serving bowl or plate and top with the green onions. Serve with green mango and porridge, if you'd like. Ta-DA! That's it!

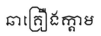

CHA KDAM KROEUNG
STIR-FRIED CRAB + KROEUNG

Serves 2 to 4

Three words: Dungeness crab season! When Dungeness crab season is at its peak between November and January, I stop everything, invite friends over, and make this stir-fry. That's because Dungeness crabs are so special: They're buttery, sweet, rich, and full of umami that goes so well with the umami in kroeung and fish sauce. My dad made the best version, usually around American holidays like Thanksgiving; instead of carving a big turkey or slicing a roast ham, we'd break apart crabs. The key to the stir-fry's flavor is the tomalley, or crab butter, that's in the shell. For that reason, you need to start with whole, live crabs. I include instructions on how to humanely dispatch and cook the crabs, but many fishmongers will do this for you if asked. Outside of Dungeness crab season, this is delicious with head-on shrimp or prawns.

- 2 fresh Dungeness crabs (about 4½ pounds total)
- Kosher salt
- 2 tablespoons oyster sauce
- 1 tablespoon water
- 1 tablespoon sugar
- ½ tablespoon fish sauce
- ¼ cup grapeseed or other neutral oil
- 3-inch piece ginger, peeled and thinly sliced (¼ cup)
- 2 tablespoons Master Kroeung (page 27)
- 2 bird's eye chiles, minced
- 1 bunch green onions, cut into 2-inch pieces
- Bai / Steamed Jasmine Rice (page 52), for serving

COOK THE CRABS

If the fishmonger has already steamed the crabs for you, skip to the next section, Prepare the Crabs. If not, humanely dispatch the crabs by placing them in a large container packed with ice. Refrigerate or freeze the crabs for 20 minutes. Then, working with one at a time, flip the crab over on its back. With a thin, sharp knife, pull back its apron (the triangular flap), where you'll see a hole that contains its nerve endings. Quickly and firmly pierce the crab at that point, then flip the crab over and pierce the crab between the eyes.

You can either steam or boil the crabs:

To steam: Fill a pot fitted with a steamer basket halfway with water (make sure the bottom of the basket does not touch the water). Bring the water to a simmer over medium heat. Place the crabs in the basket, cover, and steam until they're bright red, about 20 minutes. Cool, then rinse off any residue.

To boil: Bring a large pot of water to a roaring boil. Season the water heavily with salt. Grab the crabs by their two smallest back legs and quickly drop them into the boiling water. Cover and boil until the crabs are bright red, 8 to 10 minutes. While the crabs boil, fill a large bowl with ice and water. When the crabs are done, immediately submerge them in the ice bath to chill.

PREPARE THE CRABS

Remove the outer shell from each crab and set aside. (Don't throw them away! The shells contain tomalley, the delicious crab butter, that we'll need.) Remove from the crabs anything fuzzy or dark in color and discard. With a sharp knife, cut each crab right down the middle. Cut each half of the crab into three pieces, keeping the legs attached.

STIR-FRIED CRAB + KROEUNG, CONTINUED

MAKE THE CRAB BUTTER SAUCE

From the crab shells, scoop out the yellowish tomalley into a small bowl. Add the oyster sauce, water, sugar, fish sauce, and ½ teaspoon salt. Stir to combine.

LET'S COOK!

In a large wok over high heat, heat the oil. When the oil begins to shimmer, add the ginger and sauté until golden brown, about 1 minute. Add the kroeung and stir for 2 minutes, then add the crab butter sauce. Mix, and let it come to a boil. Add the crab pieces, spoon the sauce over the crab, and cook until the sauce thickens, another 10 minutes. Turn off the heat, add the chiles and green onions, and mix one more time.

Transfer the stir-fry to a large serving bowl to share family-style at the table. You can serve it as is right now, with steamed rice on the side, or do what I do and put the rice into the wok. Toss it around a bit to coat the rice with whatever sauce and bits are remaining, then serve the rice alongside the stir-fry.

However you serve it, don't be afraid to get messy and use your hands to eat the crab!

CHA KROEUNG
STIR-FRIED KROEUNG

Serves 2 to 4

I love this dish because the kroeung really shines: There's something about stir-frying it in a little bit of oil that really brings out its flavors. Plus, because it's so easy and fast to throw together, it was always one of my weeknight staples when I first moved to San Francisco. I like to stir-fry the kroeung with chicken thighs, but you can use pork, beef, or tofu, or try it with mushrooms, eggplants, cauliflower, long beans, leafy vegetables, or any vegetable that's in season, really. Holy basil is an important part of the dish; it lends a nutty quality that rounds out the flavors of the kroeung and prahok. That said, if it's not available, use lemon basil or Thai basil instead.

- 1 pound boneless chicken thighs, sliced into ¼-inch thin strips
- ½ teaspoon kosher salt
- 2 tablespoons water
- 1 tablespoon oyster sauce
- 1 tablespoon fish sauce
- 2 tablespoons grapeseed or other neutral oil
- 3 tablespoons Yellow Kroeung (page 28)
- 1 tablespoon palm sugar
- 1 teaspoon prahok
- ½ red onion, sliced ¼-inch thick (1 cup)
- 1 red Fresno chile, thinly sliced (¼ cup)
- 1 jalapeño, thinly sliced (¼ cup)
- 1 cup holy basil leaves
- Bai / Steamed Jasmine Rice (page 52), for serving

Place the chicken in a medium bowl and sprinkle the salt evenly all over the strips. Set aside for 10 to 15 minutes.

Meanwhile, in a small bowl, stir together the water, oyster sauce, and fish sauce.

In a wok over medium-high heat, heat the oil. When the oil begins to shimmer, add the kroeung, palm sugar, and prahok. Sauté until the kroeung is fragrant, about 3 minutes. Add the chicken and sauté for about 3 minutes, then add the oyster–fish sauce mixture. Sauté for about another 3 minutes, or until the chicken is well coated with the sauce and cooked through (its internal temperature should be 165°F).

Turn the heat to low and fold in the red onion, chile, jalapeño, and holy basil. Stir, then it's ready! Serve with rice alongside. Alternatively, remove everything from the wok except for the sauce. Throw the rice into the hot pan, give everything a good toss so the rice absorbs all that flavor and goodness left in the pan, then scoop it into bowls. Add the stir-fry right on top and serve. Store leftovers in an airtight container and refrigerate for up to 2 days.

នាត្រកុំដឹកអំបិល

CHA KROM TUK AMPIL

STIR-FRIED MUSSELS IN TAMARIND SAUCE

Serves 2 to 4

Located on the southwestern coast of Cambodia, the Kampot region is home to a rich bounty of seafood. One dish I love there is a tangy stir-fry made with sun-dried clams, usually served as a snack to go with cold beer or a pour of cognac over ice. After one trip, I craved it so much that I had to try to replicate it at home. The clams so popular in Cambodia aren't as easy to find here, so I use mussels instead. And while it is great to nosh on with a drink, it's also substantial enough that it could be a main dish if served with, say, Cha Tra Koun / Stir-Fried Water Spinach (page 205) and, of course, Bai / Steamed Jasmine Rice (page 52).

Kosher salt

1 pound live mussels

3 tablespoons Tuk Ampil / Tamarind Water (page 30)

1 tablespoon water

1 tablespoon oyster sauce

2 teaspoons cornstarch

1 teaspoon sugar

1 teaspoon fish sauce

2 tablespoons grapeseed or other neutral oil

4 garlic cloves, minced

1 small shallot, minced

1 cup loosely packed basil leaves

2 green onion stalks, thinly sliced

1 bird's eye chile, minced, or more if you like things spicy!

Fill a bowl with 3 cups ice water and ¼ cup salt. Stir, then submerge the mussels in the water. Soak for about 30 minutes, during which time the mussels will spit out sand. Drain, scrub the mussels, and place them in a fresh bowl of water for 10 minutes. Then remove the mussels from the water and set aside on a plate.

While the mussels soak the second time, make the slurry by mixing together the tamarind water, the 1 tablespoon water, the oyster sauce, cornstarch, sugar, fish sauce, and ½ teaspoon salt. Set aside.

Let's stir-fry! In a wok or large skillet over high heat, heat the oil. When the oil begins to shimmer, add the garlic and shallot. Stir constantly for about 15 seconds—don't let them burn. Add the slurry. When it begins to simmer, add the mussels and stir again. Cover tightly and steam for 10 minutes, or until the mussels open up (discard any that remain closed). Add the basil, green onions, and chile, and toss them all together. That's it, serve and enjoy immediately. Yum!

BAI SACH CHROUK
COCONUT PORK

Serves 6

Slices of pork soak up a coconut milk marinade overnight, then are quickly seared and served with rice. You can't get much simpler than that! The coconut milk tenderizes the pork and gives it a bit of sweetness. Once you toss the slices on the grill, the sugars will caramelize, and the most amazing aroma will call everyone to the table. It's because this dish is so simple yet so satisfying that I fell in love with it while in Cambodia, then learned how to make it when I returned to San Francisco. It's usually eaten for breakfast, but of course you can have it any time of the day. It's best to marinate the pork overnight, but if you're short on time, you can get away with giving the pork just a two-hour dip in the coconut milk.

1 (19-ounce) can coconut milk (see Note)

½ cup packed light brown sugar

½ cup Thai seasoning soy sauce

¼ cup chopped garlic (about 6 cloves)

1½ teaspoons freshly ground black pepper

½ teaspoon kosher salt

2½ pounds pork loin, cut into ⅛-inch slices

4 tablespoons grapeseed or other neutral oil

2 green onion stalks, thinly sliced

Bai / Steamed Jasmine Rice (page 52), for serving

6 Poung Mu-anh Jien / Crispy Fried Eggs (page 45)

Chrouk / Pickles (page 38), for serving

Note: The brand Mae Ploy offers coconut milk in 19-ounce cans. If not available, use a little less than 1½ (13.5-ounce) cans.

In a large bowl, mix together the coconut milk, brown sugar, seasoning soy sauce, garlic, pepper, and salt. Add the pork to the marinade, being sure to separate the slices so each piece is completely submerged in the liquid. Place in the refrigerator, covered, and marinate overnight.

In a large skillet over medium heat, heat 2 tablespoons of the oil. When the oil begins to shimmer, carefully slide in as many slices of pork as you can without overcrowding the pan. Cook the slices for about 2 minutes on each side, or until the pork is cooked through and no longer pink, then remove from the pan. Repeat with the remaining pork.

In a small frying pan or skillet over medium heat, heat the remaining 2 tablespoons of oil. When the oil begins to shimmer, add the green onions. Stir and quickly and lightly fry them until they're vibrant green and fragrant, 30 seconds.

Divide the pork and rice among the six serving plates. Add a crispy egg on top of the rice and spoon some green onion oil over the pork and egg. Enjoy with chrouk! Tightly wrap up any remaining pork in aluminum foil or place in an airtight container and refrigerate for up to 2 days.

PART IV

NYUM BAI

Favorites from the Nyum Bai kitchen

ព្រះចន្ទពេញវង់ កុំគួចចិត្ត
ខ្ញុំចង់កំរាយនៅយប់នេះ។
កុំគួចចិត្ត អ្នកភ្លឺដូចព្រះអាទិត្យ

Full moon, don't be upset
I want to enjoy this night
Don't be upset, you shine as
bright as the sun

"FULL MOON," AS PERFORMED
BY BAKSEY CHAM KRONG

In 2017, my mentor from La Cocina pointed me to a space at the Fruitvale Public Market in Oakland. Set back from a two-lane street, the area had a certain grittiness that reminded me fondly of my old Mission neighborhood and, to some extent, Stockton. The space itself was long and narrow, with room for twenty-five inside, plus a patio that could fit another twenty-five. My neighbors would include a woman who sold lush potted plants, a churro vendor, and a panadería. Across the street was a high school and Fruitvale Village, which housed businesses, offices, apartments, a library, and a weekly farmers' market.

After four years of catering and pop-ups, I saw this as a chance to settle down and give Nyum Bai a permanent home.

The menu, I decided, would include not just dishes popular at my various pop-ups but also dishes I loved but rarely saw in Bay Area Cambodian restaurants, like somlaw machoo kroeung, braised beef in a tamarind broth tinged yellow from kroeung. I didn't know how those dishes would be received, but *Fuck it,* I thought. *These are things I want to eat, these are the things I want to see in the world.*

With just my savings, a few business loans, and a Kickstarter to get us over the line, Nyum Bai opened in February 2018. We started the day playing music from the Golden Era, and it rocked on through service. We received some nice press; we won accolades. Nyum Bai was a success! But things were happening so fast, and expectations were so high, that I couldn't grasp everything going on. My team and I worked harder than ever during that time, but honestly, it was a little bit of a double-edged sword: I was too burned out without realizing it, too tired to enjoy the success and the awards, and too new to all the attention to know how to handle it. And on some level, I doubted I even properly earned all of it. I was a kid from Stuck Town! People like me aren't meant to be successful. And every time I thought about my family still in Stockton, I felt guilt for being where I was, for doing what I was doing. For being happy.

What pulled me out of it was finally forcing myself to take a step back and recalibrate and reset. I reminded myself once again why I started Nyum Bai in the first place: I wanted to have a shared language with my parents to connect with them, understand them—and, in doing so, better understand myself. I also had wanted to spread my love for Khmer cuisine and culture with anyone and everyone interested, and help others, too, who struggled to talk to their parents or elders. There was still so much I wanted to share and learn. My mission wasn't over. It was just the beginning.

As for connecting with my parents, my mom had visited my pop-ups a few times, but I think she thought I was going through a phase. Fair, I had gone through a lot of phases. I think she realized it was real when she came to the restaurant. It was about two weeks after I opened, and she had the kuy teav Phnom Penh. After that first visit, my parents took the two-hour drive from Stockton to Nyum Bai often. One of the last meals I served to my father was the kuy teav. He had one bowl. Then, uncharacteristically, another one. And then, even more surprisingly, he asked for one to go. Through my mother, he told me he was proud of what I was doing. That he was proud of me.

The very last time I last saw my dad was a month after opening. He was in the hospital, really, really sick. When I left, the doctor said he was going to be fine. He just needed to eat and watch his blood pressure.

Two days later, he was gone. He left a note before he passed away. The note was to my mom. It was a letter of apology. He hoped in his death, she could be free.

The vision I had at the Angkor Wat all those years ago came to pass. I followed my heart. In return, life guided me to the right path. Through Nyum Bai, I began to better understand myself and my family, and honor everything my mother did for us.

We closed Nyum Bai in 2022. It wasn't an end, though: I opened Lunette Cambodia in the Ferry Building in San Francisco in 2024. Lunette Cambodia is the next chapter, so far unwritten, a continuation of what I set out to do that day in 2012 at that noodle stall in Phnom Penh. Khmer food and culture has been in the shadow for too long, and it's been more than ready to come out of the darkness. I hope through my food and this book, I could nudge the spotlight over our way and stretch our collective understanding of Cambodia beyond the usual discourse that begins and ends with the genocide. And on a more personal level, I hope all of this can inspire, too: if you're like me, maybe this food will be a key to unlock the language to talk to your parents or grandparents about heavy subjects and to ask questions you've always felt but never were able to put into words. And I hope through food we can discover, or rediscover, ourselves and have pride in Khmer culture, too.

I still don't have all the pieces for what my parents went through. I've come to accept that this is a lifelong process and that there are some things about their experiences that I simply will never know. And that's okay. I can appreciate what they have shared with me and how cooking has set us on a path toward healing. Funnily enough, while I make the food of my childhood day in and day out, my mom is cooking something totally different: burgers. She's a grill cook at a burger spot now, and she's very proud of her skills. She's invited all of us kids over for burger night a few times. She lines up all the ingredients, just like she does at the restaurant, then grills and assembles the burgers for everyone. She's happy.

Playlist

"I'm Leaving,"
MOL KAMACH AND BAKSEY CHAM KRONG

"Koh Huer Te Eng,"
MEAS SAMON

"Chunm Oun 31,"
PEN RAN

"Cold Sky,"
ROS SEREYSOTHEA

"Pepito Mi Corazón,"
KEO MONTHA WITH THE KHMER ORCHESTRA

"Duang Netra,"
SINN SISAMOUTH

"Pkor Lorn Palin,"
ROS SEREYSOTHEA

"Tep Moke Jus,"
KEO MONTHA

RECIPES FROM NYUM BAI

The menu at Nyum Bai generally offered a few snacks, a salad or two, some noodle dishes, lots of rice, and something sweet to end the meal. This chapter is full of favorites from the restaurant that I've reworked so you can easily make them at home, including prahok ktiss, which I serve with seasonal veggies;[1] amok;[2] jien cho-yah;[3] and the dish that started me on this journey, kuy teav Phnom Penh.[4]

Nyum bai!

[1] Prahok Coconut Pork Dip (page 195).
[2] Fish Soufflé (page 215).
[3] Crispy Pork Egg Rolls (page 196).
[4] Pork Noodle Soup (page 213).

PRAHOK KTISS
PRAHOK COCONUT PORK DIP

Serves 8

Prahok ktiss was the most popular item at Nyum Bai, and I was told it was life changing. I love that it became one of the restaurant's signature dishes, because this pork dip captures so much about what I'm trying to do—which is to show you that Khmer food is so delicious! It's also an excellent example of how the classic Khmer duo of prahok and kroeung is used with coconut milk. There are a lot of flavors going on at the same time here, but the dip perfectly hits that note between sweet, salty, and acidic. Because it's served with crunchy raw vegetables, even the textures are balanced. Note that the ground pork needs to be at least 50 percent fat; that nice fat layer helps with the consistency and flavors of the dip and prevents it from being too dry.

½ cup grapeseed or other neutral oil

1 cup Yellow Kroeung (page 28)

½ cup prahok

¼ cup minced garlic (10 to 12 cloves)

2 tablespoons tamarind powder, or 4 tablespoons tamarind paste

½ cup palm sugar

2½ pounds ground pork, 50% fat

1 cup Bok Mtes / Chile Paste (page 31)

3 (13.5-ounce) cans coconut milk

Generous ¼ cup bird's eye chiles, destemmed

Sliced cucumbers, cabbage, carrots, lettuce, Thai eggplants, and any other seasonal, raw, crunchy vegetables, for serving

Bai Kadang / Rice Crackers (page 55), Bai / Steamed Jasmine Rice (page 52), or both, for serving

In a large wide pot or deep skillet over medium heat, heat the oil. When the oil begins to shimmer, add the kroeung, prahok, and garlic and sauté together until aromatic, about 5 minutes. Add the tamarind and palm sugar. Keep sautéing until the mixture glistens, 5 to 10 minutes.

Add the pork and chile paste. Stir and cook, breaking up the pork with a spoon or chopsticks as you do so, until the pork is about halfway cooked through, about 10 minutes.

Add the coconut milk and chiles, then lower the heat to a simmer until a thin layer of fat floats on top and the texture of the dip is similar to a ragù, about 30 minutes. Transfer to a bowl and serve with veggies and rice. Store leftovers in an airtight container and refrigerate for 1 week.

MAKE A RICE BOWL!

After you make the prahok ktiss, some of the sauce will remain at the bottom of the pot. Throw in some rice to soak it up, then scoop it into bowls. Add a bit of the dip and an egg on top for a great one-bowl meal.

ເຈຽຮແສຍຣ

JIEN CHO-YAH
CRISPY PORK EGG ROLLS

Makes 40 egg rolls

You will not be able to stop eating these egg rolls! They're filled with ground pork plus a few other ingredients that set them apart from others. For one thing, I add a lot of pepper, because I like that pronounced pepper flavor. Then glass noodles and creamy taro give the filling a little body and texture. For the wrapper itself, I like the ones from Menlo (I think they stay crisper than others when fried), but if you have a favorite, of course use that instead. This recipe makes enough egg rolls for a party, because egg rolls are party food; plus, they're always fun to make with friends on a Sunday. Invite everyone over to help make the filling and catch up on all the gossip while rolling the rolls. And even if you're serving less than a big party, I think it's worth making the whole batch anyway. You always can freeze what you don't fry.

- 2½ pounds ground pork
- ½ cup oyster sauce
- 3 tablespoons + 1 teaspoon sugar
- 2 tablespoons freshly ground black pepper
- 1 tablespoon + 1 teaspoon fish sauce
- 2½ teaspoons kosher salt
- 1½ to 2 ounces glass noodles
- 2 pounds taro
- ½ green cabbage, shredded (4 cups)
- 1 yellow onion, finely diced (2 cups)
- 4 garlic cloves, minced
- 40 (8 by 8-inch) egg roll wrappers
- 1 egg, beaten
- Grapeseed or other neutral oil, for frying
- Tuk Trey Piam / Fish Sauce Dressing (page 37; optional), for serving

To make the filling, in a very large bowl mix together the ground pork with the oyster sauce, sugar, pepper, fish sauce, and salt. Set aside.

Place the noodles in a medium bowl and cover with warm water. Soak for about 5 minutes to soften, then drain and pat dry well. This is important: The noodles must be dry so the rolls won't burst when frying. Once dried, cut the noodles into 1-inch segments. Place the noodles in the bowl with the pork.

Peel the taro to remove its tough brown skin. If necessary, trim away any pink speckles on the white flesh. Shred the taro using a T-peeler or a food processor with the shredder disc, or use a sharp knife to thinly slice the taro into rounds or planks. Then stack them and cut them into matchsticks. Add the taro to the bowl with the pork, then add the cabbage, onion, and garlic. Mix everything until well incorporated.

Let's roll up the jien cho-yah! Peel and separate the egg roll wrappers. Cut them in half diagonally to form two triangles and keep them covered under a damp paper towel so they won't dry out as you roll.

Take a wrapper and lay it out so the longest side of the triangle is nearest to you. Spread 2 tablespoons of the filling into a 4-inch log about ½ inch from the side closest to you, leaving some space on either side of the log. Fold the left and right sides toward the center. Then fold up the bottom and roll, as tightly as you can, up toward the top of the triangle. As you approach the top, brush it with the beaten egg, then complete the roll. Place the egg roll, sealed side down, on a tray or plate and repeat with the remaining wrappers. If you want to freeze any of the egg rolls, now's the time to do it. See Freezing the Egg Rolls below.

Line a sheet pan with a few paper towels and set aside.

In a deep pot over medium-high heat, heat 1½ inches of oil to 375°F. If you don't have a thermometer, place the tip of a wooden chopstick in the oil. If tiny bubbles immediately form and sizzle around the chopstick, the oil is ready. If the oil begins to smoke, though, it's too hot; lower the heat and test it again in a minute. Working in batches to avoid overcrowding the pot (the egg rolls won't get crispy if crowded), fry the egg rolls until they're crisp and golden brown, about 4 minutes. Drain on the prepared sheet pan. Serve with the fish sauce dressing for dipping if you'd like. And eat!

FREEZING THE EGG ROLLS

Arrange uncooked egg rolls in a single layer in a resealable freezer bag, or wrap them tightly in plastic wrap, then place in your freezer. They'll keep for 1 month. To cook, fry them right out of the freezer—no need to thaw first. They'll take 5 minutes, instead of 4 minutes, to cook through.

ញាំក្រូចថ្លុង
NGYOM KROCH THLONG

POMELO SALAD WITH FISH SAUCE DRESSING

Serves 4

This salad is such a delight. In Cambodia, pomelo salads are popular at restaurants all year long. Here in the United States, though, I like to wait until the citrus season—late fall through the winter—for pomelos to arrive at the market. That's part of the fun: You don't expect to have something refreshing and tart-sweet in the middle of a cold snap, but that's exactly what this salad brings to the table. When picking a pomelo, choose a large heavy one, as you'll have to peel several inches of rind to get to the fruit. Once the fruit is peeled, try your best to remove as much of the bitter white pith and membrane as possible. And while the pomelo is the star, I love the other parts of the salad, too, especially the savory and umami flavors of the shrimp and the dressing, as well as the contrast of textures between the pomelo and the crunchy garnishes. If you want, take this up a notch by adding some fresh crabmeat, too.

¼ cup dried shrimp

¼ cup freshly grated coconut (see Fresh Coconuts Are the Best, page 229) or store-bought shredded unsweetened coconut

1 quart water

1 teaspoon kosher salt

12 medium shrimp (about 6 ounces), without tails, peeled, and deveined

1 big pomelo, peeled and segments separated

1 English cucumber, or 2 Persian cucumbers, unpeeled, deseeded, and thinly sliced

1 to 2 bird's eye chiles (depending on your desired spice level), minced

½ cup Tuk Trey Piam / Fish Sauce Dressing (page 37)

2 cups loosely packed mix of Thai basil, cilantro, and mint leaves

¼ cup salted peanuts, chopped

¼ cup Khtoem Krahm Jien / Crispy Shallots (page 44) or store-bought

In a small bowl, submerge the dried shrimp in warm water and soak until softened, about 15 minutes, then drain. Use a mortar and pestle to break down the shrimp, or a knife to chop it into smaller pieces.

While the shrimp soaks, in a small frying pan or skillet over low heat, toast the coconut, stirring or shaking the pan frequently, until golden brown, about 5 minutes. Transfer to a small bowl to cool.

Separately, fill a large bowl with ice and water and set aside.

In a medium pot, bring the water and salt to a boil, then add the shrimp. When the shrimp turn pink and opaque, about 7 minutes, immediately transfer them to the ice bath. Once the shrimp are cooled, remove them from the ice bath and pat dry.

To assemble the salad, place the dried shrimp, toasted coconut, poached shrimp, pomelo, cucumber, and chile in a large bowl. Pour in the dressing and gently toss. Garnish with the herbs, peanuts, and fried shallots. Serve.

ញាំត្រយ៉ាងចេក
NGYOM TRAYONG JENK

BANANA BLOSSOM SALAD

Serves 4 to 6

Some dishes come and go, but this one is forever. I put ngyom trayong jenk on the menu early in my pop-up days, and it's been a rare constant in a whirlwind of changes since then. Once you make the salad, you'll see why it never has left the menu: It's refreshing, healthy, and a fun surprise for those who aren't familiar with how delicious banana blossoms can be. When prepping the blossoms, note that the thick purple leaves (the bract) are not edible, so you can either discard them, or you can do as many Khmers do and use them to plate the salad. Once the bract is removed, you'll see tightly packed, creamy yellow petals—those are the edible parts, and once you reach them, work fast: The petals will oxidize and discolor very quickly. Dropping them immediately into a bowl of water with some lime juice will help keep their color.

3 tightly packed cups sliced banana blossoms (from 1 to 2 blossoms) (see How to Slice Banana Blossoms, page 202)

2 cups shredded poached chicken (see page 32)

1 cup mung bean sprouts

1 cup loosely packed mix of Thai basil, cilantro, and mint leaves

2 bird's eye chiles, minced (optional)

1 red bell pepper, thinly sliced

1 small shallot, thinly sliced

¾ cup Tuk Trey Piam / Fish Sauce Dressing (page 37)

1 tablespoon shallot oil (see page 44; optional)

¼ cup crushed salted peanuts

¼ cup Khtoem Krahm Jien / Crispy Shallots (page 44) or store-bought

In a large bowl, gently mix together the banana blossoms, chicken, bean sprouts, herbs, chiles (if using), bell pepper, shallot, dressing, and (if using) the shallot oil. Divide the salad among the purple banana leaves you set aside or transfer to a large plate. Pile the peanuts and fried shallots right on top and serve immediately.

Variation: Instead of chicken, try shrimp! Peel and devein 8 medium shrimp (without tails). Drop them into boiling water and cook until they're pink and opaque, about 7 minutes, then immediately pull them out and place them in a bowl of iced water. Pat them dry and add to the salad.

HOW TO SLICE BANANA BLOSSOMS

As you slice the blossoms, they'll release a sticky sap, so have a damp towel nearby to wipe the knife as needed.

Fill a large bowl with cold water and add ½ cup fresh lime juice (from 4 to 5 limes). Set aside.

With your hands, peel the thick purple layers from the banana blossoms as well as the small cluster of florets between each layer until you reach the yellow leaves in the center. Discard the florets. Reserve the purple leaves for plating if you'd like, or discard.

Turn to the yellow leaves: These can be tough and hard to chew, so slice them as thinly as you can crosswise for more pleasant eating. As you do so, immediately drop them into the lime water to preserve their pretty color. Continue until you have as much as you need, then drain and pat the leaves dry. They're ready to go!

NGYOM SACH MU-ANH
CHICKEN CABBAGE SALAD

Serves 4 to 6

This salad! It's the first Khmer salad I learned how to make, the first salad I put on my menu when I was catering and doing pop-ups, the salad that introduced Khmer food to so many people. It's full of color and texture from carrots, cucumbers, bell pepper, cabbage, herbs, crushed peanuts, and a fish sauce dressing, so what's not to love? Be sure to slice the cabbage very thinly so the strands won't be too tough to eat (a mandoline is helpful here). I also add poached chicken, but you could add almost any protein you want; my mom, for instance, adds thin slices of boiled pork belly tossed in rice powder (see page 134), and other versions throw in boiled chicken feet. You always see this salad at birthday parties and gatherings because it travels so well; if you want to take it with you, too, pack the dressing separately and combine everything together at the party.

½ cup Tuk Trey Piam / Fish Sauce Dressing (page 37)

2 tablespoons fresh lime juice

2 bird's eye chiles, minced (optional)

2 carrots, peeled

3 cups poached shredded chicken (see page 32)

¼ head green cabbage, thinly sliced (2 cups packed)

¼ head red cabbage, thinly sliced (2 cups packed)

1 English cucumber, or 2 Persian cucumbers, unpeeled, sliced into ¼-inch coins

1 red bell pepper, cut into thin strips

1 cup mix of fresh Thai basil, cilantro, and mint leaves

3 tablespoons crushed salted peanuts

In a small bowl, combine the dressing, lime juice, and chiles (if using). Set aside while you prepare the rest of the salad.

Fill a large bowl with ice water. Using a peeler (a T-peeler is best), shave the carrots from root to stem to achieve thin curls. As you do so, place the curls in the ice water so they keep their shape and stay crisp. When done, drain and dry the carrots as best you can with a clean kitchen towel or paper towel.

Place the carrots in a large bowl. Add the chicken, both cabbages, cucumber, bell pepper, and herbs. Using tongs, gently mix everything together. Right before serving, add the peanuts and dressing and mix one final time.

CHA TRA KOUN
STIR-FRIED WATER SPINACH

Serves 4

This stir-fried water spinach was super popular at Nyum Bai! With the sweetness of water spinach mixed with the saltiness of the fermented soybeans, it's packed full of flavor yet is versatile enough to go well with pretty much everything on the table. When shopping for the water spinach, look for beautiful bright green bunches with long, thin stalks. You'll need a whole pound for this; it may seem like too much for your wok or skillet, but once the spinach begins to cook and wilt, it will be easy to manage. I stir-fry the spinach with chicken stock, but any stock you have will do.

1 pound water spinach (also called morning glory, tra koun, ong choy, and rau muống)

2 tablespoons grapeseed or other neutral oil

3 garlic cloves, minced

1 tablespoon salted soybeans (preferably Yeo's brand)

1 teaspoon fish sauce

1 teaspoon sugar

¼ cup Somlaw Mu-anh / Chicken Broth (page 32) or store-bought

Bai / Steamed Jasmine Rice (page 52), for serving (optional)

Slice off the bottom 3 inches of the water spinach stems and discard or compost. Pick the leaves from their stems, give them a good wash, and set them aside in a colander to drain. Feel the stems: If they're a little tough, give them a squeeze to soften (which will make for more pleasant eating). Slice the stems into 3-inch lengths, then wash and place them next to the leaves in the colander to drain.

In a wok or medium frying pan over medium-high heat, add the oil. When it begins to shimmer, add the garlic and sauté, stirring until fragrant, about 30 seconds; then add the salted soybeans, fish sauce, and sugar. Stir, then add the water spinach stems and cook, uncovered, until the stems wilt, about 5 minutes. Add the broth and stir. Add the leaves and cook them down until they soften, just a minute or two. Transfer everything to a large platter and enjoy immediately as is or with steamed jasmine rice, if desired.

ឆា ត្រប់

CHA TROUP

CHARRED EGGPLANTS WITH PORK + SHRIMP

Serves 2 to 4

Smoky sweetness from charred eggplants is everything. This is a dish that I always love ordering at Khmer restaurants because everyone almost always does it very well. And I loved that folks ordered it at Nyum Bai, too! Many versions of cha troup, including my mom's, mash the eggplant with the ground pork and shrimp; I like to split the eggplants open and spoon the pork and shrimp right on top instead. I very much prefer using Chinese eggplants for this, as charring really brings out their lovely creamy, sweet flavors.

2 large Chinese or Japanese eggplants

2 tablespoons oyster sauce

1½ teaspoons Thai seasoning soy sauce

1 tablespoon palm sugar

1 tablespoon fish sauce

Freshly ground black pepper

2 tablespoons grapeseed or other neutral oil

5 garlic cloves, minced

8 ounces ground pork or chicken

4 ounces medium shrimp, without tails, peeled, deveined, minced

2 green onion stalks, sliced

Bai / Steamed Jasmine Rice (page 52), for serving

Char the eggplants by placing them directly over a low open flame, being sure to rotate them to char on all sides, 6 to 7 minutes. Alternatively, if you don't have a gas stove (or want to avoid the smoke!), preheat the oven to 450°F. Pierce the eggplants with a fork a few times all over, then place them on a sheet pan and roast for 40 minutes, rotating the eggplants every 10 minutes so they char evenly. Transfer the eggplants to a large bowl and cover with plastic wrap to steam. Set aside.

In a small bowl, make the sauce by stirring together the oyster sauce, seasoning soy sauce, palm sugar, fish sauce, and 1 teaspoon pepper.

In a wok or large skillet over high heat, heat the oil. When the oil begins to shimmer, add the garlic. Sauté until fragrant, about 1 minute, then add the pork. Sauté for 5 minutes, breaking up the pork as it cooks. Then add the shrimp and sauce. Keep things moving in the wok until the pork and shrimp are cooked through (the shrimp should turn pink), 5 to 10 minutes. Turn off the heat.

Let's eggplant! The steam should have loosened the eggplants' skin, which makes peeling them much easier. Peel all the skin. Place the eggplants on a large plate and slice them in half lengthwise to split them open. Spoon the pork and shrimp on top. Sprinkle the sliced green onions on top of the pork and shrimp and finish with a touch more pepper. Serve with rice. Store leftovers in an airtight container and refrigerate for up to 1 day.

ឆា ល្ពៅ
CHA LAPOV

STIR-FRIED PUMPKIN WITH PORK

Serves 4

In the mid-sixteenth century, Portuguese traders visited Cambodia, then sailed forth to Japan. Among the goods they shared with the Japanese was a variety of abóbora, or "pumpkin" in Portuguese. History is fuzzy on whether the traders sourced the pumpkin from Cambodia, or if the Japanese merely associated the pumpkin with the traders' previous stop; in any case, in Japan, "Cambodia" eventually merged with "abóbora" to give the pumpkin its name: kabocha (funnily enough, here in the States, kabocha is sometimes called Japanese pumpkin!). It's less clear when kabocha made its way from Mesoamerica to Cambodia, but it has long been a part of Khmer cooking. I like using kabocha for so many things, like here, where it's stir-fried with pork.

½ small (2- to 3-pound) kabocha, peeled and deseeded

2 tablespoons water

1 tablespoon oyster sauce

1 tablespoon fish sauce

½ teaspoon kosher salt

2 tablespoons grapeseed or other neutral oil

2 tablespoons minced garlic

8 ounces ground pork or chicken

1 tablespoon palm sugar or granulated sugar

1 cup Somlaw Mu-anh / Chicken Broth (page 32) or store-bought

1 egg

2 green onion stalks, sliced

1 teaspoon freshly ground black pepper

Bai / Steamed Jasmine Rice (page 52), for serving

Cut the kabocha into ⅛-inch slabs or matchsticks until you have about 2 cups. Set aside.

In a small bowl, stir together the water, oyster sauce, fish sauce, and salt. Set aside.

In a wok over medium-high heat, heat the oil. When the oil begins to shimmer, add the garlic and sauté until fragrant, about 30 seconds. Add the sauce, pork, and palm sugar and sauté until aromatic, 5 to 7 minutes. Add the kabocha and stir, then add the broth. Crack in the egg, lower the heat to medium, and cover. Cook until the kabocha is tender, about 10 minutes.

Uncover and stir the egg into the pumpkin and pork. Add the green onions and pepper. Serve with rice. Store leftovers in an airtight container and refrigerate for up to 2 days.

THE GOLDEN ERA

If I had a time machine, I would go back to mid-1960s Phnom Penh. That was when Cambodia was, for the first time in centuries, completely independent. From about the fifteenth century on, the country was either invaded or under the threat of invasion by neighbors Vietnam and Thailand. In 1863, France declared Cambodia its protectorate and ruled for nearly a century until 1953, when Cambodia finally gained its independence.

When that happened, King Norodom Sihanouk was on the throne. He was really into the arts and was super into music, fronting his own family band and touring all over the country. Under his rule, the country's arts and culture flourished, and it was in this golden era of cultural production that Khmer rock was born.

My parents did not have a lot in common, but the one thing they did share was a love for the music of the Golden Era. Those vintage tracks brought such joy to my family, and when I began researching the Golden Era, I was struck by how *fun* everything was. Influenced by Elvis and the Beatles—who, of course, were themselves heavily influenced by gospel music, Motown, and R&B—Khmer musicians created their own distinctive style of rock, combining synthesizers and electric guitars with Cambodian music traditions and folding in bossa nova and other influences from around the world. They were a group of like-minded artists who were both of their time and also ahead of their time. Listening to their music moves me so much that I get goose bumps every time. It brings me so much joy and makes me so proud to be Khmer.

Many of the singers of the era are now household names. There was Ros Sereysothea, who sang everything from old-school classics to progressive rock. And every Khmer kid grew up with the King of Khmer rock and pop, Sinn Sisamouth. He was definitely the first Khmer singer I remember listening to. I was just a kid, so I didn't really know who he was; I just knew he was special because of the effect he had on my parents. They could have been fighting all day, but when my dad put a Sinn Sisamouth tape in the cassette player, the room would transform from cold to warm, tense to relaxed, sad to light. Sisamouth was a highly prolific songwriter and a crooner with a lush, tender, smooth, beautiful voice, and he and Sereysothea often sang duets together. When he sang ballads about young love, you could practically see him onstage, hair slicked back, dressed impeccably in a keen tuxedo, mic in hand, in full command. And then you'd hear his fiery adaptations of "Love Potion Number 9" or of the Animals' version of "House of the Rising Sun"—often adding his own compositions or lyrics—and then just want to get up and rock out.

The Golden Era came to a tragic end in the mid-1970s, when the Khmer Rouge seized power. So many of these singers and musicians, including Sisamouth, disappeared or were killed during the genocide. But somehow their music made their way to Khmer households all over America. We got ours thanks to my dad, who came across tapes of the music every once in a while at Khmer markets.

Those tapes also made their way to the hands of music collectors, filmmakers, and archivists who have helped to keep the music alive (*Don't Think I've Forgotten* is an excellent documentary about the era). The music from this era is a time capsule, a moment when there was love, creativity, prosperity, joy in the air. It was that possibility, and those pure feelings of freedom and fun, that I wanted to capture when I opened Nyum Bai. So the beats of Khmer rock became the soundtrack for the restaurant. With so much destroyed in various wars and migrations, many of these songs have become valuable pieces of documentation about how life once was. And as much as this era was a moment in the past, it can be a glimpse into the future, too: It is possible to have these beautiful moments again.

គុយទាវភ្នំពេញ
KUY TEAV PHNOM PENH
PORK NOODLE SOUP

Serves 8

This is it: the soup that started it all. Kuy teav Phnom Penh is named, of course, after the capital city, and there you'll find it at street stalls all over. And it was at one of those stalls in 2012 that I decided, right in the middle of my bowl, to start Nyum Bai. It's probably not a coincidence that I had this epiphany over this specific noodle soup; of the many things my mom made for us when I was a kid, kuy teav was a favorite. On weekends, she would make a huge pot of it for my brothers, friends, and me. When I moved out, this bowl of comfort is what I longed for the most.

To make kuy teav, you'll make the broth with the pork bones. The broth simmers for nearly 5 hours in total, but other than checking in to skim the fat and other impurities, you don't have much to do during that time. I garnish my kuy teav with pork, bean sprouts, cilantro, green onions, black pepper, lime, and hot sauce, but part of the fun of this dish is customizing the toppings exactly the way you'd like.

PORK BROTH

3 pounds pork neck bones, cut into 1- to 2-inch chunks

8 quarts water

½ cup dried shrimp, rinsed

1½ cups peeled and cut (2-inch chunks) daikon

4 ounces pork shoulder

3 tablespoons sugar

1 tablespoon kosher salt, plus more as needed

2-inch piece pickled or preserved salted radish, rinsed with warm water (from about ½ radish) (see Note 1)

1 large yellow onion, halved through the stem

3 cilantro sprigs

¼ cup + 1 tablespoon fish sauce, plus more as needed

ASSEMBLY + SERVING

12 ounces mung bean sprouts

1 pound thin, flat rice noodles

Khtoem Jien / Garlic oil (see page 42)

16 Prahut / Pork Meatballs (page 222)

1 bunch cilantro, leaves picked

Sliced green onions

Freshly ground black pepper

Quartered limes

Tuk Trey Mtes / Fish Sauce + Chile (page 33)

Jien BawnKwang / Crispy Shrimp Fritters (page 121) or mini savory crullers (optional)

Chrouk Mtes Khtoem / Pickled Garlic Chile (page 35)

Note 1: The pickled (or preserved) salted radish I use here is from Thailand. It's brown in color and shouldn't be confused with the bright yellow Japanese pickled daikon radishes called takuan. It's found primarily at Southeast Asian markets, or online, usually packaged in plastic whole or shredded. For this recipe, choose the whole radish. Popular brands include JHC, but if not available, look for another Thai brand.

PORK NOODLE SOUP, CONTINUED

MAKE THE BROTH

Rinse the bones and add them to the pot. Add the 8 quarts water and bring to a boil. Immediately lower the heat so the water is at a bare simmer. Do not let it come to full boil again; it must stay at a bare simmer, or you'll end up with a thick, oily broth—not good!

Add the shrimp to the pot, along with the daikon, pork shoulder, sugar, salt, radish, and onion. Simmer for 30 minutes, uncovered, then remove the pork shoulder and set aside. Once the pork has cooled, refrigerate it until ready to serve.

Meanwhile, keep the broth at a simmer for 3½ hours longer, uncovered, skimming often as needed to remove any fat or scum that rises to the top.

After 4 hours, the broth should be mostly clear. If it's not, skim again. Add the cilantro sprigs and simmer for 30 minutes longer, then remove the cilantro and add the fish sauce. Taste and season with additional fish sauce or salt if needed. Turn off the heat.

PREPARE THE NOODLES, ASSEMBLE THE BOWLS, AND SERVE

Bring a medium pot of water to a boil.

Meanwhile, remove the pork from the fridge and cut it into ⅛-inch slices. Then, divide the bean sprouts among the serving bowls.

Place a handful of noodles in a noodle basket or small strainer. Submerge the noodles completely in the boiling water, then immediately lift up the basket. The noodles need to just soften; if they haven't, submerge them once or twice more (this process will prevent the noodles from overcooking and becoming sad and mushy).

Assemble one bowl at a time (see Note 2). Immediately place the cooked noodles in a bowl on top of the bean sprouts. Drizzle garlic oil over the noodles, then top with a few slices of pork and 2 of the pork meatballs. Ladle the hot broth over the top of noodles. Garnish with cilantro, green onions, and a dash of pepper. Serve with a wedge of lime, fish sauce and chile, and (if using) a fritter. Assemble and serve the rest of the bowls the same way. Place the pickled garlic chile on the table for everyone to help themselves. Store leftover broth in airtight containers and freeze for up to 3 months.

Note 2: Unless the stock is added quickly to the noodles, the noodles will clump. Cooking the noodles individually and assembling the bowls one by one will prevent that from happening.

អាម៉ុក
AMOK
FISH SOUFFLÉ

Serves 4

Amok can be traced back to the Khmer Empire, where it was served to the king and the royal court. And you can see why: With the fish nestled in banana leaves and gently steamed until it puffs up like a soufflé, it looks so elegant and refined, and it tastes so light even as it's custardy and rich. There are dishes similar to amok in other Southeast Asian cultures, including Thailand's hor mok (which may or may not have originated before amok), but Cambodia's version seems to be especially well known. It's so well known, in fact, that some call it the country's national dish. Honestly, though, I wouldn't go that far, because amok isn't an everyday dish in most Khmer households. Instead, it's more often reserved for holidays and special occasion feasting. Still, it's well worth the effort any time the mood strikes or when you want to serve something impressive. I like to cook and present the amok in handmade banana baskets secured with toothpicks, but if you don't have banana leaves, you can use 4-ounce ramekins instead. Also, while amok is usually made with fish, you can substitute chicken, shrimp, mushrooms, or a hearty vegetable like cauliflower.

- 1 fingerroot, cut into small pieces
- ¼ cup Master Kroeung (page 27)
- ½ cup coconut milk, plus more for drizzling
- 2 tablespoons Bok Mtes / Chile Paste (page 31)
- 1 tablespoon fish sauce
- 1 tablespoon palm sugar or granulated sugar
- 1 teaspoon prahok
- 1 teaspoon kosher salt
- 1 pound cod or other firm whitefish, skin removed and patted dry, cut into 1-inch pieces
- 2 eggs, lightly beaten
- 8 banana leaves
- 3 cups kale, collard greens, or other dark leafy green
- 2 makrut lime leaves, center veins removed, thinly sliced
- 1 to 2 bird's eyes chiles, chopped

Place the fingerroot and kroeung in a mortar and smash them together with the pestle until blended. Alternatively, pulse them in the bowl of a food processor a few times until blended. Transfer the mixture to a large bowl and add the coconut milk, chile paste, fish sauce, palm sugar, prahok, and salt. Stir to combine, then add the fish. Coat the fish in the mixture, then add the eggs and stir well to combine.

Wipe both sides of the banana leaves with a damp cloth, then cut each one into a round 12 inches in diameter. Turn the stovetop heat to low and hold the leaves right above the burner for a few seconds, flipping and rotating them a few times, just until they're soft and pliable. Alternatively, place them in a 200°F oven for about 3 minutes to soften. (If you skip this step, the leaves will tear rather than fold when you work with them.)

FISH SOUFFLÉ, CONTINUED

To make a banana cup, place a leaf on the counter, arranging it so the lines on the leaf (its veins) run horizontally. Place another leaf right on top of that leaf, this time arranging it so the veins run vertically. (Stacking the leaves so the veins are perpendicular to each other will help make the banana cup more sturdy and prevent any leaks when steaming.)

To make a cup, fold one side of the leaves up about 3 inches. Then fold an adjacent side up 3 inches, overlapping the two sides to form a pleat. Secure the pleat with a toothpick. Work your way around the leaves, folding, pleating, and securing with a toothpick, until you've made a little banana cup that's about 3 inches in diameter. Cute, right? Repeat with the other banana leaves.

Divide the greens among all the banana cups and use a slotted spoon to add the fish right on top of each.

Fill a pot fitted with a steamer basket halfway full of water (make sure the bottom of the basket does not touch the water). Bring the water to a simmer over medium-low heat. Place the banana cups in the basket and cover (be sure to keep the water at a simmer so the eggs become custardy and don't overcook). Steam until the eggs just start to set, about 10 minutes, then spoon some coconut milk right on top of each cup. Cover once more and steam until the fish is cooked through, no longer translucent, and firm to the touch, about 10 more minutes. Top with the lime leaves and as many chopped chiles as you and your guests would like (more chiles, more heat!) and serve. The amok are best the day they're made, but store any leftovers in an airtight container and refrigerate for up to 1 day. Re-steam until warmed through, a few minutes, before serving.

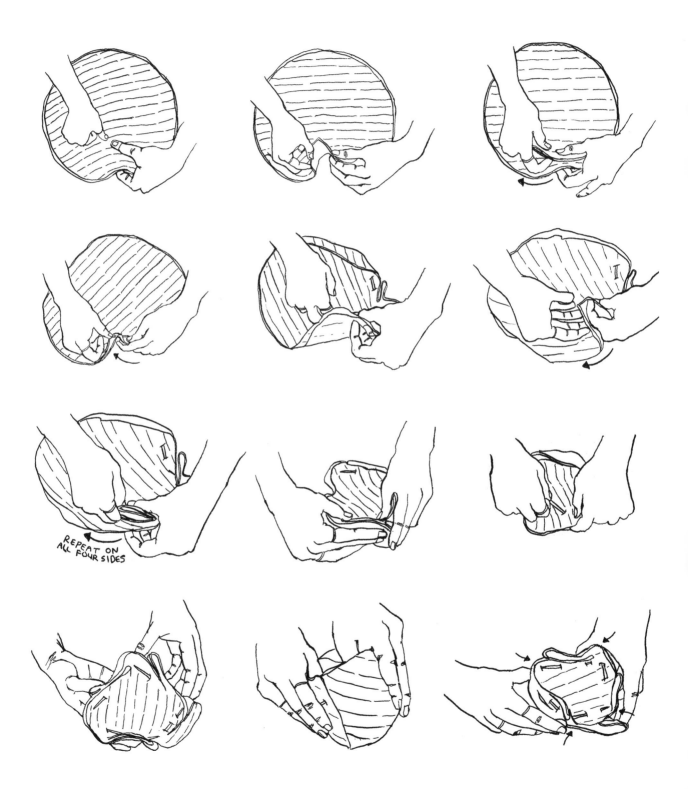

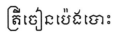

TREY JIEN BAN POUH

CRISPY FISH WITH SIMMERED SUMMER TOMATOES

Serves 2 to 4

Trey jien ban pouh is the dish to make during tomato season. I can't remember the first time I had it, but I definitely remember the crunch of the nicely crisped fish, the sweet umami of the stewed tomato sauce, the tangy sourness of the fish sauce dressing. One day, partly because I craved it and partly because it was summer and we had extra cherry tomatoes, I re-created it for Nyum Bai, and it was the perfect way to showcase our bounty. I like a little burst of tomato flavor with each bite, so I simmer the tomatoes just long enough for them to soften, but not so long that they completely lose their shape. If you prefer a smoother sauce, simmer the tomatoes a few minutes longer. A fish fillet makes prep easier and faster, but if you want to impress, a whole fish is the way to go.

TOMATO SAUCE

2 tablespoons grapeseed or other neutral oil

4 garlic cloves, minced

1 small shallot, thinly sliced (½ cup)

2 cups cherry tomatoes, halved

1 small red bell pepper, diced into 1-inch cubes (½ cup)

1 bird's eye chile, minced

½ cup Tuk Trey Piam / Fish Sauce Dressing (page 37)

1½ pounds catfish or cod fillet, skin removed

Kosher salt

1 cup cold water

½ cup rice flour (preferably Bob's Red Mill)

1 cup grapeseed or other neutral oil, for frying

1 cup loosely packed cilantro leaves

2 green onion stalks, thinly sliced

Bai / Steamed Jasmine Rice (page 52), for serving

MAKE THE TOMATO SAUCE

In a medium skillet over medium-high heat, heat the oil. When the oil begins to shimmer, add the garlic and shallot and sauté until fragrant and the garlic is golden brown, 40 seconds to 1 minute. Add the tomatoes, bell pepper, and chile. Sauté until the bell pepper softens, about 5 minutes, then add the dressing. Lower the heat to medium and simmer for about 10 minutes; the tomatoes should soften and everything should smell so nice and fragrant. Turn off the heat and set aside while you fry the fish.

MAKE THE CRISPY FISH

Pat the fish dry and season both sides with a pinch of salt.

In a medium bowl, whisk together the cold water and rice flour until the mixture is about the consistency of pancake batter.

Set a wire rack on a sheet pan, then layer a large plate with a few paper towels. Place both next to the stove.

In a medium or large cast-iron skillet over medium heat, heat the oil to 375°F. If you don't have a thermometer, drop a bit of batter into the oil, and if it puffs up, the oil is ready to go. Dip the fish into the batter and gently shake off any excess. Carefully place the battered fish in the oil and fry for about 5 minutes, flipping halfway through, until the fish is firm and cooked through. Transfer the fish to the rack and sprinkle it with a little more salt. Cool for 2 minutes, then place it on the paper towel to drain. Place the fish on a large platter or plate, spoon the tomato sauce on top, top with the cilantro and green onions, and serve with rice. It will be best the day it's made, but the fish and sauce can be stored together in an airtight container and refrigerated for up to 1 day.

KHO
CARAMELIZED PORK BELLY

Serves 4

This kho was popular at Nyum Bai, and it's a dish that, like Cha Sach Mu-anh Kyai / Chicken + Caramelized Ginger (page 99), makes me oul (which is the Khmer way of saying that I eat it so fast I can hardly breathe). A kho is a braise where the sauce is made from caramelizing sugar; the goal is to caramelize it until it turns a reddish mahogany-brown color. My mom always says if you don't achieve the right color, it's not a proper kho! There is always a danger of going too long and burning it, but as long as you keep the heat no higher than medium and stir constantly, you'll be fine. And once you get the hang of the technique, it makes for a very easy weeknight dish. This is similar to the Vietnamese version of pork kho, though we add seasoning soy sauce and star anise in the braising liquid. I like to include daikon in this kho because it soaks up the sauce so well. That said, not all Khmer khos include it; fried tofu and bamboo shoots do the same, so feel free to add them to your kho, too.

2 tablespoons Thai seasoning soy sauce

2 tablespoons oyster sauce

1 teaspoon kosher salt

1 teaspoon freshly ground black pepper

1½ pounds pork belly, skin on or off, cut into 2-inch cubes

BRAISING SAUCE

2½ tablespoons palm sugar

2 cups water

2-inch piece ginger, peeled and smashed

3 garlic cloves, smashed

1 star anise pod

2 teaspoons Thai seasoning soy sauce

2 teaspoons fish sauce

1 teaspoon kosher salt

4 eggs

9 ounces daikon, peeled and sliced into ½-inch coins (1½ cups)

Let's first make a marinade. In a large bowl, combine the seasoning soy sauce, oyster sauce, salt, and pepper. Add the pork belly and toss gently in the marinade to coat. Set aside.

MAKE THE BRAISING SAUCE

In a heavy pot over medium heat, stir the palm sugar with a wooden spoon. And keep stirring—you'll need to stand and stir and almost burn the sugar until it's reddish and deeply brown in color and starts to smell nutty and sweet, about 8 minutes. Add the marinated pork belly and give everything a good stir again. Add the water, ginger, garlic, star anise, seasoning soy sauce, fish sauce, and salt, and stir to combine. If at any point you find some sugar that has crystallized on the spoon, submerge it in the liquid and it'll melt.

Increase the heat to high. When the liquid comes to a boil, reduce to low and cover. Simmer until the pork starts to take on a nice brown color, about 20 minutes.

While the pork simmers, soft-boil the eggs. Fill a small pot with water and set it over high heat. When the water reaches a boil, gently add the eggs, then set a timer for 7 minutes. Meanwhile, fill a large bowl with ice and water and set it next to the stove. Once the timer goes off, immediately transfer the eggs to the ice bath. Once they're cool enough to handle, peel and set aside.

When the pork has simmered for about 20 minutes, uncover and simmer until the sauce has reduced by about 10 percent, about 20 minutes more. Add the daikon, cover, and cook for 10 more minutes. Finally, add the eggs and cook until the daikon is tender and the eggs turn into hard-boiled eggs, about another 10 minutes. Serve! Store leftovers in an airtight container and refrigerate for up to 3 days.

ប្រហុិត

PRAHUT

PORK MEATBALLS

Makes 36 meatballs, serves 6

We came up with these meatballs at Nyum Bai after playing around with the idea of combining our egg roll filling with the filling in shumai, a popular dim sum dish. After experimenting, we landed on these, which are lighter and less dense than other types of meatballs. They're also very peppery, with some crunch and sweetness from jicama. I suggest making the filling the night before you plan to cook; it'll not only break up the work, but the long chill will help with the shaping. Once cooked, the meatballs bring an extra layer of flavor and texture to Kuy Teav Phnom Penh / Pork Noodle Soup (page 213). They're also a great snack or appetizer!

- 1½ pounds ground pork shoulder
- ½ small jicama, minced (1 cup)
- 2 tablespoons minced yellow onion
- 4 garlic cloves, minced
- 2 green onion stalks, thinly sliced
- 1 shallot, minced
- 1 tablespoon sugar
- 1 tablespoon Thai seasoning soy sauce
- 1 tablespoon freshly ground black pepper
- 1½ teaspoons kosher salt
- ½ teaspoon cornstarch
- Grapeseed or other neutral oil, for greasing

In a large bowl, mix together the pork, jicama, onion, garlic, green onions, shallot, sugar, seasoning soy sauce, pepper, salt, and cornstarch until well combined. Cover and refrigerate for at least 1 hour, preferably overnight.

When you're ready to roll, scoop out about 1½ tablespoons of the pork mixture, form it into a ball, and place it on a sheet pan. Repeat with the remaining filling, then freeze the meatballs for 2 hours (the chill will help the meatballs keep their shape when cooked).

Fill a pot fitted with a lightly oiled steamer basket halfway with water (make sure the bottom of the basket does not touch the water). Bring the water to a simmer over medium-low heat. Working in batches to avoid overcrowding the basket, place as many meatballs as you can in the steamer without overcrowding. Cover and steam until the meatballs are cooked through (a toothpick inserted into middle of the meatball should come out clean; you also can cut one in half to make sure the center is no longer pink), about 20 minutes.

They're ready to serve right away. To store, cool them completely, then place in an airtight container and refrigerate for up to 3 days, or in the freezer for up to 1 month.

Variation: To turn these meatballs into a great stand-alone appetizer or a party snack, bake them instead. Place the meatballs on a sheet pan and bake at 425°F (or 400°F if you have a convection oven). Cook until browned and cooked through, 12 to 15 minutes.

ឡុកឡាក់
LOC LAK

STIR-FRIED BEEF CUBES

Serves 2 to 4

The French loved the deep, rich flavor of Kampot peppercorns, and during their colonial rule, they used them generously in dishes like this one. Because beef was expensive at the time, loc lak was pretty much just for the French and the upper classes. Since then, it's become more accessible, and today it's pretty common to find loc lak served with french fries or fried eggs in the capital. Because the peppercorns are the real star of the dish, it's worth sourcing black Kampot peppercorns if you can (see page 146); otherwise, use freshly ground black peppercorns. The beef will have the most flavor if it marinates overnight, but if you're in a hurry, you can marinate it for as little as 30 minutes. The tomatoes and eggs are optional for plating, but they add a little extra specialness to the feast of the dish. Serve with lots of steamed rice!

½ cup Shaoxing cooking wine

½ cup Thai seasoning soy sauce

1½ tablespoons palm sugar

1 tablespoon oyster sauce

2 garlic cloves, grated

1 teaspoon freshly ground black pepper (preferably Kampot peppercorns)

1 pound tri-tip, cut into 1-inch cubes

2 tablespoons grapeseed or other neutral oil

1 small red onion, sliced

1 bunch watercress

1 ripe tomato, thickly sliced (optional)

2 to 4 Poung Mu-anh Jien / Crispy Fried Eggs (page 45) or soft-boiled eggs (optional)

Bai / Steamed Jasmine Rice (page 52), for serving

½ cup Tuk Krauch Chhma + Ambel + Mrech / Lime + Salt + Pepper Sauce (page 36), for serving

In a large bowl, combine the cooking wine, seasoning soy sauce, palm sugar, oyster sauce, garlic, and pepper. Add the beef, stir to coat it in the marinade, and refrigerate for at least 30 minutes, preferably overnight.

In a wok or a large skillet over high heat, heat the oil. When the oil begins to shimmer, add the beef (reserve the sauce). Stir and stir, searing the beef on all sides, about 5 minutes. Add the red onion and ½ cup of the marinating sauce and toss with the beef for 2 minutes for medium-rare, or 5 minutes for well-done. Turn off the heat.

To serve, arrange the watercress on a large plate or platter and layer the tomato on top, then the beef. Place the fried eggs right on top of the beef. (If you've soft-boiled the eggs, quarter them lengthwise and arrange them around the platter.) Spoon the sauce from the wok all over. Everyone gets a bowl or plate of rice and their own little dish of the lime sauce for dipping the beef. Store leftovers in an airtight container and refrigerate for up to 2 days.

DONUT SHOP

To end, some things sweet

ស្រលាញ់ អូ ស្រលាញ់
គ្មានអ្នកណាអាចគេចពីវាទេ!

Love oh Love
There isn't anyone that
can escape it!

FROM PEN RAN'S "THERE'S
NOTHING TO BE ASHAMED OF"

This chapter is full of sweets. All kinds of sweets! From coconut waffles to cakes made of cassava to palm sugar–filled sesame balls, these are sweets and desserts that I loved eating in Stockton and Cambodia, plus a few that became beloved at my restaurant. There's also the OG Khmer donut, made of rice flour and glazed with palm sugar. But that's only partly the reason why this part is called "The Donut Shop."

Donut shops are a big part of the Khmer American story. For us, donut shops are places of survival, places of resilience, places of bonding.

Khmer Americans operate the overwhelming majority of donut shops in California and parts of Texas. Most credit Bun Tek Ngoy with laying the foundation to the Khmer donut empire. In 1975, he and his wife, Suganthini, fled Cambodia with their two children and landed in Southern California. After falling in love with American donuts and learning the trade as a manager at a Winchell's Donut House, he opened dozens of donut shops across California.

As he expanded, Ngoy sponsored Cambodian refugees for immigration and hired them to work in his shops. Many eventually set out on their own, and they replicated Ngoy's model, teaching other Khmer refugees and immigrants the trade and American culture. I get a little emotional thinking about this: Everybody in this story saw and experienced the inhumanity of war. And yet, in their new country, Khmers collaborated and helped one another survive, adjust, and thrive.

Today, second-generation Khmer Americans are taking over their family shops, introducing new flavors and outfitting their donuts with creative icing and decorations. The Khmer American legacy will live on. So next time you're at a donut shop in California or Houston or any other place home to a Khmer community, take a look: Is there an altar with a Buddha statue? Offerings of fruit in the back? If so, there's a good chance it's Khmer owned. Say "sousdey!"[1] and you will see the family's beaming smiles in appreciation.

RECIPES FROM THE DONUT SHOP

If I had a donut shop, I'd fry up maple bars and glazed twists and old-fashioneds. But I think I'd add the sweets in this chapter to the case, too, binding sticky rice with palm sugar and coconut milk to make bai treap,[2] griddling spheres of coconut custard for nom krouk,[3] and, of course, frying up some nom kong.[4] Can you imagine a Khmer donut next to an American one? Happiness.

Playlist

"Duang Netra,"
SINN SISAMOUTH

"Pkor Lorn Palin,"
ROS SEREYSOTHEA

"Tep Moke Jus,"
KEO MONTHA

"Pel Del Oun Khleat,"
SINN SISAMOUTH

---

[1] "Hello!"
[2] Palm Sugar Sticky Rice (page 228).
[3] Savory Coconut Custard (page 239).
[4] Palm Sugar–Glazed Donuts (page 243).

BAI TREAP
PALM SUGAR STICKY RICE

Serves 4 to 6

This is a low-effort, high-reward sweet similar to a Rice Krispies treat and is just as easy to make. Sticky rice is mixed together with gooey palm sugar, grated coconut, and coconut milk, then flattened into a baking dish to set (*treap* means "to flatten" in Khmer). The sticky rice is steamed with a pandan leaf, which I like to tie into a knot, partly because in doing so you'll naturally massage the leaf and release its oils and aromas and partly because the knot is easy to remove after the rice is cooked. And it's cute! The sticky rice is then topped with shredded coconut, which should be grated fresh. The store-bought packages of dried coconut flakes won't add nearly as much flavor. Note that before cooking the rice, you'll need to soak it overnight first, so plan accordingly.

2 cups uncooked glutinous rice, soaked in plenty of water overnight at room temperature

1 pandan leaf, tied into a knot

1 cup freshly grated coconut (from ½ a coconut) (see Fresh Coconuts Are the Best, page 229)

¾ cup palm sugar

1 cup coconut milk

¾ teaspoon kosher salt

3 tablespoons toasted sesame seeds

Drain and rinse the rice. If your rice cooker has a setting for glutinous or sticky rice, add the rice to the inner pot, place the pandan right on top, and cook according to the cooker's instructions. Otherwise, fill a pot fitted with a steamer basket halfway with water (make sure the bottom of the basket does not touch the water). Bring the water to a simmer over medium-heat. Place the rice in the basket, doing your best to spread it out as evenly as possible. Add the pandan leaf right on top of the rice. Cover and steam until the rice is cooked, 40 to 50 minutes.

As the rice steams, make the sauce. In a medium saucepan over medium heat, combine ½ cup of the grated coconut, the palm sugar, coconut milk, and salt. Cook just until the sugar dissolves, about 5 minutes, then remove from the heat.

When the rice is cooked, remove and discard the pandan, then transfer the rice to the saucepan. Stir, breaking up the rice to avoid clumping, until it's fully coated in the sauce. Transfer the rice to a 6 by 6-inch baking dish and flatten it out evenly. Sprinkle the top with sesame seeds.

Cool completely, then cut the rice into squares or rectangles. Top with the remaining ½ cup of grated coconut and serve. This sticky rice is best eaten the day it's made, but you can store leftovers, covered, at room temperature for 1 night.

FRESH COCONUTS ARE THE BEST

Freshly grated coconut is always much more flavorful and vibrant than the preshredded coconut or flakes at the market. In recipes like Nom Pla Ai / Mochi with Palm Sugar + a Lot of Coconut (page 231), where there are so few ingredients, I really encourage you to grate the coconut yourself. It makes a huge difference in the end. Plus, you'll gain delicious and nutritious coconut water!

To start, first pick up a mature coconut (a mature coconut has a hard brown outer husk; young coconuts, on the other hand, have a white, spongy exterior and aren't best for grating). Hold the coconut over a bowl with your nondominant hand. With the back of a heavy cleaver or a mallet, tap around its equator until it cracks open. The bowl will catch the coconut water. Keep tapping around until the coconut breaks in half and all its water has been collected.

To shred the coconut, use a grater specifically designed for that purpose (available at many Asian markets or online; it'll be clear on the label that it's intended for grating or scraping coconuts), or wedge a butter knife between the outer shell and white flesh, and run it all around the coconut until you've separated the two. Use a peeler to remove any bits of brown skin remaining on the flesh, then shred the coconut with a grater or mince it with a knife. Then you're ready to go! Store leftover grated coconut in a resealable bag and refrigerate for 1 week, or freeze for up to 1 month. The coconut water is best enjoyed immediately, but you can pour it into an airtight container and refrigerate for up to 2 days.

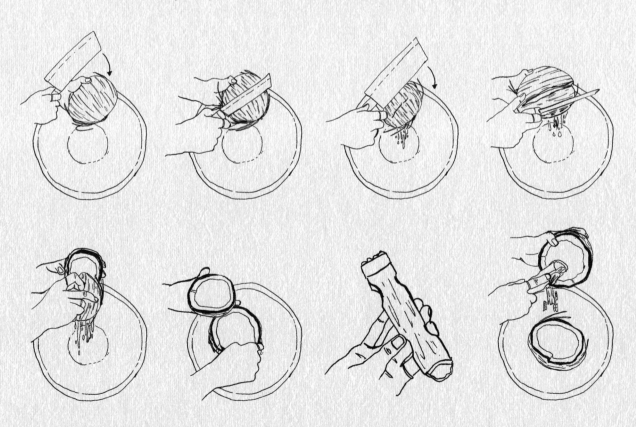

នំផ្លែអាយ
NOM PLA AI
MOCHI WITH PALM SUGAR + A LOT OF COCONUT

Makes 60 mini or 20 larger mochi balls

There's a nickname for this dessert: husband killer! As the story goes, a woman caught her husband cheating. In revenge, she made him his favorite dessert, a big pile of nom pla ai. He immediately started eating them, one right after the other. Depending on the storyteller, he died either from choking or from the extremely hot temperature of the boiled mochi and its palm sugar filling. Either way, it's both a cautionary tale about eating too fast (and infidelity) and a good way to sum up how much we love nom plai ai. There's so much flavor packed in this five-ingredient dessert. Traditionally, they're quite small, so they can take a bit of work to make; if you want to save some time, you can form them larger without sacrificing any flavor. I do suggest you take the time to shred a coconut yourself, though: The key to nom pla ai is in the generous coating of shredded coconut right at the end. I know it's easier to grab a package of preshredded flakes from the store, but please pick up the fruit instead so you can grate it fresh. It's a bit more work, but trust me, it makes a big, big difference.

- ½ cup palm sugar
- 2 cups glutinous rice flour
- 1 teaspoon kosher salt
- 1 scant cup lukewarm water
- 3 cups freshly grated coconut (from 1 coconut; see Fresh Coconuts Are the Best, page 229)

Pulse the palm sugar in the bowl of a food processor a few times, then process on low briefly until it comes together into a nice paste. Alternatively, use a heavy knife to finely chop the palm sugar into small pieces.

In a large bowl, combine the rice flour and salt. Slowly add the water, combining it with the flour as you do so to form a dough. Knead the dough in the bowl until it's one big smooth ball, similar to the texture of Play-Doh.

For mini nom pla ai, scoop out ½ teaspoon of dough and flatten it between the palms of your hands into a small round about ½-inch thick. Firmly place ½ teaspoon of palm sugar in the center, then carefully fold up the sides of the dough and gently roll it in your hands to form a ball, making sure the sugar is completely sealed in. For larger nom pla ai, follow the same steps using 1 tablespoon of dough and 1 teaspoon of palm sugar.

Place the nom pla ai on a large plate or sheet pan and repeat with the remaining dough and palm sugar.

Bring a medium pot of water to a boil. Meanwhile, spread the grated coconut on a large plate or sheet pan.

When the water is boiling, drop in as many mochi balls as you can without overcrowding the pot; make sure, too, that the water stays at a boil. When the mochi balls float to the top, about 5 minutes for the mini nom pla ai and about 7 minutes for the larger ones, they're ready! Fish them out with a slotted spoon and roll them around the bed of grated coconut to generously coat them with the flakes. Resist the temptation to try one right away, because the palm sugar filling inside will still be very, very hot! Instead, set them aside to cool completely, then serve. Cover leftovers with plastic wrap or transfer to an airtight container. They'll keep at room temperature for 1 day.

NOM ANSOM KHNOR

COCONUT STICKY RICE WITH JACKFRUIT + BEANS

Makes 16 pieces

Jackfruit grows in Cambodia year-round. With a weight up to 60 pounds and a spiky exterior, it can seem extra intimidating... but it's really such a softie inside: Sweet and almost nutty, it's a delightful fruit, perfect for desserts like this one. Nom ansom khnor is commonly offered to monks and made for holidays like the Khmer New Year. Back when we lived in Stockton, our neighbors would come together to make it. Some prepared the banana leaves; others cooked the sticky rice or cut up the jackfruit. At the very end of the assembly line, wrappers bundled and readied them for steaming. You can do the same at home with your family and friends!

1½ cups glutinous rice, soaked overnight at room temperature

1 cup coconut milk

½ cup cane sugar

½ teaspoon kosher salt

1 cup packed thinly sliced fresh jackfruit (see Note), or 1 (14-ounce) can jackfruit in syrup, rinsed and thinly sliced

¼ cup canned black beans or kidney beans (optional)

¼ cup freshly grated coconut (see Fresh Coconuts Are the Best, page 229), or store-bought unsweetened coconut flakes

16 banana leaves, cut into 6 by 6-inch squares

Note: Asian markets often offer precut wedges of fresh jackfruit, especially when the fruit is in season between late spring and early fall. The smallest wedge available likely will be more than enough for this recipe. Remove the seeds before cutting the flesh into thin slices.

Drain and rinse the soaked rice under cold water. Set aside.

In a medium saucepan over medium heat, heat the coconut milk, sugar, and salt. Stir until the sugar dissolves, about 10 minutes. Add the rice, jackfruit, beans (if using), and grated coconut. Stir until the rice completely absorbs the coconut milk and becomes sticky and pasty, 10 to 15 minutes.

Now, let's make the ansom!

Wipe both sides of the banana leaves with a damp cloth or paper towel. Turn the stovetop heat to low and hold the leaves right above the burner for a few seconds, flipping and rotating them a few times, just until they're soft and pliable. Alternatively, place them in a 200°F oven for about 3 minutes to soften. (If you skip this step, the leaves may tear when you work with them.)

Place a leaf on the counter, positioning it so the lines on the leaves are horizontal. Scoop about ¼ cup of the rice mixture and place it on the center of the leaf. Spread it out slightly, then pick up the bottom of the leaf and fold it up and over the rice. With the bottom of the leaf folded over the rice, tug the rice downward gently, then roll the leaf upward; the goal is to have a nice, tight roll, like a log. When you finish the roll at the top edge, fold in the right and left sides, then roll the log over so the packet is now seam side down, with the sides tucked underneath. (If the flaps don't stay closed, tie it closed with kitchen twine.) Repeat with the remaining banana leaves.

Fill a pot fitted with a steamer basket halfway with water (make sure the bottom of the basket does not touch the water). Bring the water to a simmer over medium-low heat. Place all the ansom seam side down in the basket, cover, and steam until the lovely aroma of jackfruit and coconut permeates the kitchen and the rice is soft and sticky, about 40 minutes. Serve! Store unwrapped ansom at room temperature, uncovered, for up to 3 days.

ចេកខ្ទិះ
JEAK KTISS
BANANA TAPIOCA PUDDING

Serves 4

Bananas are used for all sorts of desserts in Cambodia, and I really love this one, where the bananas are simmered in coconut milk and combined with tapioca pearls. The sweet is popular throughout the year, but especially during Khmer New Year and other celebrations. In Cambodia, you'll find it made with creamy baby bananas called namva, but any banana at the market will work as long as it's ripe. Be sure to stir the mixture, or it'll clump.

- 2½ cups coconut milk
- 1 teaspoon kosher salt
- 3 tablespoons sugar
- 2 ripe bananas, peeled and cut into 2-inch chunks
- 1½ tablespoons small tapioca pearls
- Crushed salted peanuts, for garnish

In a medium pot over medium-high heat, bring the coconut milk, salt, and sugar to a boil, then add the bananas. Lower the heat to medium-low and simmer until the milk thickens slightly, about 15 minutes, then drop the heat to low.

Add the tapioca pearls and stir and keep stirring for about 10 minutes so the mixture doesn't clump. Turn off the heat and that's it! Garnish with crushed peanuts and serve. Store leftover pudding in an airtight container and refrigerate for up to 3 days.

NOM LAPOV
PUMPKIN PUDDING

Serves 4

I have a soft spot for nom lapov, because it was the first Khmer dessert I learned how to make and it was one of the first sweets I served at my pop-ups. It's so comforting: Whenever I make it, I'm reminded of hazelnuts and warm pumpkin pie. You can grate the gourd yourself or use canned puree, similar to pumpkin pie. Freshly grated kabocha will give the mixture some texture and crunch, but it will be a little drier than the canned puree. If you prefer a smoother, more pudding-like filling or want to save time, use canned pumpkin puree instead.

¼ cup + 2 tablespoons freshly grated coconut (see Fresh Coconuts Are the Best, page 229) or store-bought unsweetened coconut flakes

¼ cup + 1 tablespoon cane sugar

½ teaspoon kosher salt

1 small kabocha or pumpkin, grated (2 cups) (see Note), or 1 (15-ounce) can pumpkin puree

½ cup + 1 tablespoon Thai rice flour

¼ cup coconut cream, plus more as needed

8 banana leaves, cut into 5-inch rounds or 5 by 5-inch squares

Note: Smaller kabocha and pumpkins tend to have flesh that's softer and easier to grate than those larger in size. A serrated T-peeler is best for grating the kabocha into nice strands.

In a large bowl, stir together the grated coconut, sugar, and salt. Add the pumpkin, rice flour, and coconut cream. Stir until well combined and easily spreadable. If you're using fresh kabocha and the filling seems dry, add more coconut cream, 1 tablespoon at a time, until the filling has the texture of a nice, thick paste.

Wipe both sides of the banana leaves with a damp cloth or paper towel. Turn the stovetop heat to low and hold the leaves right above the burner for a few seconds, flipping and rotating them a few times, just until they're soft and pliable. Alternatively, place them in a 200°F oven for about 3 minutes to soften. (If you skip this step, the leaves may tear rather than fold when you work with them.)

Place ¼ cup of the pumpkin mixture in the center of the leaf. Fold the top, bottom, and sides of the leaf over the mixture to completely wrap it up like an envelope. To make sure nothing escapes during cooking, wrap the whole banana leaf packet in aluminum foil. Repeat with the remaining leaves.

Fill a pot fitted with a steamer basket halfway with water (make sure the bottom of the basket does not touch the water). Bring the water to a simmer over medium-low heat. Place all the pudding packets in the steamer (if necessary, stand them upright like books on a shelf so they all fit), cover, and steam until the pudding is set and no longer runny, about 40 minutes. They'll be super hot, so cool first before serving warm or completely cooled. Store leftovers in an airtight container and refrigerate for up to 3 days. To serve again, simply resteam them for a few minutes to warm them up.

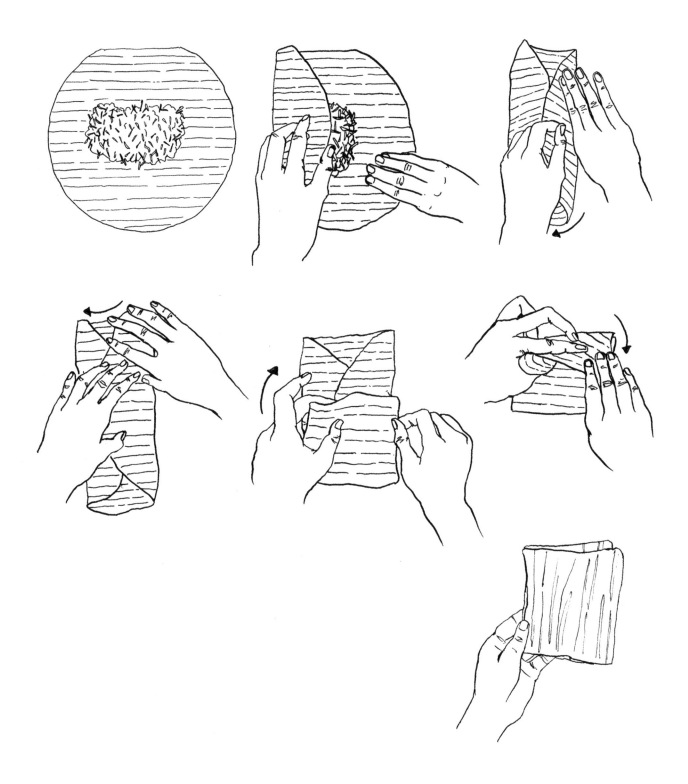

ជំក្រុក់

NOM KROUK
SAVORY COCONUT CUSTARD

Serves 4 to 6

With all the rice you make for this book, you're bound to have some leftovers. And when you do, make nom krouk! Crisp on the outside and soft and custardy on the inside, this is a popular snack in Cambodia, especially in the capital. You can't miss it: It's cooked in a griddle pan dotted with little round cups to drop in and cook the batter. Nom krouk is very similar in appearance to khanom krok, the Thai sweet, though not exactly in flavor: While both blend rice and coconut to make the batter, nom krouk is more savory, intended to be wrapped in lettuce and dipped in fish sauce. To make nom krouk, you do need that particular pan. If you have the pan to make ebelskiver or takoyaki, that will work perfectly. Otherwise, pick one up from a Southeast Asian market or online. You may want to start by cooking just a few nom krouk to get the hang of the process, then make more as you feel more confident.

2½ cups cold cooked rice

1 cup water

1 cup coconut milk

2 tablespoons sugar

1 teaspoon kosher salt

2 green onion stalks, thinly sliced

½ cup Thai rice flour

Grapeseed or other neutral oil, for greasing

1 head butter lettuce, leaves separated

1 cucumber, unpeeled, very thinly sliced

1 bunch Thai basil

1 tablespoon crushed roasted salted peanuts

1 cup Tuk Trey Piam / Fish Sauce Dressing (page 37)

In a blender, blend the rice with the water, coconut milk, sugar, and salt until it becomes a smooth paste. Add the green onions and rice flour and mix well using a spoon or whisk.

Brush each cup of the nom krouk pan with oil, then place the pan over medium-high heat. When the oil begins to shimmer, pour the batter nearly to the top of each cup. Cover and cook until crispy, about 5 minutes.

Loosen a nom krouk with a spoon and use another spoon to rotate it 90 degrees to stand it up on its side, crispy side out. Add a neighboring nom krouk into the cup, standing it so the two together form a ball. Repeat with the other nom krouk. Let the two halves sit for about a minute to fuse together and finish cooking.

Place the nom krouk on a large plate or platter along with the lettuce, cucumber, and basil. In a small bowl, combine the peanuts with the dressing. Bring everything to the table, and everyone can dive right in. Wrap the nom krouk in lettuce, cucumbers, and basil, then dip it into the dressing. YUM.

NOM POUM
COCONUT WAFFLES

Makes 6 waffles

With a batter of coconut cream and palm sugar and a big shower of toasted coconut flakes to finish, these waffles are less of a breakfast dish and more of a coconutty, fun snack or dessert. In Cambodia, you'll see vendors oiling their waffle irons as they make them to order, tucking the cooked waffle into banana leaves so you can hold it as you walk (though I never get very far before walking right back to the vendor for another one!). The waffles are the absolute best when they're fresh and hot with their edges still crisp, so serve them as soon as you pop them out of the waffle maker.

¼ cup freshly grated coconut (see Fresh Coconuts Are the Best, page 229) or store-bought unsweetened coconut flakes

½ cup palm sugar

3 eggs

1 cup coconut cream

1½ cups Thai rice flour

¼ cup tapioca flour

1 teaspoon baking powder

½ teaspoon kosher salt

4 tablespoons (½ stick) unsalted butter, melted

Banana leaves, for serving (optional)

In a small skillet or frying pan over medium heat, toast the grated coconut until golden brown, then transfer to a small bowl.

In a small pot over low heat, melt the palm sugar, stirring, until it's nice and gooey, 5 to 10 minutes.

In a medium bowl, beat the eggs until the yolks break, then mix in the coconut cream. Add the palm sugar and stir until well combined. Add the toasted coconut, rice flour, tapioca flour, baking powder, and salt. Whisk until the mixture is the consistency of pancake batter and no lumps of flour remain.

Preheat the waffle iron. Brush both sides with butter and add ½ to ¾ cup of the batter, depending on the size of your waffle maker. Follow the manufacturer's instructions for cooking the waffles. When done, they should be cooked through and crisped around the edges.

If you have banana leaves, wipe both sides clean with a damp cloth or paper towel.

When the waffle is done, wrap it in a banana leaf. That's it! Serve. Brush some more butter onto the waffle maker and continue making waffles with the remaining batter.

NOM BAK BEN
CASSAVA CAKE

ដំឡូងដក់បិន

Serves 4 to 6

Cassava cake is a dessert you'll often see at Buddhist temples during gatherings and holidays like New Year's. The starchy cassava soaks up coconut cream, condensed milk, and evaporated milk to produce a dense, rich cake with a nicely caramelized crust and a soft, chewy interior. I use fresh cassava (which may be labeled "yuca" at the market), but frozen shredded cassava also works; just thaw it first and squeeze out as much water as you can before adding it to the other ingredients.

1 pound cassava

3 eggs

Scant 1 cup coconut cream

½ cup + 3 tablespoons sweetened condensed milk, plus extra for drizzling

Scant 1 cup evaporated milk

1 teaspoon kosher salt

Grapeseed or other neutral oil, for greasing

Preheat the oven to 350°F.

Trim both ends of the cassava and discard. Then, using a sharp knife or vegetable peeler, remove the thick outer skin and the white inner peel just underneath. Remove any pinkish spots or blemishes, too. Rinse the cassava, then use a grater to shred it into a bowl (avoid shredding into the core—it's very fibrous and tough!). Discard the core. Once shredded, you should be left with about 2 packed cups.

Gently squeeze the shredded cassava to remove any excess liquid. Place it in a medium bowl and add the eggs, coconut cream, sweetened condensed milk, evaporated milk, and salt. Stir until everything is nicely combined.

Brush an 8 by 8-inch baking dish with oil. Add the batter, then bake until it's golden brown on top and a toothpick inserted into the cake comes out pretty clean, about 1 hour. If the top isn't a nice even golden brown color, transfer it to the broiler, set on low, just until caramelized.

Transfer the cake to a cooling rack and let cool for 10 minutes. Cut the cake into slices, drizzle some condensed milk over each slice, and serve. Store leftovers in an airtight container and refrigerate for up to 3 days.

ដំកង់

NOM KONG
PALM SUGAR-GLAZED DONUTS

Makes 8 donuts

Although most donut shops in California and some parts of Texas are owned by Khmer and Khmer Americans, you're more likely to find them selling American-style donuts than the OG Khmer donut. Khmer donuts are less sweet than American donuts and are made of rice flour rather than wheat. You'll find these donuts stacked high at street stalls all over Cambodia, sticky with a glaze of palm sugar and topped with sesame seeds. They're easy to make at home, too, and so good fresh and hot from the fryer. Note that when you are glazing the donuts, you should keep the melted palm sugar warm. If it cools even slightly, it won't adhere to the donut.

DONUTS
1 cup glutinous rice flour
¼ cup Thai rice flour
2 tablespoons granulated sugar
1 teaspoon baking powder
½ teaspoon kosher salt
½ cup cold water

GLAZE
½ cup palm sugar
1 tablespoon water

Grapeseed or other neutral oil, for frying

1 tablespoon toasted sesame seeds

MAKE THE DONUTS

In a medium bowl, whisk together the glutinous rice flour, Thai rice flour, granulated sugar, baking powder, and salt. Gradually pour in the cold water, whisking as you do so, until thoroughly combined and the dough has the consistency of Play-Doh. Let it sit (no need to cover) while making the glaze.

MAKE THE GLAZE

In a small skillet or sauté pan over low heat, combine the palm sugar and water. Melt the sugar, stirring occasionally, until it has the consistency of a glaze. Keep it at the lowest heat possible to keep warm while you fry the donuts.

In a medium Dutch oven or other heavy pot over high heat, heat 4 inches of oil to 350°F. If you don't have a thermometer, place the tip of a wooden chopstick in the oil. If tiny bubbles immediately form and sizzle around the chopstick, the oil is ready. As it heats, divide the dough into eight pieces. Roll one piece out into a 3-inch log, then bring the ends together to form a ring. Repeat with the remaining dough.

Place a wire rack on a sheet pan and set it next to the stove. Working in batches to avoid overcrowding the pot, carefully drop the donuts into the oil. Fry until golden brown, about 2½ minutes, then flip and fry the other side until nice and browned, too, about another 2½ minutes or so. Using a spider or a skimmer, transfer the donuts from the oil onto the wire rack.

Once the donuts are cool enough to handle, dip the top of each into the melted palm sugar (the palm sugar will be hot, so be careful), then place them back on the rack, glaze side up. After glazing all the donuts, glaze them once more in the same order and then one more time after that. Each donut should be glazed a total of three times. Sprinkle the sesame seeds on top and serve.

NOM KROUCH
SESAME BALLS

Makes 10 sesame balls

The literal translation of *krouch* is "orange," as in the fruit, because the bumpy, squishy texture of these fried balls of dough is very similar to the peel of an orange! Here, as in Cambodia, you'll usually find them filled with steamed mung beans. At Nyum Bai, though, we filled them with little spheres of palm sugar that melt and coat the interior of the dough when fried. It was a huge hit with everyone. Once they are fried, it's impossible to have just one. And really, you can have so much fun with this and fill it with anything you want. Once you fill and seal the sesame balls, they will need to be frozen for a few hours; if you don't, and instead fry right away, the filling may burst. If you really want to plan ahead, you can freeze and store them in a resealable freezer bag or airtight container up to a week in advance.

- 2 cups glutinous rice flour, plus more for dusting
- ¼ cup cane sugar
- 2 teaspoons baking powder
- 1 teaspoon kosher salt
- 1 cup coconut milk
- ½ cup white or black (or both!) untoasted sesame seeds
- ¾ cup palm sugar, cut or broken into ½-inch cubes
- Grapeseed or other neutral oil, for frying

In a medium bowl, mix together the rice flour, sugar, baking powder, and salt. In a slow stream, add the coconut milk, combining it with the dry ingredients until it just starts to resemble a dough. Lightly dust the dough with flour and knead it until it's smooth and has the consistency of Play-Doh. Set aside at room temperature (no need to cover).

Fill a small bowl with cold water. Separately, place the sesame seeds in a shallow bowl or plate. Finally, place a sheet pan or large plate next to the sesame seeds.

Scoop out ¼ cup of dough, shape it into a ball, then flatten it with the palms of your hands into a thin round about 3 inches in diameter. Place 2 teaspoons palm sugar (or 1 cube) right in the center and wrap the dough all around it. Roll it back into a smooth ball, taking care that you've really sealed in the palm sugar (otherwise, the filling will escape while frying).

Dunk the ball completely into the cold water, then drop it into the sesame seeds. Roll the dough around until it's completely covered in the seeds, then place it on the sheet pan. Repeat with the remaining dough and palm sugar.

Transfer the sheet pan to the freezer and freeze the balls of dough for at least 2 hours, or overnight, before frying.

In a medium Dutch oven or heavy pot over medium-low heat, heat 5 inches of oil. As the oil heats, place a wire rack on a sheet pan and set aside.

When the oil reaches 350°F, add the sesame balls in batches to avoid overcrowding the pot. (If you don't have a thermometer, place the tip of a wooden chopstick in the oil. If tiny bubbles immediately form and sizzle around the chopstick, the oil is ready.) Fry for 6 minutes, then rotate them and continue to fry until golden brown, 6 to 8 more minutes. Using a slotted spoon or strainer, pull them out and place on the rack. The sesame balls will be hot and the sugar inside will be extremely hot, so be careful—let them cool a bit before serving. They're best eaten the day they're made, but you can store leftovers on the counter for up to 2 days. There's no need to cover them, but if you do, be sure to completely cool them first.

SOURCES + FURTHER READING

Daguan, Zhou. *Customs of Cambodia*. Translated by Solang and Beling Uk. DatASIA, 2016.

De Monteiro, Longteine, and Katherine Neustadt. *The Elephant Walk Cookbook: Cambodian Cuisine from the Nationally Acclaimed Restaurant*. Houghton Mifflin Harcourt, 1998.

Gu, Alice, dir. *The Donut King*. Logan Industry in association with Scott Free Productions, 2019.

Long, Sorey, and Kanika Linden. *Ambarella: Cambodian Cuisine*. White Tara Limited, 2013.

Nguon, Chantha, with Kim Green. *Slow Noodles: A Cambodian Memoir of Love, Loss, and Family Recipes*. Algonquin Books, 2024.

Peyok, Dee. *Away from Beloved Lover: A Musical Journey Through Cambodia*. Granta Books, 2023.

Pirozzi, John, dir. *Don't Think I've Forgotten: Cambodia's Lost Rock and Roll*. Argot Pictures, 2014.

Rotanak, Ros, and Nataly Lee. *NHUM: Recipes from a Cambodian Home Kitchen*. Rotanak Food Media, 2019.

ACKNOWLEDGMENTS

Writing this cookbook was an emotional process because it made me slow down and truly reflect on my life. I'm grateful to know how so many people have helped me on my journey.

I had a dream once to share Khmer food with everyone, to bring light. It seemed impossible then: I had no clue how to cook or start a business. I had no resources. But I knew in my bones that I had to do it. I had to start. I had to try. Yes, it was very crazy of me, but there was the underlying force that pushed me through it all: love.

Love made me yearn to understand my mom; love meant honoring my folks and ancestors. Love led me to believe in myself; love led me to my truth. Love led to healing intergenerational trauma. Love led me to my purpose and this life I have now, always reppin' Khmer culture. And, of course, it was all my love for Khmer food—almost an obsession—that drove everything.

Nyum Bai started fifteen years ago, and, as you read, it wasn't an easy start. Despite the obstacles, fear, doubts, pain, and tears, one constant pushed me along, and it was still love.

It was love that brought these friends into my life who helped make my dream come true. Without love, none of this would exist.

In no particular order, sending love to:

My La Cocina family, present and past, especially the crew circa 2014, and especially Geets and Daniella, who gave me the first catering gig. The entrepreneurs there who continue to inspire me every day. And Caleb, Leticia, Blake, Marcella, Emiliana, and Aniela, who all believed in me when I didn't believe in myself.

Women's Initiative, who taught me how to write my first business plan back in 2012!

Rica, my book agent. Thank you for handling all the (not so fun) business aspects in this process and truly hearing out my vision.

To Bryant Terry, Claire Yee, Betsy Stromberg, Gabby Ureña Matos, and the rest of the 4C team, thank you for believing in my vision and making it a reality. I felt so supported and seen. And thank you, Bryant, for all the small pep talks. I feel so honored to have you as a mentor.

Everything felt right with my quad D girls: Nicola, the extraordinary photographer, who was so thoughtful in every way. Fanny, Allison, and Michelle for the attention to all the details and fun vibes when it comes to food and prop styling. Smells so good, looks so good, and tastes so good. All Dreamy!

Tien, we have been on this cookbook journey since 2021. How did you stand to listen to me talk for so long? You're a wizard. When my words were just jumbled up, you found a way to tell the story in the truest way possible. So happy that we had our first HOPR together. Happy moments.

Michelle Minori and Diep Tran, thank you for your recipe-testing skills.

The amazing Lunette Cambodia crew who held down the shop while I was away working on the cookbook.

The Khmer community, who believes in helping one another out and celebrating joy.

The beautiful friends and aunties I met in Cambodia who helped shape my cooking identity.

Friends who supported my journey back then and now. I see you, and I love you.

Boramy, who has been my ride or die since day one.

Christine Wong, who gave me a place to live when I was at my lowest low.

Carla Mannix, who helped with Nyum Bai's branding starting way back when NB was just a dream. Thank you always for coming through with the last-minute flyers. I don't think anyone understands my aesthetic better than you. I will cherish our Cambodia trip until the end of time.

Nak Bou, your art leaves me speechless. Your dedication to your craft is unmatched. I love how we just sync up with ideas. This book would not be the same without your illustrations. To more collaboration and cheers to our mitapheap! La hay, La houm for life.

The team behind Nyum Bai's Kickstarter: Thanks for believing in me when I didn't have anything. I will always remember the hours you all volunteered to design, build, and help tell my story. I was very lucky.

Nyum Bai crew, the ones who are still currently in my life. Thank you for your trust.

To all the friends who volunteered during my pop-up days. I see you all, and I love you.

To my family and ancestors, this book is for you. You have taught me how to live with a pure heart and to face life with compassion, kindness, and love. Ah kun. I don't doubt that the life I have now is because of the good deeds and karma that were passed down from my mom and ancestors.

ABOUT THE CONTRIBUTORS

Nite Yun was born in a refugee camp after her parents escaped wartorn Cambodia. Her family eventually moved to California, where she grew up listening to her father's Khmer rock 'n' roll music and learned to cook traditional Cambodian dishes from her mother. Inspired by trips to Cambodia to learn about her heritage, Nite dedicated herself to bringing the flavors of Cambodian food back to the Bay Area. She opened her first restaurant, Nyum Bai, in Oakland in 2018 and now runs Lunette in San Francisco. Nite has been recognized as one of *Time* magazine's 100 Most Influential People and named a *Food & Wine* Best New Chef 2019, was a recipient of the Vilcek Foundation Prize for Creative Promise in Culinary Arts, 2019, and was featured on Netflix's *Chef's Table* in 2024. She lives in San Francisco with her French bulldog queen, Nola.

Tien Nguyen is a food and culture writer. She is the coauthor of several cookbooks, including the *New York Times* bestseller *L.A. Son: My Life, My City, My Food* with chef Roy Choi and the IACP-nominated *Sohn-mat: Recipes and Flavors of Korean Home Cooking*. Her work also has been honored by the Association of Food Journalists. She teaches food journalism at the University of Southern California and lives in Los Angeles.

INDEX

Note: Page references in *italics* indicate photographs.

A

Amok / Fish Soufflé, 216–17, *217*

B

Bai Kadang / Rice Crackers, *54,* 55
Bai Mu-anh / Poached Chicken + Ginger Rice with Spicy, Limey Fish Sauce, 150–51
Bai Sach Chrouk / Coconut Pork, *186,* 187
Bai / Steamed Jasmine Rice, 52
Bai Treap / Palm Sugar Sticky Rice, 228
Banana blossoms
  Ngyom Trayong Jenk / Banana Blossom Salad, 200, *201*
  slicing, 202
Banana leaves, 22
Banana Tapioca Pudding / Jeak Ktiss, *234,* 235
Bangkea Dot Tuk Kampot / Grilled Freshwater Prawns in Kampot Sauce, *112,* 113
Beans
  Nom Ansom Khnor / Coconut Sticky Rice with Jackfruit + Beans, 232
  Smolaw Koko / Stirring Soup, *132,* 133–34
  Trey Jien Juen / Whole Fish with Ginger + Salted Beans, *96,* 97
Beef
  Curi Saraman / Saraman Curry, *136,* 137–38
  Kuy Teav Kho Ko / Caramelized Beef Stew, 139–40
  Loc Lak / Stir-Fried Beef Cubes, 223
  Mee Ka-Tung / Stir-Fried Egg Noodles with Gravy, 94–95
  Nom Pachok Kampot / Kampot Noodles with Coconut Fish Sauce Dressing, *142,* 143
  Plea Sach Ko / Beef Carpaccio Salad, 77
  Sach Ko Ang / Kroeung Beef Skewers, *66,* 67
  Sgnor Chuong Kho / Cozy Oxtail Soup, 169
  Somlaw Machoo Kroeung / Tamarind Kroeung Soup, *84,* 85–86
  Tuk Prahok / Prahok Dipping Sauce with Seared Rib Eye, 73–74, *75*
Bok La Hong / Green Papaya Salad, 76
Bok Mtes / Chile Paste, 31
Bor Bor / Plain Porridge, 53
Bor Bor Sach Mu-anh / Chicken Porridge, 148, *149*
Broth, Chicken / Somlaw Mu-anh, 32
Buns, Steamed Pork / Nom Pow, 68–69

C

Cabbage
  Jien Cho-Yah / Crispy Pork Egg Rolls, 196–97
  Mee Cha / Student Noodles, 174
  Ngyom Sach Mu-anh / Chicken Cabbage Salad, 203
  Nom Pow / Steamed Pork Buns, 68–69
  Plea Sach Ko / Beef Carpaccio Salad, 77
  Sgnor Chuong Kho / Cozy Oxtail Soup, 169
Cake, Cassava / Nom Bak Ben, 241
Cambodia, 104–5
Carrots
  Chrouk / Pickles, 38, *39*
  Kuy Teav Kho Ko / Caramelized Beef Stew, 139–40
  Sgnor Chuong Kho / Cozy Oxtail Soup, 169
  Somlaw Chap Chai / Celebration Soup, 87–88, *89*
Cassava Cake / Nom Bak Ben, 241
Ceviche, Khmer / Pleay Trey, *78,* 79
Cha Dau Fu Kh-Chai / Quick Stir-Fry with Fried Tofu + Chives, 161
Cha Kdam Kroeung / Stir-Fried Crab + Kroeung, *180,* 181–82
Cha Kroeung / Stir-Fried Kroeung, 183
Cha Krom Tuk Ampil / Stir-Fried Mussels in Tamarind Sauce, 184, *185*
Cha Lapov / Stir-Fried Pumpkin with Pork, *208,* 209
Cha Mee Sou / Peppery Stir-Fried Glass Noodles with Yuba, 92, *93*
Cha Mouk Mrech Baitang / Stir-Fried Squid with Green Peppercorns, 144, *145*
Cha Port / Stir-Fried Corn, *108,* 109
Cha Sach Mu-anh Kyai / Chicken + Caramelized Ginger, 99–100
Cha Tra Koun / Stir-Fried Water Spinach, 205
Cha Trek Sak / Stir-Fried Cucumbers with Black Pepper + Egg, *166,* 167
Cha Troup / Charred Eggplants with Pork + Shrimp, 206, *207*
Chicken
  Bai Mu-anh / Poached Chicken + Ginger Rice with Spicy, Limey Fish Sauce, 150–51
  Bor Bor Sach Mu-anh / Chicken Porridge, 148, *149*
  Cha Kroeung / Stir-Fried Kroeung, 183
  Cha Sach Mu-anh Kyai / Chicken + Caramelized Ginger, 99–100
  Curi Sach Mu-anh / Chicken Curry, *90,* 91
  Mu-anh Doat Cola / Coca-Cola Chicken, *152,* 153
  Ngyom Sach Mu-anh / Chicken Cabbage Salad, 203
  Ngyom Trayong Jenk / Banana Blossom Salad, 200, *201*
  Sach Mu-anh Boungk / Stuffed Chicken Wings, 164–65
  Sach Mu-anh Jien / Fried Chicken Wings, *64,* 65
  Sgnor Sach Mu-anh / Chicken Lime Soup, 168
  Somlaw Mu-anh / Chicken Broth, 32
Chile paste
  Bok Mtes / Chile Paste, 31
  Red Kroeung, 28
Chiles
  Bok La Hong / Green Papaya Salad, 76
  Bok Mtes / Chile Paste, 31
  Chrouk Mtes Khtoem / Pickled Garlic Chile, *34,* 35
  Kampot Sauce, *112,* 113
  Prahok Dipping Sauce, 73–74, *75*
  Tuk Trey Mtes / Fish Sauce + Chile, *33,* 34
Chives + Fried Tofu, Quick Stir-Fry with / Cha Dau Fu Kh-Chai, 161
Chrouk Khtoem / Pickled Garlic, *40,* 41
Chrouk Mtes Khtoem / Pickled Garlic Chile, *34,* 35
Chrouk / Pickles, 38, *39*
Coca-Cola Chicken / Mu-anh Doat Cola, *152,* 153
Coconut
  Bai Treap / Palm Sugar Sticky Rice, 228
  fresh, grating, 229
  Nom Ansom Khnor / Coconut Sticky Rice with Jackfruit + Beans, 232

Nom Lapov / Pumpkin Pudding, 236
Nom Pla Ai / Mochi with Palm Sugar + a Lot of Coconut, *230,* 231
Nom Poum / Coconut Waffles, 240
shredded, 20
Coconut cream, 16
    Natang / Coconut, Pork + Dried Shrimp Dip, 117
    Nom Bak Ben / Cassava Cake, 241
    Nom Poum / Coconut Waffles, 240
Coconut milk, 16
    Bai Sach Chrouk / Coconut Pork, *186,* 187
    Coconut Fish Sauce Dressing, *142,* 143
    in Khmer food, note about, 27
    Nom Ansom Khnor / Coconut Sticky Rice with Jackfruit + Beans, 232
    Nom Krouch / Sesame Balls, 244, *245*
    Nom Krouk / Savory Coconut Custard, *238,* 239
    Pot Ang / Grilled Corn with Coconut Milk + Green Onion, 160
    Prahok Ktiss / Prahok Coconut Pork Dip, *194,* 195
    Somlaw Machoo Ktiss Ban Kong / Shrimp Tamarind Coconut Soup, 170, *171*
Corn
    Cha Port / Stir-Fried Corn, *108,* 109
    Pot Ang / Grilled Corn with Coconut Milk + Green Onion, 160
Crab, Stir-Fried, + Kroeung / Cha Kdam Kroeung, *180,* 181–82
Crackers, Rice / Bai Kadang, *54,* 55
Cucumbers
    Cha Trek Sak / Stir-Fried Cucumbers with Black Pepper + Egg, *166,* 167
    Chrouk / Pickles, 38, *39*
    Mee Kola / Cold Noodles with Cucumber Relish + Dried Shrimp, 175–76, *177*
    Somlaw Kraung Chnuk / Soup Outside the Pot, 82, *83*
Curi Sach Mu-anh / Chicken Curry, *90,* 91
Curi Saraman / Saraman Curry, *136,* 137–38
Custard, Coconut / Nom Krouk, *238,* 239

D

Daikon
    Kho / Caramelized Pork Belly, *220,* 221
    Kuy Teav Kho Ko / Caramelized Beef Stew, 139–40
    Somlaw Chap Chai / Celebration Soup, 87–88, *89*
Dips + spreads
    Kapeek Pow / Smoked Fish + Shrimp Tapenade, 163
    Natang / Coconut, Pork + Dried Shrimp Dip, 117
    Prahok Dipping Sauce, 73–74, *75*
    Prahok Ktiss / Prahok Coconut Pork Dip, *194,* 195
    Tuk Kroeung / Tinned Mackerel with Prahok, 72
Donuts, Palm Sugar–Glazed / Nom Kong, *242,* 243
Donut shops, 226
Dressings
    Coconut Fish Sauce Dressing, *142,* 143
    Tuk Trey Piam / Fish Sauce Dressing, 37
Dried shrimp, 16
    Kapeek Pow / Smoked Fish + Shrimp Tapenade, 163
    Mee Kola / Cold Noodles with Cucumber Relish + Dried Shrimp, 175–76, *177*
    Natang / Coconut, Pork + Dried Shrimp Dip, 117
    Nom Pachok Kampot / Kampot Noodles with Coconut Fish Sauce Dressing, *142,* 143

E

Eggplants
    Cha Troup / Charred Eggplants with Pork + Shrimp, 206, *207*
    Prahok Dipping Sauce, 73–74, *75*
    Smolaw Koko / Stirring Soup, *132,* 133–34
    Somlaw Machoo Kroeung / Tamarind Kroeung Soup, *84,* 85–86
Egg Rolls, Crispy Pork / Jien Cho-Yah, 196–97
Eggs
    Bai Sach Chrouk / Coconut Pork, *186,* 187
    Cha Lapov / Stir-Fried Pumpkin with Pork, *208,* 209
    Cha Trek Sak / Stir-Fried Cucumbers with Black Pepper + Egg, *166,* 167
    Kho / Caramelized Pork Belly, *220,* 221
    Mee Cha / Student Noodles, 174
    Mee Ka-Tung / Stir-Fried Egg Noodles with Gravy, 94–95
    Mee Kola / Cold Noodles with Cucumber Relish + Dried Shrimp, 175–76, *177*
    Poung Mu-anh Jien Ka-Lok / Egg Ribbons, *46,* 47
    Poung Mu-anh Jien / Crispy Fried Eggs, 45
    Sa-om Poung Mu-anh Jien / Sa-om Omelet, 71
    Somlaw Kraung Chnuk / Soup Outside the Pot, 82, *83*

F

Fermented fish paste. *See* Prahok
Fingerroot
    about, 22
    Green Kroeung, 29
Fish sauce, 16
    Bai Mu-anh / Poached Chicken + Ginger Rice with Spicy, Limey Fish Sauce, 150–51
    Coconut Fish Sauce Dressing, *142,* 143
    Kampot Sauce, *112,* 113
    Ngyom Kroch Thlong / Pomelo Salad with Fish Sauce Dressing, *198,* 199
    Tuk Trey Mtes / Fish Sauce + Chile, 33, *34*
    Tuk Trey Piam / Fish Sauce Dressing, 37
Fritters, Crispy Shrimp / Jien BawnKwang, 121

G

Galangal, 22
    Master Kroeung, *26,* 27–29
    Prahok Dipping Sauce, 73–74, *75*
Garlic, 22
    Chrouk Khtoem / Pickled Garlic, *40,* 41
    Chrouk Mtes Khtoem / Pickled Garlic Chile, *34,* 35

Garlic, *continued*
    Kampot Sauce, *112,* 113
    Khtoem Jien / Crispy Garlic Oil, 42, *43*
    Master Kroeung, *26,* 27–29
    Prahok Dipping Sauce, 73–74, *75*
    Sach Chrouk Ang / Garlic + Pepper Pork Ribs, 101
Ginger, 23
    Bai Mu-anh / Poached Chicken + Ginger Rice with Spicy, Limey Fish Sauce, 150–51
    Cha Sach Mu-anh Kyai / Chicken + Caramelized Ginger, 99–100
    Trey Jien Juen / Whole Fish with Ginger + Salted Beans, *96,* 97
Glutinous rice flour, 20
Green Kroeung, 29
Green mangoes, 23
    Ngyom Svay / Green Mango Salad with Dried Smoked Salted Fish, 124, *125*
    Somlaw Kraung Chnuk / Soup Outside the Pot, 82, *83*
    Trey Jien Svay / Green Mango Salad with a Crispy Fish Fillet, *122,* 123
Green onions
    about, 23
    Pot Ang / Grilled Corn with Coconut Milk + Green Onion, 160
Green papaya, 23
    Bok La Hong / Green Papaya Salad, 76
    Chrouk / Pickles, 38, *39*
    Smolaw Koko / Stirring Soup, *132,* 133–34

H

Holy basil
    Cha Kroeung / Stir-Fried Kroeung, 183
    Prahok Kop / Buried Prahok, *114,* 115–16, *116*

J

Jackfruit + Beans, Coconut Sticky Rice with / Nom Ansom Khnor, 232
Jeak Ktiss / Banana Tapioca Pudding, *234,* 235

Jicama
    Nom Pung Jien / Crispy Toast with Pork + Jicama, *118,* 119
    Prahut / Pork Meatballs, 222
Jien BawnKwang / Crispy Shrimp Fritters, 121
Jien Cho-Yah / Crispy Pork Egg Rolls, 196–97

K

Kabocha
    Cha Lapov / Stir-Fried Pumpkin with Pork, *208,* 209
    Nom Lapov / Pumpkin Pudding, 236
    Smolaw Koko / Stirring Soup, *132,* 133–34
    Somlaw Prahor / Countryside Soup, 135
Kampot Sauce, *112,* 113
Kapeek Pow / Smoked Fish + Shrimp Tapenade, 163
Khmer
    Golden Era, 210–11
    identifying as, 13
    re-creating nearly lost dishes, 172–73
Kho / Caramelized Pork Belly, *220,* 221
Kho Trey / Caramelized Fish with Tomatoes, *178,* 179
Khtoem Jien / Crispy Garlic Oil, 42, *43*
Khtoem Krahm Jien / Crispy Shallots, 44
Kroeung
    Cha Kdam Kroeung / Stir-Fried Crab + Kroeung, *180,* 181–82
    Cha Kroeung / Stir-Fried Kroeung, 183
    Green, 29
    in Khmer food, note about, 27
    Master, *26,* 27–29
    Red, 28
    Sach Ko Ang / Kroeung Beef Skewers, 66, *67*
    Somlaw Machoo Kroeung / Tamarind Kroeung Soup, *84,* 85–86
    Yellow, 28
Kuy Teav Kho Ko / Caramelized Beef Stew, 139–40
Kuy Teav Phnom Penh / Pork Noodle Soup, *212,* 213–14

L

Lemongrass, 23
    Master Kroeung, *26,* 27–29
    Mu-anh Doat Cola / Coca-Cola Chicken, *152,* 153
    Prahok Dipping Sauce, 73–74, *75*
    Prahut Trey / Lemongrass Fish Cakes, 110, *111*
Lime
    Bai Mu-anh / Poached Chicken + Ginger Rice with Spicy, Limey Fish Sauce, 150–51
    Kampot Sauce, *112,* 113
    Sgnor Sach Mu-anh / Chicken Lime Soup, 168
    Tuk Krauch Chhma + Ambel + Mrech / Lime + Salt + Pepper Sauce, 36
Lime leaves
    Master Kroeung, *26,* 27–29
    Prahok Dipping Sauce, 73–74, *75*
    Sgnor Sach Mu-anh / Chicken Lime Soup, 168
Loc Lak / Stir-Fried Beef Cubes, 223

M

Mackerel, Tinned, with Prahok / Tuk Kroeung, 72
Makrut lime leaves. *See* Lime leaves
Meatballs, Pork / Prahut, 222
Mee Cha / Student Noodles, 174
Mee Ka-Tung / Stir-Fried Egg Noodles with Gravy, 94–95
Mee Kola / Cold Noodles with Cucumber Relish + Dried Shrimp, 175–76, *177*
Mu-anh Doat Cola / Coca-Cola Chicken, *152,* 153
Mochi with Palm Sugar + a Lot of Coconut / Nom Pla Ai, *230,* 231
Mushrooms
    Prahok Kop / Buried Prahok, *114,* 115–16, *116*
    Somlaw Chap Chai / Celebration Soup, 87–88, *89*
    Somlaw Machoo Ktiss Ban Kong / Shrimp Tamarind Coconut Soup, *170, 171*
    Somlaw Prahor / Countryside Soup, 135
Mussels, Stir-Fried, in Tamarind Sauce / Cha Krom Tuk Ampil, *184,* 185

N

Natang / Coconut, Pork + Dried Shrimp Dip, 117
Ngyom Kroch Thlong / Pomelo Salad with Fish Sauce Dressing, *198, 199*
Ngyom Mee Sou / Potluck Glass Noodle Salad, *126,* 127
Ngyom Sach Mu-anh / Chicken Cabbage Salad, 203
Ngyom Svay / Green Mango Salad with Dried Smoked Salted Fish, 124, *125*
Ngyom Trayong Jenk / Banana Blossom Salad, 200, *201*
Nom Ansom Khnor / Coconut Sticky Rice with Jackfruit + Beans, 232
Nom Bak Ben / Cassava Cake, 241
Nom Kong / Palm Sugar–Glazed Donuts, *242,* 243
Nom Krouch / Sesame Balls, 244, *245*
Nom Krouk / Savory Coconut Custard, *238,* 239
Nom Lapov / Pumpkin Pudding, 236
Nom Pachok Kampot / Kampot Noodles with Coconut Fish Sauce Dressing, *142,* 143
Nom Pachok Somlar Khmer / Rice Vermicelli with Fish Chowder, *128,* 129–30
Nom Pla Ai / Mochi with Palm Sugar + a Lot of Coconut, *230,* 231
Nom Poum / Coconut Waffles, 240
Nom Pow / Steamed Pork Buns, 68–69
Nom Pung Jien / Crispy Toast with Pork + Jicama, *118,* 119
Noodles
　Cha Mee Sou / Peppery Stir-Fried Glass Noodles with Yuba, 92, *93*
　glass, about, 16
　Kuy Teav Phnom Penh / Pork Noodle Soup, *212,* 213–14
　Mee Cha / Student Noodles, 174
　Mee Ka-Tung / Stir-Fried Egg Noodles with Gravy, 94–95
　Mee Kola / Cold Noodles with Cucumber Relish + Dried Shrimp, 175–76, *177*
　Ngyom Mee Sou / Potluck Glass Noodle Salad, *126,* 127
　nom pachok, preparing, 131
　Nom Pachok Kampot / Kampot Noodles with Coconut Fish Sauce Dressing, *142,* 143
　Nom Pachok Somlar Khmer / Rice Vermicelli with Fish Chowder, *128,* 129–30
　Sach Mu-anh Boungk / Stuffed Chicken Wings, 164–65
Nyum Bai, 190–93

O

Oil, Crispy Garlic / Khtoem Jien, 42, *43*
Omelet, Sa-om / Sa-om Poung Mu-anh Jien, 71
Oyster sauce, 16

P

Palm sugar, 19
Pantry goods, 16–20
Peanuts
　Nom Pachok Kampot / Kampot Noodles with Coconut Fish Sauce Dressing, *142,* 143
　Sach Mu-anh Boungk / Stuffed Chicken Wings, 164–65
Peppercorns, 19
　Cha Mouk Mrech Baitang / Stir-Fried Squid with Green Peppercorns, 144, *145*
　Cha Trek Sak / Stir-Fried Cucumbers with Black Pepper + Egg, *166,* 167
　Kampot, about, 146
　Kampot, colors and flavors, 147
　Loc Lak / Stir-Fried Beef Cubes, 223
　Sach Chrouk Ang / Garlic + Pepper Pork Ribs, 101
　Tuk Krauch Chhma + Ambel + Mrech / Lime + Salt + Pepper Sauce, 36
Pickles
　Chrouk Khtoem / Pickled Garlic, *40,* 41
　Chrouk / Pickles, 38, *39*
Pineapple
　Somlaw Machoo Ktiss Ban Kong / Shrimp Tamarind Coconut Soup, 170, *171*
Plea Sach Ko / Beef Carpaccio Salad, 77
Pleay Trey / Khmer Ceviche, *78,* 79
Pomelo Salad with Fish Sauce Dressing / Ngyom Kroch Thlong, *198, 199*

Pork
　Bai Sach Chrouk / Coconut Pork, *186,* 187
　Cha Lapov / Stir-Fried Pumpkin with Pork, *208,* 209
　Cha Mee Sou / Peppery Stir-Fried Glass Noodles with Yuba, 92, *93*
　Cha Trek Sak / Stir-Fried Cucumbers with Black Pepper + Egg, *166,* 167
　Cha Troup / Charred Eggplants with Pork + Shrimp, 206, *207*
　Jien Cho-Yah / Crispy Pork Egg Rolls, 196–97
　Kho / Caramelized Pork Belly, *220,* 221
　Kuy Teav Phnom Penh / Pork Noodle Soup, *212,* 213–14
　Natang / Coconut, Pork + Dried Shrimp Dip, 117
　Ngyom Mee Sou / Potluck Glass Noodle Salad, *126,* 127
　Nom Pow / Steamed Pork Buns, 68–69
　Nom Pung Jien / Crispy Toast with Pork + Jicama, *118,* 119
　Prahok Kop / Buried Prahok, *114,* 115–16, *116*
　Prahok Ktiss / Prahok Coconut Pork Dip, *194,* 195
　Prahut / Pork Meatballs, 222
　Sach Chrouk Ang / Garlic + Pepper Pork Ribs, 101
　Sach Mu-anh Boungk / Stuffed Chicken Wings, 164–65
　Smolaw Koko / Stirring Soup, *132,* 133–34
　Somlaw Chap Chai / Celebration Soup, 87–88, *89*
　Trey Prama / Pork + Salted Cod Loaf, 120
Porridge
　Bor Bor / Plain Porridge, 53
　Bor Bor Sach Mu-anh / Chicken Porridge, 148, *149*
Pot Ang / Grilled Corn with Coconut Milk + Green Onion, 160
Potatoes
　Curi Sach Mu-anh / Chicken Curry, *90,* 91
　Sgnor Chuong Kho / Cozy Oxtail Soup, 169
Poung Mu-anh Jien Ka-Lok / Egg Ribbons, *46,* 47
Poung Mu-anh Jien / Crispy Fried Eggs, 45

Prahok, 19
   in Khmer food, note about, 27
   Prahok Dipping Sauce, 73–74, *75*
   Prahok Kop / Buried Prahok, *114,* 115–16, *116*
   Prahok Ktiss / Prahok Coconut Pork Dip, *194,* 195
   Tuk Kroeung / Tinned Mackerel with Prahok, 72
   Tuk Prahok / Prahok Dipping Sauce with Seared Rib Eye, 73–74, *75*
Prahut / Pork Meatballs, 222
Prahut Trey / Lemongrass Fish Cakes, 110, *111*
Prawns, Grilled Freshwater, in Kampot Sauce / Bangkea Dot Tuk Kampot, *112,* 113
Pudding
   Jeak Ktiss / Banana Tapioca Pudding, *234,* 235
   Nom Lapov / Pumpkin Pudding, 236
Pumpkin
   Cha Lapov / Stir-Fried Pumpkin with Pork, *208,* 209
   Nom Lapov / Pumpkin Pudding, 236

R

Red Kroeung, 28
Rice, 20
   Bai Kadang / Rice Crackers, *54,* 55
   Bai Mu-anh / Poached Chicken + Ginger Rice with Spicy, Limey Fish Sauce, 150–51
   Bai Sach Chrouk / Coconut Pork, *186,* 187
   Bai / Steamed Jasmine Rice, 52
   Bai Treap / Palm Sugar Sticky Rice, 228
   Bor Bor / Plain Porridge, 53
   Bor Bor Sach Mu-anh / Chicken Porridge, 148, *149*
   in Cambodia, 48
   Nom Ansom Khnor / Coconut Sticky Rice with Jackfruit + Beans, 232
   Nom Krouk / Savory Coconut Custard, *238,* 239
   rules of, 49
   Toasted Rice Powder, 134
   white jasmine, preparing, 50
Rice flour, 20

S

Sach Chrouk Ang / Garlic + Pepper Pork Ribs, 101
Sach Ko Ang / Kroeung Beef Skewers, 66, *67*
Sach Mu-anh Boungk / Stuffed Chicken Wings, 164–65
Sach Mu-anh Jien / Fried Chicken Wings, *64,* 65
Salads
   Bok La Hong / Green Papaya Salad, 76
   Ngyom Kroch Thlong / Pomelo Salad with Fish Sauce Dressing, *198,* 199
   Ngyom Mee Sou / Potluck Glass Noodle Salad, *126,* 127
   Ngyom Sach Mu-anh / Chicken Cabbage Salad, 203
   Ngyom Svay / Green Mango Salad with Dried Smoked Salted Fish, 124, *125*
   Ngyom Trayong Jenk / Banana Blossom Salad, *200, 201*
   Plea Sach Ko / Beef Carpaccio Salad, 77
   Pleay Trey / Khmer Ceviche, *78,* 79
   Trey Jien Svay / Green Mango Salad with a Crispy Fish Fillet, *122,* 123
Salt, 20
San Francisco, CA, 156–57
Sa-om Poung Mu-anh Jien / Sa-om Omelet, 71
Sauces. *See also* Dressings
   Kampot Sauce, *112,* 113
   Prahok Dipping Sauce, 73–74, *75*
   Tuk Krauch Chhma + Ambel + Mrech / Lime + Salt + Pepper Sauce, 36
Seafood
   Amok / Fish Soufflé, 216–17, *217*
   Cha Kdam Kroeung / Stir-Fried Crab + Kroeung, *180,* 181–82
   Cha Krom Tuk Ampil / Stir-Fried Mussels in Tamarind Sauce, 184, *185*
   Cha Mouk Mrech Baitang / Stir-Fried Squid with Green Peppercorns, 144, *145*
   Cha Troup / Charred Eggplants with Pork + Shrimp, 206, *207*
   Jien BawnKwang / Crispy Shrimp Fritters, 121
   Kapeek Pow / Smoked Fish + Shrimp Tapenade, 163
   Kho Trey / Caramelized Fish with Tomatoes, *178,* 179
   Natang / Coconut, Pork + Dried Shrimp Dip, 117
   Ngyom Kroch Thlong / Pomelo Salad with Fish Sauce Dressing, *198,* 199
   Ngyom Mee Sou / Potluck Glass Noodle Salad, *126,* 127
   Ngyom Svay / Green Mango Salad with Dried Smoked Salted Fish, 124, *125*
   Nom Pachok Somlar Khmer / Rice Vermicelli with Fish Chowder, *128,* 129–30
   Pleay Trey / Khmer Ceviche, *78,* 79
   Prahut Trey / Lemongrass Fish Cakes, 110, *111*
   Somlaw Kraung Chnuk / Soup Outside the Pot, 82, *83*
   Somlaw Machoo Ktiss Ban Kong / Shrimp Tamarind Coconut Soup, 170, *171*
   Somlaw Prahor / Countryside Soup, 135
   Trey Jien Ban Pouh / Crispy Fish with Simmered Summer Tomatoes, *218,* 219
   Trey Jien Juen / Whole Fish with Ginger + Salted Beans, *96,* 97
   Trey Jien Svay / Green Mango Salad with a Crispy Fish Fillet, *122,* 123
   Trey Prama / Pork + Salted Cod Loaf, 120
   Tuk Kroeung / Tinned Mackerel with Prahok, 72
Sesame Balls / Nom Krouch, *244, 245*
Sgnor Chuong Kho / Cozy Oxtail Soup, 169
Sgnor Sach Mu-anh / Chicken Lime Soup, 168
Shallots
   Khtoem Krahm Jien / Crispy Shallots, 44
   Master Kroeung, *26,* 27–29
Shrimp
   Cha Troup / Charred Eggplants with Pork + Shrimp, 206, *207*
   Jien BawnKwang / Crispy Shrimp Fritters, 121
   Natang / Coconut, Pork + Dried Shrimp Dip, 117
   Ngyom Kroch Thlong / Pomelo Salad with Fish Sauce Dressing, *198,* 199

Ngyom Mee Sou / Potluck Glass Noodle Salad, 126, 127
Somlaw Machoo Ktiss Ban Kong / Shrimp Tamarind Coconut Soup, 170, 171
Shrimp, dried. See Dried shrimp
Shrimp paste, 20
    Kapeek Pow / Smoked Fish + Shrimp Tapenade, 163
    Red Kroeung, 28
Smolaw Koko / Stirring Soup, 132, 133–34
Somlaw Chap Chai / Celebration Soup, 87–88, 89
Somlaw Kraung Chnuk / Soup Outside the Pot, 82, 83
Somlaw Machoo Kroeung / Tamarind Kroeung Soup, 84, 85–86
Somlaw Machoo Ktiss Ban Kong / Shrimp Tamarind Coconut Soup, 170, 171
Somlaw Mu-anh / Chicken Broth, 32
Somlaw Prahor / Countryside Soup, 135
Soufflé, Fish / Amok, 216–17, 217
Soups + stews
    Curi Sach Mu-anh / Chicken Curry, 90, 91
    Curi Saraman / Saraman Curry, 136, 137–38
    Kuy Teav Kho Ko / Caramelized Beef Stew, 139–40
    Kuy Teav Phnom Penh / Pork Noodle Soup, 212, 213–14
    Nom Pachok Somlar Khmer / Rice Vermicelli with Fish Chowder, 128, 129–30
    rice, about, 16
    Sgnor Chuong Kho / Cozy Oxtail Soup, 169
    Sgnor Sach Mu-anh / Chicken Lime Soup, 168
    Smolaw Koko / Stirring Soup, 132, 133–34
    Somlaw Chap Chai / Celebration Soup, 87–88, 89
    Somlaw Kraung Chnuk / Soup Outside the Pot, 82, 83

Somlaw Machoo Kroeung / Tamarind Kroeung Soup, 84, 85–86
Somlaw Machoo Ktiss Ban Kong / Shrimp Tamarind Coconut Soup, 170, 171
Somlaw Prahor / Countryside Soup, 135
Soy sauce, 20
Spinach
    Somlaw Prahor / Countryside Soup, 135
Stockton, CA, 58–61

T

Tamarind
    Cha Krom Tuk Ampil / Stir-Fried Mussels in Tamarind Sauce, 184, 185
    Somlaw Machoo Kroeung / Tamarind Kroeung Soup, 84, 85–86
    Somlaw Machoo Ktiss Ban Kong / Shrimp Tamarind Coconut Soup, 170, 171
    Tuk Ampil / Tamarind Water, 30
Tapenade, Smoked Fish + Shrimp / Kapeek Pow, 163
Tapioca Banana Pudding / Jeak Ktiss, 234, 235
Taro
    Jien Cho-Yah / Crispy Pork Egg Rolls, 196–97
    Somlaw Prahor / Countryside Soup, 135
Toast, Crispy, with Pork + Jicama / Nom Pung Jien, 118, 119
Tofu, Fried, + Chives, Quick Stir-Fry with / Cha Dau Fu Kh-Chai, 161
Tomatoes
    Kho Trey / Caramelized Fish with Tomatoes, 178, 179
    Somlaw Kraung Chnuk / Soup Outside the Pot, 82, 83
    Trey Jien Ban Pouh / Crispy Fish with Simmered Summer Tomatoes, 218, 219

Trey Jien Ban Pouh / Crispy Fish with Simmered Summer Tomatoes, 218, 219
Trey Jien Juen / Whole Fish with Ginger + Salted Beans, 96, 97
Trey Jien Svay / Green Mango Salad with a Crispy Fish Fillet, 122, 123
Trey Prama / Pork + Salted Cod Loaf, 120
Tuk Ampil / Tamarind Water, 30
Tuk Krauch Chhma + Ambel + Mrech / Lime + Salt + Pepper Sauce, 36
Tuk Kroeung / Tinned Mackerel with Prahok, 72
Tuk Prahok / Prahok Dipping Sauce with Seared Rib Eye, 73–74, 75
Tuk Trey Mtes / Fish Sauce + Chile, 33, 34
Tuk Trey Piam / Fish Sauce Dressing, 37
Turmeric
    Green Kroeung, 29
    Yellow Kroeung, 28

W

Waffles, Coconut / Nom Poum, 240
Water spinach
    Cha Tra Koun / Stir-Fried Water Spinach, 205
    Somlaw Machoo Kroeung / Tamarind Kroeung Soup, 84, 85–86

Y

Yellow Kroeung, 28
Yuba
    Cha Mee Sou / Peppery Stir-Fried Glass Noodles with Yuba, 92, 93
    Somlaw Chap Chai / Celebration Soup, 87–88, 89

4 COLOR BOOKS
An imprint of the Crown Publishing Group
A division of Penguin Random House LLC
1745 Broadway
New York, NY 10019
4colorbooks.com
penguinrandomhouse.com

Text copyright © 2025 by Yoeun Yun
Photographs copyright © 2025 by Nicola Parisi
Illustrations copyright © 2025 by Kann "Nak" Bou

Penguin Random House values and supports copyright. Copyright fuels creativity, encourages diverse voices, promotes free speech, and creates a vibrant culture. Thank you for buying an authorized edition of this book and for complying with copyright laws by not reproducing, scanning, or distributing any part of it in any form without permission. You are supporting writers and allowing Penguin Random House to continue to publish books for every reader. Please note that no part of this book may be used or reproduced in any manner for the purpose of training artificial intelligence technologies or systems.

4 COLOR BOOKS and the 4 Color Books colophon are registered trademarks of Penguin Random House LLC.

All lyrics of Cambodian songs on pages 58, 104, 156, 190, and 226 translated by Nate Hun.

Typefaces: Tightype's Moderat, Danh Hong's Moul Pali, Mark Simonson Studio's Proxima Sera, and VJ-Type's Sud

Paper texture by Octavio Parra/Shutterstock.com

Library of Congress Cataloging-in-Publication Data
Names: Yun, Nite, author. | Nguyen, Tien, author. | Parisi,
Nicola (Photographer), photographer. | Bou, Nak, illustrator.
Title: My Cambodia: a Khmer cookbook / by Nite Yun with Tien Nguyen;
photographs by Nicola Parisi; illustrations by Nak Bou.
Identifiers: LCCN 2024044055 (print) | LCCN 2024044056 (ebook) |
ISBN 9781984863379 (hardcover) | ISBN 9781984863386 (ebook)
Subjects: LCSH: Cooking, Cambodian. | Asian American cooking. | LCGFT: Cookbooks.
Classification: LCC TX724.5.C16 Y86 2025 (print) | LCC TX724.5.C16
(ebook) | DDC 641.59596—dc23/eng/20241029
LC record available at https://lccn.loc.gov/2024044055
LC ebook record available at https://lccn.loc.gov/2024044056

Hardcover ISBN: 978-1-9848-6337-9
Ebook ISBN: 978-1-9848-6338-6

Editor-in-Chief: Bryant Terry | Acquiring editor: Claire Yee
Production editor: Abby Oladipo | Editorial assistant: Gabriela Ureña Matos
Art director: Betsy Stromberg | Production designers: Mari Gill and Faith Hague
Production: Jane Chinn | Prepress color managers: Nick Patton and Hannah Hunt
Food stylist: Fanny Pan | Food stylist assistant: Allison Fellion
Prop stylist: Nicola Parisi | Prop stylist assistant: Michelle Prochnow
Copy editor: Jude Grant | Proofreaders: Nancy Inglis and Penelope Haynes
Indexer: Elizabeth Parson
Publicists: Felix Cruz and David Hawk | Marketer: Monica Stanton

Manufactured in China

10 9 8 7 6 5 4 3 2 1

First Edition

The authorized representative in the EU for product safety and compliance is Penguin Random House Ireland, Morrison Chambers, 32 Nassau Street, Dublin D02 YH68, Ireland, https://eu-contact.penguin.ie.

"Nite beautifully weaves past and present, Cambodia and California, and nostalgia and innovation into one intricate canvas of the Khmer experience in America. With each comforting and delicious dish, she honors the oral traditions of her elders, her peers, and the community she builds. I want to eat and experience every single flavor and feeling in this book!"

—REEM ASSIL, award-winning chef and author of *Arabiyya*

"*My Cambodia* is a soulful journey that is undeniably deep and personal. Nite proudly champions Cambodian cuisine by way of her delicious chronicles that are real and uncompromising. After reading and cooking through her book, you cannot help yourself from cheering for Nite."

—JAMES SYHABOUT, chef and owner of Commis and author of *Hawker Fare*

"This cookbook is a marvel. When I first had Nite's food, I was struck by the clarity and boldness of the flavors of her cooking. The recipes in *My Cambodia* evoke the same feeling of awe: Every recipe has a sense of home and a love and respect for the food that shaped her. The recipes are easily achieved in any home, often with just a handful of ingredients. With this book, you're under the tutelage of a generous, patient, and masterful teacher."

—DIEP TRAN, James Beard Award–winning writer, founder of the Banh Chung Collective, and former chef/owner of Good Girl Dinette